SOUTH AFRICAN PREDICAMENT

SOUTH AFRICAN PREDICAMENT

The Economics of Apartheid

F. P. SPOONER

FREDERICK A. PRAEGER, *Publisher*

New York

BOOKS THAT MATTER

Published in the United States of America in 1961
by Frederick A. Praeger, Inc., Publisher
64 University Place, New York 3, N. Y.

Library of Congress Catalog Card Number: 61-11021

Printed in the United States of America

CONTENTS

5

FOREWORD

SOUTH AFRICA has been in the news a great deal since the
Second World War. Its once fair name has been badly
seared by the winds of adverse criticism that have blown upon
it from the four corners of the earth. Naturally enough, most of
this criticism is resented in South Africa, and certainly much of
it has been ill-informed and unfair: but where there is smoke
there is fire, and it cannot be claimed that all is well within the
country. Yet while much of the criticism can be ignored by
South Africans only at their own peril, at the same time it
would be as well if the criticism could be more sympathetic and
constructive, in view of the particularly difficult problems which
confront the country.

Apart from its wealth in precious minerals, which are being
taken from the earth as rapidly as possible by the best means that
modern science can devise, the country is not particularly rich
in natural resources. Yet within its borders there are four
distinct racial groups – the Whites, the Africans, the Indians,
and the Coloureds – all determined to retain their racial
characteristics in this one country, which all insist is their only
homeland. But the divisions go even further than this. Among
the Whites there are the Afrikaners, derived mainly from the
early Dutch and French settlers and speaking a distinct language,
the English-speaking people, largely descendants of British
colonists, and a fair proportion of Jews from all parts of Europe.
Among the Africans there are at least four distinct ethnic
groups, which have yet to shed their historical antagonisms.
The Indians include both Hindu and Moslem; and the
Coloureds – hitherto the most tragic section of the population –
are a heterogeneous people springing from varying mixtures of
African and Malay slaves, Hottentots and Whites.

To weld these diverse elements into a nation is a formidable
task, and it is little wonder that in the process there is friction,

9

bitterness and hatred. It is all very well for those who live in
countries less complicated racially to point accusing fingers at
South Africa, but the behaviour of peoples generally suggests
that the eager critics would probably not have done much better
themselves in such a complex, multi-racial country. In the
circumstances, while many South Africans are prepared to
accept much of the criticism from abroad as well-meaning and
even necessary, a good deal of it unfortunately serves to aggravate the problems rather than help in their solution. There are
in the Union many shades of opinion on the racial issues,
ranging from those who, for reasons satisfactory only to themselves, insist that their particular section and outlook should
dominate the affairs of the country, to those who, in seeking a
just solution, are prepared to make considerable sacrifices in
the interests of all concerned. The hope of the country lies,
however, in some middle course, some compromise between the
extremes – and the achievement of this is necessarily a delicate
matter, easily upset by unfair and ill-informed criticism from
overseas.

I have hesitated in choosing a title for this book. Under present
conditions it is almost impossible to give a completely unbiased
account of South African conditions. Outsiders, often after
spending but a few weeks in the country, write airily of its
people and its problems – usually with inadequate knowledge
of the facts, and with even less understanding of the feelings and
aspirations of the peoples within its borders. The South African,
on the other hand, White or non-White, in writing of his
country, will more likely than not taint his account with the
feelings, aspirations and prejudices prevalent among that
section of the community to which he belongs.

The history of the country has been unfortunate, in that its
outstanding episodes have sharpened rather than modified the
differences between the various sections. At no time has the
country been called upon to meet an invasion or to face a crisis
of which the various races could make common cause. Even in
the three wars in which, in this century, South Africa has
been engaged, the dangers have been insufficient to efface

the differences: in fact, the wars have actually aggravated them.

It would be virtually impossible to write about the country in terms that would meet with the approval of all sections of the population. Indeed, the most accurate and truthful book that could be written would in one way or another give offence to the susceptibilities of every section – for there have been rights and wrongs in varying degrees in all sections. While, therefore, this book will almost certainly offend many in the country, I believe nevertheless that my background and experience, from a lifetime spent in the country's service, enable me to give as balanced an account of the situation as can be given.

I am South African born. So were my parents before me. My father's people were English, who came to settle in the old Cape Colony over a hundred years ago; my mother's were Afrikaners whose ancestry dated back to the early settlers of the Cape. I grew up and went to school in a country town whose population was predominantly Afrikaner, and graduated at a leading Afrikaans university. I was articled to the Cape Town branch of a leading London firm of chartered accountants, and then entered the public service of the Union. After serving the State in a professional capacity for twenty years, I became a director of public companies, and as such, for the past fifteen years, I have identified myself with the post-war industrial development of the country. In the public service my colleagues were mainly Afrikaners, on the boards of public companies mainly English-speaking, and I have lived in various parts of the country and worked in various capacities among both sections of the White population.

My parents were of the generation of the prominent Boer generals – Botha, Smuts and Hertzog. Their early lives were undoubtedly influenced by the intense antagonisms that culminated in the Anglo-Boer War. Yet, despite the fact that they were drawn from opposing camps, their marriage survived the conflict. In fact, the bonds were strengthened by the respect each had for the other's people. The coming of Union was regarded by them as the opening of a new era, in which erstwhile foes would shed past antipathies to begin life anew in the

interests of a happy and prosperous South Africa. Although I
was still young at the time, I well remember my father's elation
when Louis Botha was appointed the first Prime Minister of the
Union. In contrast, our neighbours, who were Afrikaners,
regretted that Merriman's claim had been overlooked. These
sentiments were typical of the atmosphere which prevailed
then and in which I was brought up – an atmosphere of mutual
respect and trust, of give and take, and of implicit faith in the
future and fair name of the new Union of South Africa.

Recently we have celebrated the first half-century of the
Union. During these years the country has grown in stature
and economic strength, despite its being involved in two world
wars. Fortunately, in both world wars, the country fought on the
side of the victors, thereby earning valuable opportunities for
development. But what of the spirit of co-operation, tolerance
and trust that imbued the first years of Union? Does it still
exist? Unhappily, it seems to have vanished over the years, for
at no time have I been conscious of greater uneasiness or concern for the future of South Africa than at present. There may
be diverse reasons for this deterioration in spirit, but impartial
opinion will surely apportion the greatest blame to a section of
the Afrikaner people. They, unfortunately, have succumbed
once more to their nineteenth-century outlook – cult of privilege, as I describe it – under which they claim divine right to
rule and exploit the country in the interests primarily of the
Afrikaner people. Accordingly, they have entrenched themselves in power by shady devices, and shrug off criticism in the
name of patriotism. Fellow-Afrikaners who do not side with
them are branded as traitors; English-speaking South Africans
are slighted as un-South African because of their sentimental
attachment to the Commonwealth; and non-Whites are regarded as a menace in the country, to be kept apart at all costs
and to be cast into jail on the slightest provocation. It is little
wonder that uneasiness and concern are felt everywhere.

If criticism from abroad is to help matters it must take into
account the diverse elements of the population and the wide
range in their degrees of civilization. Talk of universal suffrage

and social integration serves only to encourage extremism and embarrass, even thwart, those who seek a just and balanced solution of the country's problems. Under present conditions in South Africa, universal suffrage can result only in giving power to those least equipped to govern – and any system that brings about such a result must surely be condemned.

White South Africans of all shades of opinion will, therefore, understandably oppose – and oppose with their blood – the extension of universal suffrage to the country. Moreover, it is highly probable that even the non-Whites – Africans, Coloureds or Indians – who have advanced in the scale of civilization, would oppose it, if only they could be sure of recognition and fair treatment by the Whites: for they too must realize that their status and achievements must be imperilled if votes were given to the large body of primitive Africans, who would inevitably succumb to those who made the biggest (and most irresponsible) promises.

Nor can social integration be supported in the Union in its present stage of development. All communities suffer in great or less degree from racial prejudices. This is an innate human frailty, which becomes cruelly apparent when subjected to compulsion. Thus the forcing of integration, no less than the forcing of segregation, leads only to bitterness and resentment. Most racial groups in the Union would be quite happy to confine themselves to their respective social circles, if fairly treated and not made subject to discriminatory legislation. It is not social apartheid in itself that is the evil in South Africa, but the fact that it is forced down the throats of the non-Whites in an often unjust and callous manner by ill-considered and reactionary legislation. Had the past efforts of the white man in South Africa been directed towards narrowing the gap between White and non-White living standards instead of the reverse, the innate racial prejudices would have tended to mellow rather than sharpen.

While White South Africans generally resent outside criticism, they will never be free of it so long as sections of the community are not properly consulted or adequately represented.

And the criticism will be all the sharper while one section arrogates to itself divine favours and a monopoly of patriotism. But if criticism there must be, let it be specific, well founded, and directed at the evil deeds and words that cause hurt and suffering, particularly to the underprivileged. It is not necessary to destroy the theatre because bad films are being shown in it. And the proffered remedies of universal suffrage and social integration would mean exactly that. Moreover, such talk unsettles the minds of primitive natives, causing them to believe that they have moral claims by virtue of their numbers only. On the other hand, the absence of universal suffrage and social integration throws all the more responsibility on the ruling classes to see that the people who do not enjoy these privileges are justly and fairly treated.

Unfortunately, as this book will disclose, there is a great deal that is unfair and unjust in South Africa at the present time. This in the long run will inevitably bring its own punishment. The book refers to this also. If outside criticism could but assist well-wishers in the country to remedy these ills before it is too late, it would indeed be invaluable. How this can be achieved is not clear, but if criticism be temperate and sympathetic, it could no doubt help in eliminating those evils that threaten the happiness and future of all who have made South Africa their homeland – White and Black alike.

The thought that South Africa has recently celebrated its fiftieth anniversary of Union brings back memories of that eventful episode in the history of the country – the advent of Union. At the time, a pageant was staged in Cape Town depicting the principal historical events from the first landing of European settlers to the establishment of Union itself. This latter was portrayed in a spectacular 'Grand Finale', in which scene the evil spirits that had haunted the country's past were being chased into the sea by happy young South Africans bearing the fruit and other products of this smiling land. This scene aptly reflected the spirit that pervaded the country at that time – a spirit of goodwill and tolerance, envisaging a new start without the ghosts of the past.

The memory of this scene has, in its turn, raised speculative thoughts of how best to present the spirit that broods over the Union today, after a half-century of existence. In my mind's eye I visualize a scene like the following: there are the same faces which fifty years ago, young and smiling, followed the evil spirits from the arena; they are not smiling now, but harassed and worried, on foot no longer, but in motor-cars driven hither and thither without any clear sense of direction. The reason for their uneasiness soon becomes clear: the evil spirits have returned – not from the sea, but out of the land – and there seems to be more of them the farther one ventures from the coast. They taunt those in the cars with gesticulations that seem to urge the drivers in the direction of the sea. The significance of this becomes more ominous when on the landscape there appear multitudes of young people, toiling, sweating, badly clothed, some underfed, yet all laughing and singing. Their skins are black, not white, and they sing about Africa, which very word they stress with fervour. They do not seem to hold the evil spirits in fear, and the spirits for their part seem eager to keep out of their way.

This vision brings to mind another extraordinary episode in the history of South Africa. Some hundred years ago a young African maiden named Nongquase received a message in a dream, from one of her tribal ancestors, to the effect that the tribe should slaughter all its livestock and destroy its crops. This done, the sun would on an appointed day move from west to east and the white man would then be driven into the sea, leaving the land in the possession of the Blacks. The stock and crops were duly destroyed, but on the appointed day the sun did not change its course, nor were the white men pushed into the sea. Instead the tribe, after great privation, had to be saved from starvation by the intervention of the white man. This was indeed a disaster for Nongquase's tribe; but the thought arises whether the blunder did not lie in the interpretation of the dream rather than in the dream itself. For in the affairs of nations a hundred years and more may be but the equivalent of a few days or weeks in the lives of mortals. If, for instance, the

destruction of stock and crops were but symbolical of the sacrifices that would have to be endured, and the change in the
direction of the sun but an exhortation to seek salvation in the
East and not the West, could not the vision of the flight of the
white man still be fulfilled? A disturbing thought, no doubt,
but an utterly fantastic belief, say most South Africans – and I
am inclined to agree. But is it any more fantastic than the vision
of apartheid so dear to the present ruling clique in the country?

PART ONE

A brief survey of the country, its history and its people

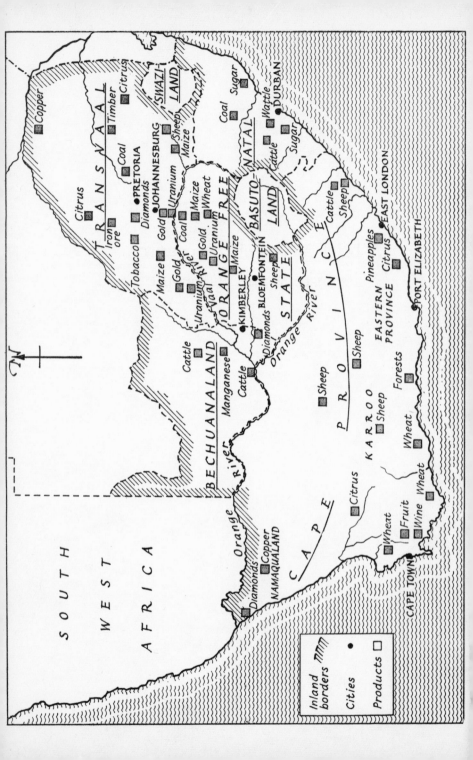

I

PHYSICAL FEATURES

SOUTH AFRICA is a land of contrasts: it has fertile plains and valleys, and also large stretches of sheer desert; it holds highly-civilized peoples, and also hordes of primitive folk; many inhabitants have fair hair and blue eyes, but many more have brown or black skins; in some parts of the country it rains in the winter, in other parts in the summer; many languages are spoken throughout the land and some of the territories that geographically and economically comprise South Africa are in fact not under the administration of its government. There is nothing homogeneous about the country or its people, and it is dangerous to generalize about it.

Visitors landing at Johannesburg, Cape Town or Durban are impressed by the air of prosperity in the city. Handsome buildings line the main streets, heavy traffic moves to and fro, the people in the principal thoroughfares are well dressed and the shops well stocked with high-quality goods from all over the world. A stroll in the better residential suburbs will reveal a standard of housing unsurpassed in any part of the world. On the outskirts modern factories will be seen, in which up-to-date machines are humming. From the hill-tops skirting Johannesburg one gets a vista of large mine dumps, which rise in testimony of the intense activity thousands of feet down in the bowels of the earth. Cape Town and Durban, again, are flanked by large harbours at which a continuous stream of liners, tankers and cargo vessels call. All these cities, moreover, have up-to-date airports – especially Johannesburg, which is an international terminal. In this respect these three South African cities are well equipped by international standards, and compare favourably with medium-sized cities elsewhere.

Cape Town, the most southerly city in Africa, is the original gateway through which Western civilization entered South Africa. It stands at the foot of Table Mountain – one of the most prominent landmarks in the world, whose majestic beauty has been appreciated by mariners for over three hundred years. Today the suburbs of Cape Town sprawl over the Cape Peninsula in an area of unsurpassed loveliness and temperate climate, where life is pleasant for both resident and holiday-maker.

The Cape Province

The immediate hinterland of Cape Town is the winter-rainfall area known as the Western Province, or Boland in the language of the Afrikaners. It is a land of beautiful mountains and valleys with perennial streams and rivers. To the immediate north and east of the Cape Peninsula the valleys are studded with beautiful fruit farms from which a thriving trade is conducted in deciduous fruits, and wines, for both export and local use. The climate is Mediterranean and virtually ideal for those accustomed to European conditions. To the west and east of the fruit-growing area lie the principal wheatlands of South Africa. The farmers here, too, are relatively prosperous, for besides their annual wheat crops they run woolled sheep and dairy cows, which feed on the stubble left on the lands after reaping and at the same time contribute towards the fertilization of the fields. The Western Province was first settled by Dutch and Huguenot agriculturists about three hundred years ago and is therefore the first area to have been opened up in South Africa by Europeans. The descendants of these early settlers are still largely in possession of the fertile lands of the Province. Farther on towards the north-west the land becomes more and more arid as the annual rainfall declines. Where it abuts on the Orange River – the border between the Union of South Africa and South West Africa – it is known as Namaqualand and, although arid, is not devoid of riches. The territory has yielded large quantities of copper and diamonds, and the sea off its coast is rich in fish.

Going east from Cape Town, after a short distance through fruit country one passes into a relatively narrow grain belt which runs parallel with the sea and a range of mountains some miles inland. Thereafter the landscape changes as the mountains close in towards the sea. The road through this part is called the Garden Route because of the magnificence of the scenery. The mountain slopes are wooded with indigenous trees which provide excellent timber for furniture, but agriculturally the soil is relatively poor. As the mountains recede from the coast, one enters the area known as the Eastern Province of the Cape. The principal city here is Port Elizabeth – a medium-sized town by South African standards. Through this town the early British settlers passed on their way to the areas allotted to them, which lie to the north and east of the town. This stretch of country is by no means as fertile as the Western Province and in consequence the settlers had a tough struggle for existence, intensified by the fact that the country here borders on territory occupied by African tribes, which made occupation hazardous in the early days of the settlement. In fact, in the first half of the nineteenth century this part was the scene of a number of Kaffir wars and the settlement was overrun and devastated a number of times. Beyond this are the Border districts, so called because they border on the Transkei African Reserve occupied by the Xhosa tribes.

All the way from Cape Town there is a gradual change in the climate from winter to summer rainfall, and in the Border districts the rain comes down mainly in summer. So, too, there is a gradual change in the indigenous population as one proceeds along the south-east coast from the Cape Peninsula to the Transkei: Coloureds give way to Africans, who predominate from Port Elizabeth onwards. Across the Kei River one enters African territory proper until the Natal border is reached. Here the Africans live in their primitive huts, raise inferior cattle, and scratch the surface of the earth to produce low-yielding maize crops for local consumption. In the coastal stretch of the country from Port Elizabeth to the Transkei Reserve the White farmers produce pineapples, citrus fruits and chicory, and also pasture small herds of cattle and flocks of sheep.

Crossing the mountain ranges to the north of the Western Province one enters the great plain known as the Karroo. This is an area of low rainfall and shrub. Agriculturally it produces very little, but here are raised some of the best flocks of Merino sheep to be found anywhere. The land is pastoral and produces excellent wool and mutton, but farming can be conducted only on an extensive scale, so that the plains are but sparsely populated by both humans and animals. Not only is the rainfall low in the Karroo, but the area is also devoid of running rivers. River-beds there are in plenty, but they rarely contain water and run only a few days or even hours a year. There are, however, underground sources of water on most farms which are tapped by windmill or oil pump to provide drinking water for man and beast. While in the summer months the heat can become intense, it is nevertheless dry and healthy. The winter climate is crisp, fresh and exhilarating. The Karroo, moreover, has a fascinating beauty of its own and those born there are loath to live in other parts of the country.

Towards the north-west the veld of the Karroo deteriorates until it merges with the semi-arid areas of Namaqualand and the Kalahari Desert. Due north it ends below the Orange River and the grass-lands of Griqualand West and the Orange Free State. South, east and west are the mountain ranges that separate the Karroo from the coastal regions of the Cape Province.

Natal

From the Cape Province we pass to the other erstwhile British colony, Natal. Its principal city and seaport is Durban, a place of considerable charm with a somewhat tropical climate. Durban is about half the age of Cape Town and as yet somewhat smaller. In many ways, however, it is superior to the Mother City, as Cape Town is called: it is better planned, with wider streets, many of which are lined with flowering trees.

It is also more African in character, although a large proportion of the population is of Indian origin.

Durban gives one the impression of being highly prosperous – and so, no doubt, it is. Besides being a considerable industrial centre, it is the principal holiday resort of people from the interior, both the Transvaal and the Rhodesias. It is the most important harbour in the Union, and through it passes a large proportion of the trade for the Reef and other centres. It is also the centre of the sugar industry, which stretches north and south along the coastal belt of Natal. The greenness of the country along this coast is attractive, and so are the small seaside resorts, particularly towards the south.

The sugar industry was started in these parts about a hundred years ago and was responsible for introducing the Indian community into Natal. In the early days of the industry there was an acute shortage of plantation labour, as the Africans in the surrounding territory had not as yet taken to working in the service of the White colonists, and Indians were therefore indentured for the work and have remained in the country ever since. The industry today is highly organized and relatively prosperous, and the Natal coastal strip in general, with its seaside resorts and attractive sugar estates, is well developed. The sugar belt is, however, relatively narrow, and towards the west, away from the coast, the land gradually rises to levels where the climate is unsuitable for cane-growing. Much of the land here is hilly and rather unsuitable for intensive agriculture. Large stretches bordering on the cane-lands are today African Reserves and not very productive.

Farther towards the west the terrain affords good grazing for cattle, and White settlers run large dairy herds and also slaughter stock. This part is also the site of big wattle plantations, producing large quantities of bark and extract for export to many overseas countries. To the south the rising land is soon overshadowed by the mighty peaks of the Drakensberg range, which prevents easy access to Basutoland and beyond. In the centre the mountain ranges flatten out and beyond stretch the highlands of South Africa, known as the Highveld. These highlands stretch into the Transvaal and Orange Free State and beyond the Witwatersrand and Free State goldfields. The Highveld is a relatively rich farming area; it produces good pasture for both woolled sheep and cattle and yields good crops of maize, potatoes, and even wheat. The climate is excellent both in summer and winter. While it can become hot at times, the nights are always cool, and, besides, cooling rains frequently fall during the summer months. The winters are bracing and even cold at times, and there are occasional snowfalls. The north-west of Natal runs into the mountain ranges that separate this province from Swaziland. Much of this part, although actually in the province, is African Reserve for the Zulu tribes.

Over the past one hundred and fifty years Natal has been the storm centre of South Africa. Little is known of its history before the coming of the White settlers, but the opening decades of the nineteenth century saw the fierce and bloody campaigns of the Zulu tyrant, Chaka, and his impies. The land was laid waste and soaked in human blood by his terrorist attacks upon neighbouring tribes, and also by the many purges which he carried out among his followers. Then in the late 1830s the Zulus murdered some voortrekkers, who had entered Natal over the Drakensberg from the Orange Free State in search of a new home. After avenging the death of their comrades, the voortrekkers in the main left Natal because of differences with the British, who were in occupation of the country immediately surrounding the present city of Durban.

A ding-dong struggle between the British and Zulus followed, lasting many years. This was finally settled by the defeat of the Zulus at the Battle of Ulundi, but only after considerable bloodshed on both sides in a number of skirmishes. Some years after this, several important battles between the British forces and the Boers were fought on Natal soil during the Anglo-Boer War – at Colenso in particular. It is true to say, therefore, that during the nineteenth century Natal was the principal cockpit of the struggles between many of the peoples that inhabit the Union of South Africa. Today it is the only province in which English-speaking South Africans predominate, but it is the one in which the ratio of Whites to non-Whites is lowest, and in which the bulk of the Indian population of the country lives.

The Transvaal

Johannesburg, in the Transvaal, the last of the three main ports of entry into the Union, is the youngest but also the largest city in South Africa. It is not a seaport but an air terminal, and is barely seventy years old. It has grown with amazing rapidity, and economically is the most important centre in the Union. It started as a mining camp, but soon developed into a city as the great wealth of the underlying gold reefs in its vicinity became known. Today it is the economic heart, not only of South Africa but also of the adjoining territories which with the Union make an economic entity in southern Africa.

The city is nearly six thousand feet above sea-level and enjoys an invigorating climate, providing suitable conditions for a tempo of life corresponding to that in the cities of the United States of America. While economic activity provides the foundation for the city's prosperity, Johannesburg is susceptible to the vicissitudes of the gambling public not only at home but also in London, Paris and New York. It boasts the most important Stock Exchange in the Southern Hemisphere, and prices are influenced by speculators in Europe and America. The temperament of Johannesburg is therefore somewhat mercurial; its mood is largely determined by the mood of the Stock Exchange. When prices are buoyant, Johannesburg smiles; when they slump, faces are glum and a grimness overtakes the city – but with the first indication of an upward turn, faces brighten again and optimism comes to the surface.

Many South Africans will deny the overriding importance of gold in the economy of the country, but it is plainly visible in Johannesburg. The vitality, drive and tenseness of its population are something apart from the rest of the Union, where the tempo of life is easy-going and pleasant. Johannesburg is one of the ramparts of capitalism, thriving as it does on gold – but gold has always been one of the pillars of that system. The gold-mining industry of the Transvaal and Orange Free State is directed from Johannesburg and is conducted on a highly efficient basis. On the whole, the gold reefs are not high-grade, and consequently the mines must be run efficiently to survive. They depend vitally, however, upon low-paid African labour which the industry draws from a wide area extending beyond the borders of the Union. While the engineering and executive skill employed by the mining groups is second to none, the profitability of the industry rests also upon the expert handling of the Black labour force.

Without this force the industry would be but a shadow of what it is today. By African standards these workers are generally well treated by the mining groups, although the treatment is dictated more by economic than by humanitarian considerations. The workers are fed on a carefully-balanced diet and their health maintained by excellent medical services and hospitals – not directly because of any human feeling for these people, but because such treatment materially increases the output per man-shift. In other words, it pays the mining companies and their shareholders to spend the extra sums on the feeding and care of the workers. The health of the labour force is of considerable importance to the mines, for the African in his primitive kraal, from which he is recruited for service in the mines, is usually under-nourished and does not possess the necessary stamina to stand up to hard physical work.

The human and sociological aspects of the labour employed in the mines are, however, rather disturbing, for the workers are not permitted to bring their families to the mines where they work. They are herded into compounds and remain separated from their wives and families for periods of eighteen months and more. This system of migratory African labour applies not only to the mines, but generally. The influence of the gold-mining industry, which today includes large-scale production of uranium, is felt throughout South Africa. It is the principal contributor to the high standard of living enjoyed by the Whites throughout the country, but only in Johannesburg and on the Reef is one conscious of its power and vitality.

Hence the Reef and its environs have attracted the heaviest concentration of population, both White and non-White; in this area also, manufacturing industry has developed on a larger scale than elsewhere in the Union.

The natural resources of the Transvaal are not, however, confined to gold. The province is rich in many other minerals, such as platinum, diamonds and uranium, and holds vast deposits of coal and iron ore. Agriculturally, too, the province possesses considerable wealth. All around Johannesburg large quantities of maize are produced. To the south the maize-lands stretch into the Orange Free State, where today a rich new gold-field has been discovered. To the east, both in the Transvaal and in the Orange Free State, is the Highveld, already described, and westwards, the maize belt merges into cattle country which reaches across the Bechuanaland border. To the north of Johannesburg the Highveld gradually dips into lower-lying territory, known as the Bushveld. Besides citrus, several other important crops are produced in this area. The Bushveld also stretches beyond the Highveld in the Eastern Transvaal where the scenery is magnificent and rivals the beauty of the Western Province of the Cape. Citrus for export, and vegetables for the Reef and Pretoria markets, are grown here on a large scale. The Kruger National Park is in this area on the borders of Portuguese East Africa.

The Orange Free State

Immediately to the south of the Transvaal lies the Orange Free State. In many respects, this province is similar to parts of the Transvaal in that the Highveld and Middleveld regions extend into it. Until the end of the Second World War the province was predominantly agricultural, but since then gold mining has grown and added much to its economic welfare. New towns have come into existence and the new goldfields are a hive of industry. The agricultural produce of the Free State is similar to that of the Highveld and Middleveld regions of the Transvaal – wool, maize and wheat. These regions have a reasonably pleasant climate: cold in winter and warm in summer, but the warmth tempered by the cooling showers of a summer-rainfall area. On the other hand, the Lowveld regions of the Transvaal have a mild winter but a rather torrid and humid summer. Generally speaking, both the Transvaal and the Orange Free State enjoy reasonably good annual rainfalls, although parts of these provinces are occasionally subject to drought.

This brief description of the three major cities of the Union and of the countryside about them gives a rough cross-section of that part of the country dominated by the White races. The description is perhaps rather superficial, but should give readers who have not seen the country a fairly good idea of its geography, and enable them to appreciate better the problems to be discussed in later chapters.

Black and White

On his first visit, the traveller will be struck by the high standard of living of the country's White inhabitants: everywhere he will see White men and women, well dressed, living in well-built, spacious houses and driving about in motor-cars, a large proportion of which are heavy American makes. He will find them in comfortable offices, serving in fine shops and managing factories, farms and mines – all in all, a pleasing spectacle of a people enjoying a high standard of life amid general prosperity in town and country. However, should the traveller be interested in human affairs or the economics of the country he will soon notice that all the heavy and menial labour and much of the semi-skilled manual labour is done by people with black or brown faces. These people are not so well dressed, and in many cases work in tattered clothing. On his journey through the cities, towns and countryside it will gradually occur to him how heavily the edifice of White prosperity he has seen rests upon the sweat and labour of the brown and black workers.

The dockyard navvies, the railroad gangs, the road-makers,

the delivery boys and the garbage collectors, are all brown or black. In the factories there will be many more dark-complexioned workers attending machines than Whites. On the farms he will find hardly any White workers other than the owners and their families – a black or brown worker will be driving the tractor or lorry, tending the animals, tilling the soil and reaping the crop. Down the mines the ratio of Black to White will be as high as, or even higher than, on the farms – probably ten to one. In virtually every home there will be at least one servant, a dark-skinned boy or girl, doing the household chores. In every hotel the waiters are black or brown, and so are the room attendants; the kitchen hands and most of the cooks, too. At the garages where he may pull up for petrol the pump attendants are all black. And if he should be interested in building or other construction work, he will find only Blacks doing the unskilled work and every skilled artisan white (except in parts of the Cape), with a black or brown assistant to do all the heavy work.

By this time the intelligent traveller will have realized that White prosperity and high living standards are based largely upon black and brown labour – truly a White aristocracy and a Black proletariat. Furthermore, if the traveller is European or American, he will be largely unaware of the conditions under which the non-Whites live, unless he is interested in social problems, particularly of the lower-income groups. He will stay in hotels where only Whites are residents or will visit comfortable and well-furnished homes where only Whites are hosts. In the social sphere in which such a traveller moves the non-Whites will be virtually non-existent; he will encounter them only in the role of servants.

Where, then, do the non-Whites live and play? In Cape Town and Port Elizabeth, and certain other Cape centres, the visitor will notice here and there, between houses occupied by Whites, rows of rather small, slummy-looking dwellings. In these, members of the Coloured community live. While the houses are small and shabby, they are in fact no worse than many dwellings to be found in the slum quarters of European or American cities. Indeed, in some cases the houses are actually superior to many of their counterparts in Europe, as many Coloured workers in the Cape earn good wages and some of them take considerable pride in their personal appearance and their homes.

Since the early days of settlement in the Cape it has been customary for White and non-White to live in separate areas, and the islands of non-White dwellings found today amid houses occupied by Whites are largely remnants of Coloured areas which have been surrounded by the homes of the Whites as a result of the growth of the cities and towns. New residential areas for the Coloureds have naturally been opened up in later years. These are usually on the outskirts of the towns and cities and thus some distance from the places of work of the occupants. The houses in these parts are usually small but in many cases not much inferior to those in the poorer quarters of European cities. Unfortunately, the older and the newer houses are gravely overcrowded – to some extent because of the high birth-rate among these people, but mainly because the provision of houses for Coloureds has not kept pace with the economic growth of the country: house-building has been allowed to lag to such an extent that living conditions among the Coloureds are in many instances deplorable – they have had to content themselves with self-constructed shanties pieced together from scraps of tin-plate and timber from discarded packing cases, erected on unused stretches of land which in winter are often waterlogged and where no amenities for sanitation exist.

These areas are festering sores which breed crime and disease and are certainly no credit to the authorities nor to White South Africa in general. But it cannot be said that the Coloured community of the Cape has not been provided with playing fields, and indeed, the amenities available for recreation among the Coloureds are superior to those provided for many White communities in both Europe and America. Living and social conditions similar to those of the Coloured people in the Cape Province are found among the Indians of Natal – except that the Indians, on the whole, have succeeded in maintaining a better standard among their poorer families.

Africans in the cities

The lot of the city- and town-dwelling Africans throughout South Africa is, if anything, worse than that of the Coloureds and Indians. While the African has for many years been in the employ of the Whites, he is relatively a new-comer as a city dweller. Previously the bulk of the Africans working in the towns and cities had their homes in the Reserves or on the farms, and sought work away from home only intermittently. This state of affairs has been undergoing a gradual change for some time, with the result that today large numbers of Africans have no ties with the rural areas and have settled with their wives and families in the towns. This does not mean that the migratory form of labour is decreasing, for most African labour is still in this category. But without the authorities fully realizing the implications, more and more African families drifted to the cities. This movement was speeded up during the Second World War because of the insistent demand for industrial labour. Until some years back the native Reserves were able to absorb the increasing African population, but overcrowding of these limited areas, farmed in the most primitive manner, has resulted in the land vomiting up its surplus population. And where could this surplus of women and children find a livelihood but in the towns and cities where their men worked?

This movement caught the authorities unprepared, so that for years living conditions among many African families in the cities were shockingly bad. When the authorities woke up to the task of rehousing and providing for these people in cities like Johannesburg the problem had already become one of almost unmanageable proportions. Indeed, it had become a national problem. But by then a Nationalist Government was in power and it set its face against the admission of native families as residents in the established cities and towns of the country. It decreed that, except for families already established in the cities for a number of years, African women and children were to be forced back to the Reserves and rural areas from which they had come.

Within the ambit of this policy the Government undertook to improve the living conditions of the African families permitted to remain in the cities, and embarked upon fairly extensive housing schemes. No Africans, however, were entitled to own land in these so-called White cities as a general rule; and this gave rise to considerable heartburning among Africans who held title to land and houses which they were required to surrender when moved to the new townships, as the old ones were demolished for White settlement or other purposes. But rehousing of Africans in the large cities of the Union, particularly in Johannesburg, is a major task and is being carried out relatively slowly. Meanwhile, conditions generally among African residents are still bad and in these areas there is no abatement of crime, which has reached alarming proportions.

Whether the Government's policy of encouraging only migrant labour and of preventing the settlement of African families in the cities and towns (where most work is to be found) can in the long run succeed, is open to question. Quite apart from this, the rehousing of single Africans and of the families who know no other home but in the cities is a big enough undertaking, particularly in the light of the natural increase in this population that is bound to take place. At times one doubts whether the authorities fully appreciate the magnitude of the problem, for the African population employed in a city like Johannesburg is large enough in itself to constitute a fair-sized city, and to house these people satisfactorily with the necessary amenities for health, education and sport is no task that can be accomplished by a capital outlay of one or two million pounds a year.

Africans on the land

In the country districts, housing for the non-Whites is not quite so urgent a problem. On many farms in the Cape Province and along the coastal belt of Natal, where Coloureds and Indians respectively are employed, housing standards are very much the same as in the cities of Cape Town and Durban. But overcrowding is not quite such an evil there, and on the farms there is plenty of fresh air.

On the other hand, money wages are miserably low in these parts – certainly insufficient to provide the workers' families with wholesome meals, not to mention clothes and other necessaries of life. These comments apply to Coloured and Indian labour on farms; Africans on farms live either in barracks where the labour is migratory, or in straw-and-mud huts where whole families squat on the farms of the Whites. While money wages paid to Africans on farms are extremely low, it is customary for the farmer to supply these workers with a quantity of maize or maize meal, and in some cases other simple foods, as part payment for their labour. In many cases, too, the African families are permitted to run limited numbers of livestock on the farm and to cultivate small patches of maize or kaffircorn. So, while the majority of African farm labourers are not adequately fed, their families living with them do not starve and are often better off in this respect than Africans in the cities, although the squatters do live under primitive conditions – not very different from those on the Reserves.

Yet today many of these farms are equipped with modern facilities and it is a commonplace to see Africans driving tractors and lorries and using agricultural implements of the latest design. This daily contact with modern implements and practices, which have enriched the farms materially, must in the long run influence the outlook of the African farm workers. It is too much to expect of anyone actively operating these implements that he will not become dissatisfied with primitive living conditions, while the owners of the machinery grow progressively richer because of its use. It is therefore in the interests of all concerned that the living standards of African farm workers should be gradually raised as they come in contact with, operate, and maintain, the many modern contrivances which are changing the face of the world and breaking down primitive ideas and methods.

The African Reserves

A picture of the Union of South Africa would not be complete without some reference to the African Reserves, the High Commission Territories and South West Africa. The Union proper, together with these territories, is an economic entity which for convenience could be described as Greater South Africa. The African Reserves fall within the boundaries of the Union of South Africa and, in consequence, under the control of the Union Government. A special Government department, the Department of Bantu Administration and Development, administers all the laws and regulations affecting the African population both within and without the Reserves. In recent years, as a result of a flood of new legislation affecting the Africans, the Department's functions and powers have been greatly widened, so that its activities, in its special sphere approach those exercised by a government and make it virtually a state within a state.

The principal Reserves are situated in the eastern Cape, Natal, northern and western Transvaal, and Bechuanaland. In the Transvaal in particular there are numerous small areas separated from the main bodies which make up the Reserves. This makes the administration of the Reserves as a whole a rather complicated matter. (The map on page 156 shows the location of the principal Reserves.)

The Reserves are tracts of land set aside for the exclusive use of those African tribes which live within them. Hitherto it has been possible for Whites to obtain concessions to live and trade within the areas, but the policy of the Nationalist Government is slowly to get rid of these concessions so that all trading within the Reserves is for the benefit of the Africans. Local councils exist within the Reserves which, within limits, administer the affairs of the tribes they represent. They are largely composed of the tribal chiefs and their headmen serving under the guidance of White officials of the Department of Bantu Affairs.

Provision is made under certain Union laws to increase, up to a point, the territory to be held in trust for Africans, but even if these powers are fully exercised the total area to be held in trust would not exceed thirteen per cent of the land area of the Union itself, excluding South West Africa and the High Commission Territories. In making this comparison, however, it must be pointed out that a large section of the Union under White settlement is arid and inferior land, and that most of the trust lands are in areas of good rainfall, although in parts they are rather mountainous. So the agricultural potential of the Reserves could be considerably more than thirteen per cent of the Union – probably up to about twenty per cent.

Unfortunately, very little progress has been made agriculturally in the Reserves. The Africans still live by traditional custom under the control of chiefs, who in many instances are not particularly enlightened men. Most of the land is communally held for the benefit of the numerous tribes and the methods of stock-raising and agriculture are primitive indeed, most of the work on the land being left to the care of the women. Unfortunately, too, the population in the Reserves has been rising steadily, until today it is about four million, if the migrant workers away from their homes are included. Scientific effort on any scale has been introduced only in recent years to improve pastoral and agricultural conditions, and much of this has been thwarted by superstition and suspicion among the Africans, who in many respects are still influenced by pagan beliefs and the practices of witch doctors. Education among them has not as yet made sufficient progress to rid them of these superstitions and beliefs. Consequently, the Reserves have been overstocked with cattle and the fertility of the soil impaired by ignorant farming methods, resulting in serious soil erosion.

Because of this, these areas are unable to support the large African population living in them; and a large proportion of the men find it imperative to seek work elsewhere to supplement the food supply and other requirements necessary to maintain a bare minimum living standard. A good proportion are drawn to the Witwatersrand where they obtain employment in the mines, thereby consolidating the migratory system of labour first introduced by the large mining houses. The system was subsequently encouraged by successive governments, which imposed taxes upon African huts and thus forced the inhabitants to earn money to pay the taxes.

The wheel has turned full circle, however, for today necessity forces most of this labour beyond the bounds of the Reserves to avert the threat of hunger and starvation. The problem of rehabilitating these areas has received some attention recently and an important commission appointed in 1950 has issued a voluminous report in which recommendations are made on the subject. The commission also evolved a plan for increasing the carrying capacity of the Reserves; but there is a danger that the problem has been neglected too long for the Reserves to carry a much larger population without excessive cost to the country as a whole.

The High Commission Territories

The High Commission Territories, although under the control of the British Commonwealth Relations Office, really fall within the economic boundaries of the Union. Much of the produce of these Territories is sold to and consumed in the Union, and a good proportion of the food necessary to feed their populations is drawn from it. In addition, large numbers of the male population find employment in the Union, and in fact are forced to seek work there through dire necessity. The Territories are not self-supporting and depend on the Union labour markets and food supplies.

The Territories in question are Basutoland, Swaziland and the Bechuanaland Protectorate, and their total population is approximately one and a quarter million, of which only some eight to nine thousand are White, the rest mainly Africans. Basutoland and Swaziland are mountainous, relatively small, and therefore unable to carry large populations. The rainfall in both Territories is relatively good, so that, with the aid of science and light industry, economic progress should be possible. In both there is scope for the development of hydro-electric power, but because of the terrain, transport is likely to be costly. Except for a few miles in Basutoland, neither Territory has any railways and in parts of Basutoland transport is by pack animals only. Road motor services are developing, however, and in Swaziland there is now talk of railway construction. Several farming and industrial ventures have started up in this Territory, which appears to be on the threshold of considerable development.

Many of the problems that have held back progress in the African Reserves of the Union have also been experienced in the High Commission Territories – ignorance, superstition, poor agriculture, and soil erosion. This has been the case in Basutoland in particular, and the standard of living there depends materially upon the earnings of the migratory workers who obtain employment in the Union. The Commonwealth Relations Office, however, has considerably speeded up efforts to improve education, to check erosion and to develop the Territory economically.

The Bechuanaland Protectorate covers an enormous area of over 300,000 square miles. Most of this is sandy and arid, an extension, in fact, of the Kalahari Desert. But the west and north-west, which border upon the Union and Southern Rhodesia respectively, afford good grazing for cattle. In the north along the Caprivi Strip, which belongs to South West Africa, the land is well watered and should be capable of development. The Territory has not been thoroughly prospected for minerals and there may be opportunities in this direction also. The existing population is small in relation to the size of the Protectorate and there may be scope for it to carry many times its present number.

South West Africa

South West Africa, formerly German South West Africa, also falls within the ambit of the Union from the economic point of view. It is a large territory, almost the size of the Union itself, but for the most part is desert or near-desert. The whole coastal region for fifty miles and more inland is sheer desert with hardly a blade of grass anywhere. The southern half is not much better than desert, although it does support flocks of karakul sheep which supply the valuable Persian lamb pelts – one of the principal exports. The central portion of the territory away from the coastal belt, although dry, does provide fairly good pastoral conditions, and north and north-east the land improves sufficiently to support a relatively wealthy farming community, although even here operations have to be conducted on an extensive scale.

In minerals the territory is relatively wealthy: diamonds are mined on a large scale in the southern coastal belt, while lead, vanadium, manganese and copper ores form part of the exports. The territorial waters are particularly rich in fish and support a prosperous industry. South West Africa is administered largely by the public services of the Union, but in the main its laws are enacted by its own Legislative Assembly.

It is a bit of a hybrid in this respect. The territory forms part of the Union as far as customs duties are concerned, and external affairs and defence are cared for by the Union Government. Most other government functions, however, are the responsibility of the local Assembly. The territory is represented in the Union House of Assembly by six specially-elected members. South West Africa was mandated to the Union after the First World War by the League of Nations. During the Second World War the status of the territory lacked clear definition, but the Union Government has consistently declined to admit that the present United Nations Organization has any say in its affairs. This has led to a good deal of criticism of the Union, particularly in debates in the Assembly of the United Nations.

In order to give the reader some idea of the size and population of the Union, and of Greater South Africa as defined in this chapter, the following table is included:

AREA AND POPULATION

	Union of South Africa	Greater South Africa
Area in square miles	472,359	1,083,600
Population (1957):		
Whites	3,000,000	3,070,000
Africans	9,600,000	11,200,000
Coloureds	1,350,000	1,355,000
Indians	400,000	402,000
Population per square mile	30·4	14·8

The population figures are actually estimates, but these should be reliable as the rates of growth have been fairly steady since the last census. The table shows the immense area covered, particularly by Greater South Africa and the sparseness of the population. By comparison, the area of the United Kingdom is only 94,200 square miles, but in making any comparison it should be remembered that about sixty per cent of Greater South Africa is either desert or near-desert. Over the rest of the territories there is a great variation in rainfall ranging from under ten to over fifty inches a year, but water supply is one of the major problems affecting the country, for in most areas evaporation is high and run-off heavy. If and when deserts can be made to blossom, southern Africa should benefit greatly. And who can tell what may happen with the development of nuclear power?

HISTORICAL BACKGROUND

THE history of any multi-racial society is likely to be an explosive subject. While true history should be no more than a record and an explanation of past events, the interpretation of the events is bound to differ according to the viewpoints of the various peoples that make up the society. This is particularly the case where the peoples have been in violent conflict with one another. South Africa has been no exception in this respect, and it would be virtually impossible to give a history of the country acceptable to all the diverse elements of its population today. Hitherto the history has been written almost entirely from the point of view of its White inhabitants, and the non-Whites have all too often been treated merely as barbarians or sub-human species who thwarted White settlement. In the many conflicts between the races the Whites have invariably been described as the heroes and the non-Whites as the villains. Although justified in certain circumstances, such accounts can hardly be regarded as unbiased and accurate history, and it cannot possibly be contended that the non-Whites had no valid points of view or legitimate rights in all the struggles. It is to be hoped, therefore, that future histories will accord the non-Whites better recognition than has hitherto been given them.

In this chapter only a brief account is given of those episodes in the history of the country which, more than any other, have influenced the outlook of and sharpened the antagonism among the different peoples living in the Union. It concerns mainly the differences that have arisen between the two White races in the country, for unfortunately little is known of non-White reactions to the major events over the past three hundred years.

The Dutch East India Company

Although seafarers of different nations had called at the Cape of Good Hope (as the Cape Peninsula was then termed) before 1652, the known history of South Africa really starts with the landing at Table Bay, during that year, of a party of officials of the Dutch East India Company under the leadership of Jan van Riebeeck. The object of the landing was to open up a half-way station between the Netherlands and the East, for the provision of fresh supplies to ships belonging to the Company on their way to and fro – the health and efficiency of the crews depending to a great extent upon the availability of such supplies. At that time there was no intention of colonizing the Cape, but merely of setting up an outpost where vegetables could be grown and fresh meat obtained from the indigenous population.

These people were mainly Hottentots who occupied the surrounding countryside, although bands of Bushmen also hunted in these parts. The Hottentots were a pastoral people owning considerable herds of cattle and also numbers of small stock. They lived a primitive existence, congregating in small bands or tribes and wearing practically no clothing; they were unclean in their habits and had rather undeveloped ethical and national codes. The Bushmen were an even more primitive people with virtually no possessions other than their bows and poisoned arrows. They lived by hunting game, but also by killing and stealing the cattle and small stock of the Hottentots. Consequently the two races were bitter enemies, although much alike in appearance, the main difference being the Bushmen's smaller stature.

The new settlers soon contacted and traded with the Hottentots, who proved rather unreliable and at times raided the vegetable garden and ran off with livestock belonging to the Company. In fairness, some allowance must be made for the inevitable fears of the Hottentots, primitive though they were, that the White settlers were out to deprive them of part at least of their traditional grazing grounds. The Hottentots were not regarded as a very serious menace, for, not long after the establishment of the settlement, a number of the officials wished to break away from the Dutch East India Company to farm on their own account, and they succeeded in doing so.

Independent offshoots

These independent settlers were the earliest ancestors of the Afrikaner people who today dominate the country politically. In the early years the settlers were encouraged to befriend the Hottentots, some of whom were taken into the service of the Company; but on the whole the Hottentots did not take kindly to service and preferred their independence. With time, friction mounted between the settlers and the Hottentots, who gradually withdrew further into the interior as the settlement expanded.

The Bushmen preyed upon both Hottentots and settlers and came to be regarded very much as vermin to be shot on sight. The settlers experienced many difficulties in the early days of the settlement, however, for, on the one hand, the Company wanted to maintain a monopoly of the trade with the vessels calling at Table Bay for fresh provisions and, on the other, they were frequently harassed by Hottentot and Bushman raids.

Meanwhile, because of the shortage of available labour in the settlement, the Company began to import slaves from Central Africa, Madagascar and the East. The independent settlers, too, acquired slaves, and soon afterwards their farms began to prosper, partly because of such labour and partly because of a more tolerant attitude on the part of the Company.

The number of independent settlers was augmented by the arrival in 1688 of Huguenot fugitives from France. These French Protestants, who fled from their homeland because of their religion, settled in the Paarl and Franschhoek valleys and soon became valuable additions to the settlement. Many were agriculturists skilled in the cultivation of the vine and in wine-making. They introduced the vine into the Cape and established the wine-making industry, which still flourishes in the valleys mentioned, and in other districts of the Western Province.

The administrators in the service of the Company discouraged the use of the French language in the settlement and encouraged the integration of the French and Dutch settlers. As a consequence the French, in a relatively short period, lost their language and became fully identified with the budding Afrikaner people.

Origins of the Coloureds

Another significant development occurred during these early years of settlement in the Cape. A certain amount of miscegena· tion took place between the White settlers and the Hottentots and slaves, and between slaves and Hottentots. The offspring of these unions formed the basis of the Coloured community, whose numbers today exceed one and a quarter million. Among them can still be counted pure-bred descendants of slaves and Hottentots, but generally the Coloured community is a mixture of races with a considerable amount of White blood in their veins, infused throughout the past three hundred years. Among them, too, are descendants of slaves from the East who still adhere to the Mohammedan religion. These are known as the Cape Malays.

Eighteenth-century colonialism

The Dutch East India Company governed the settlement at the Cape for nearly one hundred and forty years. As the authorities at Cape Town were Company employees and not officers of a state department of the Netherlands, they were not particularly concerned with a constructive colonial policy. Their attitude towards the independent settlers was more negative than positive: so long as the settlers obeyed the regulations issued from time to time (which in the main laid down responsibilities and obligations, and a code of behaviour) and did not trespass upon the trading activities of the Company, they were left very much to their own devices.

As the settlement grew, the Hottentots and Bushmen were

pushed further into the interior, resulting in a gradual lessening of live-stock losses because raids by these people were fewer. In addition, both townsman and farmer in the Peninsula and surrounding districts possessed slaves to do the heavy work and to assist them in beating off the intermittent raids. At times, however, the farmers and what militia there was at Cape Town had to engage in punitive expeditions to recover stolen stock or to quieten adventurous bands of aborigines.

But with slaves to do the work and with relative tranquillity in the Peninsula and immediate environs such as Stellenbosch, Paarl and Tulbagh, life in the settlement became pleasant and easy compared with conditions in Europe. The more affluent enjoyed a considerable amount of leisure and culture, which is evident to this day in beautiful homesteads and character furniture inherited from the Cape of the eighteenth century. Many of these masterpieces are the work of craftsmen among the slave population brought to the Cape from the Far East. To such an extent was the White population dependent on slave labour during the eighteenth century that any manual work was regarded as beneath the dignity of Whites. In fact, it was at times even considered *infra dig.* for any White man or woman to be employed at all. To maintain their status, they had to be owners of property or proprietors of the businesses in which they were engaged.

The frontiersmen

Large families were commonplace in those days; and, as the settlement grew, less and less land became available within its recognized boundaries for the younger sons of the landowners. As employment was not favoured, and as there appeared to be limitless land outside the confines of the settlement, many of the younger men trekked beyond the recognized borders and claimed for themselves large stretches of land upon which to graze their stock. This practice was recognized by the Dutch East India Company, which allowed the trekkers to mark off land for their own use. The size of the areas marked off was usually determined by a method of walking a horse for half an hour in each direction, and normally equalled about six thousand acres. A small annual charge, which had come to be known as 'recognition money', was made for the use of the land.

On account of the vast area covered by the holdings of the new settlers, however, the Company was unable to provide them with much protection against the predatory raids of Hottentots and Bushmen, into whose grazing and hunting grounds these pastoralists had moved. The law in many instances did not reach the newly occupied farms. As a result, the trekkers did very much as they pleased in meeting the resistance of the aborigines and in treating with them.

The process of occupying more and more land continued into the nineteenth century, but by the end of the eighteenth century the Hottentot clans in the central and eastern sections of the Cape had already been deprived of practically all the lands upon which they grazed their stock, and of the stock itself. In these parts – more particularly in the fertile eastern districts of the Cape – the position of the Hottentots soon became untenable because, in addition to the pressure from the south, they were subject to pressure from the north by the African tribes migrating southwards. Only towards the north-west were the Hottentot and Bushman clans able to survive the eighteenth century as self-supporting pastoralists and huntsmen. But the pressure from trekkers continued in this north-westerly direction throughout the nineteenth century until the Hottentots were finally pushed to the banks of the Orange River and beyond.

Having been dispossessed of their grazing lands and the stock as well, the Hottentots in the central and eastern districts had either to seek employment with the new possessors of the land or to roam the countryside which only a few years previously had supported their stock. This meant that they had either to live by thieving or to accept employment on the most disadvantageous of terms. If they were caught thieving they were severely punished, so for some time most of them accepted employment, usually without any pay beyond their keep.

They received virtually no protection from the authorities – at that time the Dutch East India Company – and were largely at the mercy of the frontier farmers, themselves by no means well off, their standards of living and culture having seriously deteriorated by comparison with those of their ancestors. The frontiersmen had been removed from civilizing influence for more than three generations and had lived for so long virtually without the law, that they had become a law unto themselves and strongly resented any interference with their customs, habits and way of life, no matter from what quarter.

Practically the only lasting contact that these frontiersmen had with the civilized world, apart from rare visits to Cape Town, was the Bible, which exerted a profound influence over their lives. To this day a section of the Afrikaner people, mainly those from the northern provinces of the Union, differ markedly in character from their relations who remained in the settled districts of the western Cape; and it was from among the frontiersmen predominantly that the Boers of the Transvaal and Orange Free State Republics were drawn.

African tribal movements

During the period of rule – about one hundred and forty years – of the Dutch East India Company at the Cape, very little was known of the happenings in the territories to the north which today form part of the Union of South Africa. Vaguely it was known that these parts, particularly along the coastal belt, were inhabited by black races, but some of the areas of the interior appeared to be only sparsely populated. From the few sources of information available, however, it is now evident that certain African tribes were pressing steadily southwards during this period. Along the coastal regions the Xhosa tribes were in the van of the movement, followed by the Zulus; but in the interior, too, various tribes were on the move.

There was much fighting among them and new groups were

formed from among the remnants of the defeated. In this manner the Basutos came into being and established themselves in the present Basutoland and in parts of the eastern Free State. So, too, various other tribes settled in Bechuanaland, Swaziland, and over scattered areas of the Transvaal. By the end of the eighteenth century the most powerful and warlike tribes were the Xhosas in the eastern Cape, the Zulus in Natal, and the Basutos in the areas mentioned. By then, too, the vanguard of the northward-trekking frontiersmen had met with the south-ward-moving Bantu and the first skirmishes had taken place on the eastern frontier.

British administration

At that time Europe was in a ferment: France and England were in conflict, and Holland was an ally of France. Outside Europe, British influence in the Far East had grown while that of Holland had declined, with the result that the Dutch East India Company was no longer the power it had been. The British, in order to safeguard their route to the East, occupied the Cape after attacking and defeating the local forces. After some years the administration was handed back to the Dutch – not to the Dutch East India Company but to the Batavian Republic. Government by the latter did not last long, for, with the success of Napoleon in Europe and the doubtful attitude of the Netherlands in these campaigns, the British once again occupied the Cape. There was no handing back after the defeat of Napoleon; the British compensated the Netherlands and continued to administer the colony.

This second occupation took place in 1806. At that time the White population of the country numbered only about twenty-five thousand, the slaves in the vicinity of thirty thousand, and the Hottentots – who by then included considerable numbers with slave and White blood in their veins – probably less, for intermittent smallpox epidemics had decimated them on several occasions. The Batavian Republic, in its effort to exercise authority, had introduced reforms which many of the colonists, especially the frontiersmen, resented. On taking over, the British continued this work, particularly the introduction of some law and order into those areas where the frontiersmen in the past had done pretty well what had suited their own interests best.

Conditions on the frontier were in a disturbed state because the vanguard of the northward-trekking Whites had for some years been in conflict with the southward-moving Bantu. Raids and counter-raids were taking place and the situation needed careful handling; in fact, open warfare had broken out on the frontier some years previously. The Kaffirs were pushed back, but an uneasy peace prevailed. In addition, the frontiersmen were having trouble with the Hottentots or Coloureds, as these people could by then be termed: as the terms of their employment by the frontiersmen were often somewhat harsh, and as there were virtually no laws regulating such employment, many of the Coloureds preferred vagrancy to employment. This led to an unhealthy state of affairs on the eastern frontier for both Whites and Coloureds.

The first British governors tried to remedy this by introducing a form of employment which tied the Coloureds to the White employers for varying periods, and by penalizing vagrancy. The task of the new rulers was, however, an unenviable one, for the development of the colony had reached a critical stage and the clash of the different races which were to occupy a common country was now becoming apparent.

After patching up the labour problem of the frontiersmen, the Administration was forced to direct its main attention to the hidden conflict that was being waged on the eastern frontier between the frontiersmen and the Africans. To ease this situation it was planned to bring out British immigrants to the country and place them on farms near the frontier so that they might serve as a buffer between the parties. At the time there was considerable unemployment in the United Kingdom as an aftermath of the Napoleonic wars. There was therefore not much difficulty in finding families willing to emigrate to the colony. Had they known before they agreed to emigrate of the trials they were to undergo, probably few would have volunteered. In some measure they must have been deceived by those responsible for their recruitment. Numbers of these immigrants were brought out, however, and settled in a virtual no-man's-land. This was the first major batch of British settlers to come to South Africa and they became known as the 1820 Settlers.

Humanitarian ideals

In the early years of the nineteenth century a humanitarian movement had come to the fore in England, possibly as a result of the guilty conscience over the exposures of the ruthlessness of the slave traffic, in which England participated in no small measure. A wave of compassion for the Black and Coloured peoples of Africa swept through Britain, influencing the policies of both Church and State. The London Mission Society, which had a number of workers in South Africa, began a campaign against the alleged ill-treatment of the Coloured workers in the eastern districts of the Cape. About that time the slave trade was abolished and a strong agitation for the total abolition of slavery in British colonies was gaining momentum. The London Mission Society asserted that the conditions under which the Coloured community on the frontier was forced to live and work were, in fact, worse than slavery. On the whole, existing records show that the slaves in the Western Province of the Cape, apart from the indignity of being slaves, were not harshly treated, so that there was in all probability a good deal of truth in the Society's assertion.

Afrikaner discontent

While, in general, opinion at the Cape supported the measures of successive British governors designed to force Coloureds to accept employment on the frontier farms and to regulate such employment, the British Government, on the advice of the Mission Society, brought pressure to bear on the governors to reverse this policy. This step proved most unpopular with the colonists, and to this day is regarded as one of the principal causes of the Great Trek northwards. Shortly after this came the abolition of slavery in the Cape, also cited as one of the causes of the trek, but as most of the slaves were held in Cape Town and surrounding districts and only a few on the eastern frontier, this was hardly a compelling reason. The third reason given for the trek was the inadequacy of the protection given to the frontiersmen against Xhosa raids into the colony; yet from 1820 the brunt of these raids must have fallen upon the British community which had been settled on the frontier during that year.

There is no question, however, but that considerable discontent was rife on the eastern frontier and dated from the time the British took over the administration of the Cape. This discontent was in large measure shared by the 1820 Settlers, who suffered severely from their own inexperience of South African conditions and the Xhosa raids. However, it sprang more from the policy of the British Government in London towards the non-Whites in the Cape (both Coloureds and Bantu), than from the acts of local governors, who made considerable efforts to appreciate and meet the viewpoints of the colonists, both British and Afrikaners.

In and around Cape Town the relationship between the established population and the Administration was much more cordial, but even in those parts the good feeling was harmed by the decision to free all slaves, and by the basis on which compensation was paid to the slave owners. Among the Afrikaner frontiersmen dissatisfaction reached such a pitch that in 1838 a large number decided to move northwards to lands beyond the border of the colony, where they would be free of the British concept of racial relationships. These frontiersmen gathered together their families and belongings and set off in covered wagons for pastures new. This was the beginning of the movement known as the Great Trek which resulted, after many hardships, in the founding of the Transvaal and Orange Free State Republics.

While the movement was doubtless intensified by the sense of injustice felt among the frontiersmen because non-Whites now ranked equally with Whites before the law and were permitted to enjoy the privileges of free men, the urge to take possession of further lands for grazing their increasing herds (an urge which had become ingrained in them during the past hundred years) certainly played an important part in this far-reaching decision to trek. The view that non-Whites had any claim to citizenship in the country was foreign to most of the established community at the Cape at the time the British took over the administration: such people were either slaves, Hottentot servants or uncivilized barbarians who were thought – more particularly by the frontiersmen – to be rightly at the mercy of the small White community then occupying the Cape.

The concept that the non-Whites had any rights at all was British, alien and intolerable; nor was it then generally accepted that these people even had any such rights. Today the verdict of the world would be overwhelmingly on the side of the British Government then in power in London; yet to this day among many Afrikaners the attitude of the Colonial Office of that time is regarded as having been oppressive, and ample justification for the desire of the frontiersmen to rid themselves of British administration. What is even more startling is the fact that among many South Africans the attitude of the frontiersmen of one hundred and fifty years ago still persists towards non-Whites. They still refuse to accept the implications of a multi-racial society.

Apart from its handling of the thorny problem of race relationships, regarded at the time as highly provocative, the British administration soon proved its superiority over that of the Dutch East India Company. In the one hundred and forty years of its rule, very little in the nature of constructive colonization was carried out by the Company; but under the British, roads and bridges were built, education was broadened and organized on a sounder footing by the importation of a number of Scottish schoolmasters, the rule of law was widened and applied with greater justice and humanity, a free press was initiated and even a university founded. It should be remembered, however, that the Company was not a state department and never really regarded colonization as its function, for its true purpose was merely the management of a refreshment station on the route to the Far East – not empire-building. Nevertheless, the rule of the Company was in many respects monopolistic, autocratic, and at times corrupt. The colony made headway under British rule despite the frequent Kaffir wars on the eastern frontier and the exodus of the trekkers to pastures beyond its borders.

The Great Trek

In the history of South Africa, the Great Trek is regarded as one of the principal episodes. The trekkers, after leaving the eastern Cape, avoided the coastal belt where the African population was thickest, and moved across the Orange River in to parts which subsequently became the Orange Free State. In these parts a number of Cape families had already settled by the time the trekkers arrived. Here the trekkers split up: some moved north across the Vaal River into the territory which was to become the Transvaal, some chose to settle between the Orange and Vaal Rivers, but the bulk crossed the Drakensberg range into the present province of Natal.

Not long after their arrival, they found that parts of the province were occupied by the warlike Zulu tribes. In fact, not twenty years previously the land here had been overrun and terrorized by the powerful Zulu chief, Chaka, and, as a result, was thinly populated. The trekkers therefore sought to acquire some of the area for settlement and entered into negotiation with Dingaan – a brother of Chaka, whom he had murdered in order to usurp the chieftainship. Dingaan received a party of trekkers under their leader, Piet Retief, but, at a given sign, the Zulus swooped down upon the unsuspecting party and, in an act of treachery, murdered them all, including the leader.

This was a serious blow to the trekkers, but they were soon avenged when they heavily defeated the Zulu impies at the Battle of Blood River. This victory removed the Zulu menace for the time being, but did not end the troubles and disappointments of the trekkers. Some years earlier, a party of British had settled in the vicinity of Durban and had claimed the surrounding area for the British Crown. The trekkers now became a threat to this settlement and, as a consequence, the British dispatched reinforcements from the Cape to defend it. The British feared that the trekkers would exert pressure upon the Zulus and other tribes in southern Natal, thereby bringing pressure in turn upon the Xhosas in the Eastern Cape – with whom the British were having constant friction but whom they hoped to pacify. They therefore extended the area under British sovereignty to include some parts of Natal occupied by the trekkers.

This, of course, was anathema to the trekkers, who had, only a few years previously, left the Cape in order to escape British rule. Many of them now left Natal, and once again they moved off – this time westwards into the present province of the Transvaal, where they joined up with those from the Cape who had trekked there originally.

The Boer republics

Those trekkers who had not entered Natal had also had hardships to face, though not quite the disappointments experienced by the others. After defeating some African tribes, particularly the Matabele, who opposed their encroachment, the trekkers settled down, ultimately founding two republics, the South African Republic (Transvaal) and the Orange Free State. Before these republics materialized, however, several minor republics were established, giving rise to considerable friction and animosity among rival groups and leaders.

In the Transvaal in particular the innate independence and insubordination to government of the former frontiersmen came to the fore, making it extremely difficult for the chosen leaders to exert the authority and impose the discipline necessary to govern with success. In the Orange Free State conditions were more harmonious, although in the early years of the settlement considerable friction arose between the Burghers and the Basutos, many of whom at that time were living within the eastern boundaries of the State. The Cape Colony intervened on a number of occasions in these disputes for fear that disturbances on the Free State-Basutoland border would spread to the unsettled and uneasy eastern Cape frontier.

At times the British administration at the Cape would side with the Burghers, and at other times with the Basutos. For a while the Free State was brought under British protection and guidance, but the vacillation of British policy, dictated from London, antagonized the Burghers and bewildered the Basutos. After some years the British decided to wash their hands of the dispute between Burgher and Basuto and allowed their interest in the territory to lapse. The upshot was the defeat of the Basutos by the Burghers and the driving of the tribesmen from the eastern plains of the Free State into the mountain areas of Basutoland, where they are today. The Basuto, in self-defence, then sought British protection, which was ultimately given. The territory was first annexed to the Cape Colony and then brought under direct British control, which survives to this day.

The question of British suzerainty over the republics established by the former frontiersmen who had trekked from British-held territory was never entirely absent from British policy in South Africa prior to the turn of the nineteenth century. The tendency to regard the republics in this light was fostered by the fact that all the approaches to them were in British hands or defended by British power. But British policy vacillated according to the party in power in Great Britain, and this unquestionably gave rise to much misunderstanding and ill-feeling among all concerned in South Africa.

The absence of a consistent policy did much to bring British administration into disfavour, both inside the Cape Colony and in the newly-formed republics. Despite this, the Cape Colony progressed steadily in many directions, due mainly to British experience and guidance in colonial affairs. On the eastern border, intermittent Kaffir wars were fought and quelled until the Xhosa resistance was finally broken in 1857, when certain of these African tribes fell victim to their own superstitions.

In 1854 the Colony was given representative government, and eighteen years later responsible government. This meant that, from then on, the making of all domestic laws was virtually in the hands of representatives elected from among the Colony's own population. Meanwhile, slow but steady progress was made in the economic sphere; the wool industry flourished, farming generally improved, and copper was mined in Namaqualand. Then overnight something happened which, with one other development, was destined to bring about a far-reaching change in the economy and character of the whole of South Africa: diamonds were discovered in Griqualand West.

Natal

In Natal also the British colony progressed slowly at first, but more quickly later as South Africa in general advanced. The colonists were surrounded by strong African tribes, the Zulus in particular, and care had to be exercised in all dealings with them. For many years the relationships were on a fairly friendly footing, but in the 1870s the Zulus reverted to their former practices, threatening all and sundry, and had to be put down by force.

In the early 1850s a significant development took place in this colony – the first sugar was produced. The industry took root and developed steadily into one of the major industries of the country. At first the pioneers were considerably handicapped by shortage of labour. The Africans at that stage could not be induced to enter the service of the Whites in sufficient numbers. As a result, the Natal administration of the day persuaded both the British and the Indian governments to agree to the export of a number of Indian coolies to the colony for the purpose of working the sugar plantations. These Indians were indentured to the growers and mill-owners for a number of years, but were given the right to settle in Natal after the expiration of their contracts. Many of them did eventually exercise this right, and thus formed the nucleus of the Indian community in Natal, which today exceeds 400,000 in number.

Being a much younger colony, Natal obtained self-government some years after the Cape. In the 1870s Zulu power, which had been weakened by the voortrekkers some thirty years earlier at Blood River, once again emerged as a menace to the surrounding tribes and settlements. On this occasion the Zulus had acquired some firearms and, by the time their power was finally broken, they had about thirty thousand highly-disciplined warriors. As a consequence, the British increased the garrison in Natal, and, as the Zulu threat appeared to be directed more against the south-eastern districts of the Transvaal than against Natal itself, significant steps were taken by Sir Theophilus Shepstone, at that time the British officer administering the government of Natal.

The Colonial balance-sheet

Before passing on to the next phase in the history of South Africa – a phase that heralded the most profound changes in the economic and political life of the country as a whole – it is appropriate to consider the viewpoints and feelings of those elements of the population which had been ground under by the steady advance of the White peoples into the interior of the country. All too little is known of the feelings of these non-White peoples, who today form eighty per cent of the population. At that time the proportion was even larger. In the early days of the White settlement these people were without doubt backward and primitive in their habits, but that does not mean that they were without feeling, or sentiments as noble as some of the best that inspired the White races of that day.

White South Africa, supported by the earlier historians, is prone to represent the Africans and also the early Hottentots as depraved, barbaric and vicious people who ravaged, thieved and destroyed the White man's possessions simply because they were depraved, barbaric and without any code of decency or humanity. These critics seldom stop to ask what they themselves would have done had the land which they and their forefathers had occupied been taken from them by force or guile these being, in many instances, inseparable from the superior civilization of that day. The Afrikaners or the English-speaking South Africans who followed them were no worse than the pioneers who opened up the Americas, Australia, and the rest of the undeveloped world. If anything, they were less ruthless, but that does not mean that the non-White populations were without grievances. On the contrary, no people would have taken lying down such encroachment upon the territory they had come to regard as theirs by right, or even conquest. Naturally they objected and resorted to such means as their inferior equipment permitted in resisting the advance of the White man.

Among White peoples the world over, such resistance would have been regarded as fully justified and been eulogized as brave or stout-hearted, had the victims been White or civilized. But in South Africa where the victims were non-White the resistance was characterized merely as deceit, theft or savagery, without any regard whatever for the feelings or rights of the victims. This attitude would not have been so bad had the victors brought material benefits and enlightenment in which the victims could have shared; but, as so often happened in the eighteenth and early nineteenth centuries, the victors merely seized the land without putting it to very much better use, and what is worse, after pushing the previous occupants off, left them to starve or steal or enter their employ, often upon rather humiliating terms.

When seen through the eyes of the non-Whites, it is not easy to escape the conclusion that the record of the White man in South Africa has not been wholly praiseworthy. Unfortunately, too little is known of the feelings, sufferings and heartbreaks of the non-Whites in their early clashes with the Whites. As they were illiterate, there are hardly any records of these experiences, but gradually the truth is dawning upon civilized people the world over, and South Africa is no exception.

On the other hand, there has been a tendency since the

Second World War to decry all efforts at colonization. While much guilt must rest upon the conscience of nations for their earlier actions in colonizing – and the Americans are no exception in this – much that is constructive and humane has been accomplished by the colonial powers during the past hundred years. A great deal of the progress that has been made in eliminating superstition and tribal massacres, in the prevention of disease, in providing education, and in raising living standards among colonial peoples during the past century, would not have happened so quickly but for the help and guidance and investments of the responsible colonial powers.

In the interest of the future welfare of all concerned, it is necessary that the question of the extension of independence to colonial peoples should be seen in perspective: life does not stand still and no race or people can be expected to accept a subservient role indefinitely in its own land; yet too rapid an emergence from primitive conditions can do more harm than good to an emergent people, the more so as there are nations only too ready to exploit their inexperience.

As far as the Union is concerned, a good deal has been done to educate and house the non-Whites, but much remains unaccomplished. A fair proportion of the Africans and a substantial proportion of the Coloureds and Indians are acquiring education and enlightenment and cannot indefinitely be treated as subject races. Unfortunately, the majority of Whites are slow to appreciate the changing circumstances and find it difficult to accept non-Whites on the basis of merit. For the past three hundred years the dividing line between enlightened and unenlightened, between civilized and uncivilized, rich and poor, master and servant, has been colour, so that the South African – the Afrikaner in particular – finds it very hard to rid himself of this complex. Let us hope that as the non-Whites emerge sufficiently to make their contribution to and explain their case in the literature of the country, their attitude and viewpoints will be better understood.

★

Anglo-Boer antagonism

We come now to the last quarter of the nineteenth century – a period which saw South Africa in convulsion. Hitherto the country had advanced at a leisurely pace; the white man had pushed north and eastwards virtually to the present boundaries of the Union. In so doing, he had broken the resistance of the Hottentots and of the various African tribes, with the exception of the Zulus. He had acquired most of the land previously used by these people to graze their stock. The Hottentots had ceased to exist as independent graziers and the Africans had been confined to limited areas where they could practise their primitive methods of agriculture. They had all been forcibly subdued by the superior techniques and equipment of the white man. The Whites were clearly masters of all the Blacks, except for the well-disciplined Zulu impies. Unfortunately, over the previous fifty years there had been considerable friction between the original White settlers, the Afrikaners and the British Colonial administration at Cape Town and Pietermaritzburg. In the older parts of Cape Colony relations were, on the whole, friendly, but to the north, particularly in the new republics, there was much antagonism towards the British.

The roots of this antagonism can be traced all too clearly to the clash over the treatment of non-Whites. The traditional Afrikaner attitude towards colour was steeped in the traditions of slavery on the one hand, and Hottentot subjection on the other, during the years that the frontiersmen had been virtually a law unto themselves. To the northern Afrikaner of that day, a non-White was a sub-human species, fit only to work in the service of the Whites; independent, he was a menace, and therefore allowed to enjoy only the minimum of rights. The British view of colour, however, was influenced by the guilty conscience which had emerged from the cruelties of the slave traffic in which the British had been extensively engaged. London was determined, therefore, that the non-Whites in its sphere of influence should be treated with justice, should be given rights and opportunities for betterment and, in fact, should enjoy a human status equal to that of the Whites where they could establish that their ability and character warranted it.

Such an outlook was pure heresy to the northern Afrikaner, and in consequence his prime object in life was to escape from British influence. This led to much friction, bitterness and hatred, for even when the northern Afrikaners, the descendants of the frontiersmen, were installed in their own republics, the British would insist upon a code of treatment of the Africans and that the Afrikaners curtail their practice of taking possession of land by forcibly driving African tribes off it. It was in this atmosphere that the far-reaching developments of the last quarter of the nineteenth century were to take place.

Mineral developments

The developments were the discovery of precious minerals – diamonds in Griqualand West and gold on the Witwatersrand – and the clash between Boer and Briton. The discovery of diamonds in 1868 brought fortune-seekers to the Cape from many parts of the world, including some forceful characters who were to play no mean part in the events that followed. It also brought many rough and undesirable characters.

The ownership of the territory in which the diamond fields were discovered formed the subject of a dispute between the Cape Colony and the Orange Free State. Logically the territory fell within the boundaries of the Free State, but the Cape based its claim upon an obscure treaty between the Colony and a tribe of half-castes called Griquas who once lived in that area. The terms of the treaty proved inconclusive, however, and the Cape, to cover its action in claiming the diamond fields, paid the Orange Free State a capital sum which proved ridiculously small for the benefits gained. The Orange Free State naturally resented the high-handed action of the Cape, which was then a British colony, and this caused a deterioration in the relationships between the Free State Burghers and the British, which until then had been not unfriendly.

★

Annexation of the Transvaal

Meanwhile, before gold had been discovered on the Witwatersrand, conditions in the Transvaal had deteriorated. At the head of the Republic was a Cape clergyman with somewhat radical views. In consequence, he was not wholly respected by the Transvaal Burghers, who were fundamentalists in their religious beliefs. In addition, partisan disputes had weakened the Republic, the finances of which were thoroughly unsound. At this juncture the Zulus, who had been undergoing rigorous military training, were causing concern to the Natal administration. It was feared that the Zulu impies would attack the eastern districts of the Transvaal and cause a crisis on the border. To avoid this, Shepstone, at that time Governor of Natal, marched into the Transvaal and annexed the territory for the British Crown – apparently with some connivance on the part of elements in the Republic.

This accomplished, the British, under Lord Chelmsford, proceeded against the armed Zulus. After suffering a severe reverse at Isandhlwana, the British forces finally defeated the Zulus at the Battle of Ulundi and so removed the threat to the Transvaal. In these campaigns the British received virtually no aid from the Burghers of the Transvaal. No sooner had the Zulu threat been removed than the Burghers started a campaign for the removal of British control from the Transvaal. A British column was surprised and badly mauled in an engagement at Bronkhorstspruit, and later a British force under General Colley was defeated on the heights of Majuba. Thus ended what has come to be known as the First Transvaal War. The British made no further attempt to retain their control of the Transvaal, and the Burghers regained their independence. The decisive defeat at Majuba and the tame surrender of the Transvaal by the British (dictated by a Liberal Government in Britain) created a bad impression among the Cape and Free State Afrikaners and caused a decline in British prestige.

★

Gold

Some years after this gold was discovered on the Witwatersrand, and when the wealth of the strike became known another major influx of fortune-seekers converged upon the mining camps at Johannesburg. The population of the town grew with amazing rapidity: the leading personalities associated with diamond-mining at Kimberley transferred much of their time and energy to the new Mecca; engineers from Britain and America gave their services in opening up the reefs; and miners were brought out from Britain to assist in the underground operations.

But with the many useful contributors to the new industry and ancillary services there also came a proportion of blackguards and crooks. Within a relatively short period the population of Johannesburg numbered almost as many as that of the rest of the Transvaal, and Paul Kruger, by that time President of the Republic, feared that the Boer population would be swamped. Accordingly, he virtually denied certain civic rights to the new population, which had come to be known as 'Uitlanders' (Outsiders). This caused much unrest among them led by a group called the Reform Committee, who raised many grievances – some real but others imaginary.

The gravamen of their charge was that the Republic drew its income overwhelmingly from gold mining and ancillary activities, which were financed and operated entirely by the Uitlanders, yet they were not permitted to become enfranchised citizens except under onerous conditions. Kruger was adamant, for he believed that the gold boom would soon pass and the industry decline, and that the Republic could be much damaged, even to the extent of being deprived of its independence, if the franchise were to be given to those who were only temporary residents. There was something to be said, at the time, for Kruger's point of view. The President had proved a strong character amid all these disturbances; but in the Cape an equally forceful personality had come to the fore – Cecil John Rhodes.

*

The Jameson Raid

While Kruger's aims were confined almost entirely to the preservation of the independence of the Transvaal, Rhodes was dreaming of a great future for a united or federated South Africa with boundaries far beyond the Zambezi. Kruger was his stumbling-block and these forceful personalities were bound to clash sooner or later.

Rhodes seized upon the grievances of the Uitlanders to further his cause, but, as events turned out, this decision gave rise to the greatest blunder of his career; indeed, not only for the career and aims of Rhodes but also for South Africa as a whole. Sponsored by Rhodes, a raid into the Transvaal was organized to coincide with an uprising by the Uitlanders in Johannesburg. The raid was to be under the command of Dr Jameson from the Bechuanaland border and its object was the overthrow of the Kruger Government. The raid proved a miserable failure owing to the impetuosity of Jameson and the fact that the Boers had been forewarned. As a consequence the uprising misfired. Jameson and the leaders of the Reform Committee were arrested; the latter were tried for high treason at Pretoria and Jameson was handed over to the British authorities for punishment. The British Government protested its ignorance of the plot and neither Jameson nor the Committee members received severe sentences.

Conspiracy, although practised in many countries at that time (as it is today), had long since been abandoned by the British as a method of dealing with opponents. Nevertheless, among the Boers and also among many Afrikaans-speaking colonials the raid was regarded as evidence of British duplicity. No single act in the history of South Africa has done more to set Boer against Briton. Its influence on moderate Afrikaner opinion was disastrous, for it played right into the hands of extremist Boer opinion. Henceforth the British were not to be trusted. The position of Rhodes as Prime Minister of the Cape became untenable; he resigned and was ordered to Britain to explain his actions and connection with the plot.

For the time being his dreams were shattered, but such was the calibre of the man that from then on he directed his main energies to the territories north of the Union, which today bear his name as their founder – the Rhodesias. Here he accomplished much and to this day is venerated because of his work and the greatness of his vision. And even in the land of his adoption, where he achieved great things but unfortunately blundered badly, he is gratefully remembered for the generosity of his will, under which his great wealth passed to the South African nation. It is said of Rhodes that his health had much to do with the blunder; he was suffering from an incurable disease and knew that his life would be short. In consequence, he grew impatient for the materialization of his ideals and succumbed to methods which proved his undoing. But the greatness of the man cannot be denied, his vision of a greater South Africa stretching from the borders of Tanganyika to the Cape of Good Hope is an ideal of much greater consequence and value to South Africa as a whole than the parochial concept of a small independent Boer republic. If in the end such a greater South Africa fails to materialize, it will be a tragedy far greater than the unfortunate raid.

Growing hostility

From the date of the raid, or even from some years before, the basic difference between northern Afrikaner and Briton – the treatment of the non-White races – became lost in the sharper antagonisms arising from the ill-feeling let loose by recent events. Thanks to gold mining, the Transvaal had become relatively prosperous and was able to spend considerable sums on guns and ammunition. This was to a large extent imported via Lourenço Marques over a newly-constructed railway linking Pretoria with that port. Largely, therefore, because of British capital and know-how, the Transvaal was acquiring arms which, in the opinion of far-seeing observers, could only be used against the neighbouring British colonies.

The Transvaal Boers, however, suspected that the British

had definite designs upon their country because of its richness in gold. Did not the agitation of the Uitlanders and the Jameson Raid point to that conclusion? Therefore the Republic had to be fully prepared and armed. The British, in their turn, became anxious because of certain international portents. Germany had become an exceedingly powerful military state and was developing a colony on the very borders of South Africa, which, since the British occupation of the Cape, had not been threatened by outside nations almost solely because of the power of the British fleet. What if Germany were to be at war with Britain? With the Boer republics armed and antagonistic, and with a large percentage of colonial Afrikaners in sympathy with these republics, the position of the British in southern Africa would be vulnerable indeed.

Relations between the Transvaal and Britain became strained and tense. The Transvaal leaders did not sense the British fears (which the subsequent trend of events in Europe justified) and Kruger, somewhat imprudently, resorted to a number of provocative actions. The British unwisely moved troops to the borders of the Republic as a result. Kruger demanded their withdrawal in an ultimatum which lapsed before the British were in a position to reply. Boer forces then invaded the British-held colonies and the unfortunate Anglo-Boer War began.

The Anglo-Boer War

For White South Africa this was the worst tragedy imaginable, for it embittered relations between these people to an extent that many Afrikaners, even sixty years after the event, still regard the British as an enemy not to be trusted or tolerated. Yet in retrospect one cannot help feeling that, with a little more understanding and toleration on both sides, the war could have been avoided. Personally, I am inclined to agree with the view of Colonel Denys Reitz expressed in his book *Commando* that, while there were rights and wrongs on both sides, the British must bear the greater responsibility for the tragedy;

they were a great and powerful nation and should have exercised greater restraint in their dealings with a small, inexperienced republic. But on both sides the personalities in command were strong, determined men – Kruger for the Boers and Rhodes and Milner for the British – and, as so often happens, such men overplay their hands and tragedy results.

In the early stages of the conflict the Boers gained a series of victories, but as more and more British troops were landed, weight of numbers began to tell. The British invaded the Transvaal and Orange Free State, and soon afterwards both Pretoria and Bloemfontein – the respective capitals – were under British control. The Boers, however, refused to surrender and decided to embark upon guerrilla warfare. While one cannot but admire the tenacity of the Boers, in retrospect this decision can be seen only as a blunder, for it ended in much hardship and tragedy. In taking this decision, the Boer leaders exposed their women and children, and their farms, to the mercy of the enemy, for the men in the field were totally unable to protect them. It was also expecting rather much from a foe that he should leave the farms with their occupants intact so that these could be used as provision centres or look-out posts against him. In self-defence, therefore, the British removed the occupants of the farms to concentration camps and burnt down many farm-houses. Unfortunately, the military authorities underestimated their responsibilities regarding the camps. Women and children were herded together in tents which in many respects were inadequate; moreover, many of the occupants were unused to communal living, and therefore untrained in the elements of hygiene. This the military authorities failed to appreciate, with the result that infectious diseases spread like wildfire, resulting in an appalling and unnecessary death-rate.

Over twenty-six thousand women and children died in these camps. This was a very high proportion of the Boer population, and the responsible authorities deserve the severest censure for allowing such a state of affairs to develop. Naturally these deaths caused great grief and bitterness among Afrikaners, and to this day are regarded by many of them as evidence of the evil intent and ruthlessness of the British. No unbiased person today believes that the deaths were the result of deliberate policy, an opinion spread about on occasion by propagandists among Afrikaner extremists. The deaths were the unfortunate result of unpreparedness, poor organization and lack of understanding of the problem. Not that such causes exonerate the responsible authorities; their guilt remains, and the concentration camp episode lingers as the ugliest scar on British stewardship in South Africa.

The war lasted three years, entering the twentieth century, and ending with the Treaty of Vereeniging in 1902. The British were victorious, but in their struggles the Boers had gained the admiration and sympathy of the world. The British took over the administration of the former republics and a new chapter in the history of South Africa began. In contemplating the events of the previous three years there was not much in which the British nation could take pride, but they soon set about making amends: in the two republics the farms were returned to the owners and generous facilities were made available to rehabilitate them so that the country could return to normal as soon as possible. The public services were reorganized on the British model and sound systems of local government introduced. The mines were restarted and business in general improved rapidly, particularly in the Transvaal.

In the meantime, a feeling of remorse and resentment came to the surface in England. At the outbreak of the war there had been considerable opposition to it, but, as the initial battles went against the British, this opposition gave way to a measure of concern, which to some extent closed the ranks with a resolve to end the campaign as quickly as possible. The long-drawn-out guerrilla warfare accompanied by considerable loss of life, and the disclosure of the deaths and suffering among Boer women and children in the concentration camps, stirred the British public against their political leaders of the day, and the Tories were swept out of office at the next general election. The incoming Liberals, many of whom had opposed the war from the outset, were sympathetic towards the Boers, and in

1905 – only three years after the termination of the war – granted both former republics responsible government. This enabled the Boer leaders to take an active part in the administration of the country.

Union

At this stage a new spirit seemed to pervade the country as a whole. Large proportions of Afrikaans- and English-speaking people throughout the four colonies were inspired by a desire to let bygones be bygones so that a fresh start could be made towards the ideal of one country stretching from Cape Town to the Limpopo. Boer leaders from the Transvaal and English-speaking leaders from Cape Colony responded to this, and a national convention was called for the purpose of thrashing out a basis for the union of the four colonies. The convention met, a constitution was hammered out which was subsequently approved by all four local parliaments as well as the British Parliament, and in 1910 the Union of South Africa became an accomplished fact.

More than a hundred years had elapsed since the British took over the administration of the Cape Colony; much misunderstanding, ill-feeling and resentment had been stirred up during those years, but throughout the period the greater spirits among the White peoples of South Africa must have realized that some form of union or federation was essential for the long-term interests of all concerned. Compromise and toleration had in the end to replace mistrust and strife if South Africa as a whole was to become prosperous and contented. The question now arises whether Union has turned to be out all that its promoters intended. The history of the years succeeding Union will give a clue to the answer.

Attitudes to the non-Whites

Since the defeat of the British force at Majuba, the original and basic difference between Boer and Briton (the treatment

of the non-White inhabitants of the country) was first intensified by the discovery of gold on the Witwatersrand and by
the influx of the Uitlanders and then obscured by the more
intense nationalism of the day. The Transvalers, and for that
matter Afrikaners generally, began to feel an upsurge of
strength, for they had a defeat of the British to their credit, and
the republics were growing in power because of the newly-
acquired wealth in gold and diamonds. Meanwhile the British,
smarting under their defeat at Majuba, were coming to realize
that the Boer republics could be a source of great embarrassment and even danger in the event of a European war with
Germany.

A spirit of British jingoism came into conflict with an awak-
ened and self-assertive Afrikaner nationalism. The climax to
this conflict was the Anglo-Boer War, and after the Peace of
Vereeniging the pervading feeling was that this antagonism
would lead nowhere and that it would be better to live down the
intense nationalisms by agreeing to live together on a basis of
compromise.

The new spirit did not in its early stages, however, take into
consideration the basic difference in outlook on the question
of colour. To some extent, also, the Uitlanders in Johannesburg
became influenced by and in a measure sympathized with the
Boer outlook on this issue. It was really only at the National
Convention, where a constitution for the Union was under
consideration, that the question of the Coloured races again
came to the fore. But this time it was not so much a difference
between Boer and Briton as one between the northern Provinces
and the Cape, where under British rule a liberal spirit on this
issue had prevailed. In fact, some of the staunchest advocates
of this liberalism were Afrikaners with the long tradition of
racial relationships at that time existing in Cape Town and
immediate surroundings.

While the northern territories were quite content with, and
even insisted on, a constitution in which the non-Whites would
have no political rights whatever, the Cape representatives
were not prepared to enter Union without the entrenchment of

those political rights which the non-Whites at that time enjoyed in their Province. A constitution was ultimately accepted by all the territories, and this provided for no non-White franchise rights in the former republics, but secured the voting rights of the non-Whites in the Cape and Natal – in the latter, however, these rights were virtually insignificant.

Afrikaner supremacy

While this compromise ensured the coming into effect of the union of the South African territories, it perpetuated the fundamental difference between the Afrikaner and British outlook on the question of the non-White races – a difference which for almost a century had split the country. Union had been established, but to bring it about English-speaking South Africa had to take on trust the Afrikaners, who henceforth would hold the majority vote. In fact, to such extent did the English-speaking South African accept the Afrikaner as a countryman that not only was he prepared to forfeit any spoils of victory and submit his future to an Afrikaner majority, but, in addition, he agreed to a heavy loading of the country vote (largely the Afrikaner vote) in favour of the city vote (largely the English-speaking vote).

This was a supreme act of faith on the part of the English-speaking South African, but at the time it was hardly questioned, so implicit was the trust that the average British descendant had in the Afrikaner leaders of the day. The English-speaking section in general welcomed the appointment of a Boer leader as the first Prime Minister of the Union. It must be added that neither of the Boer leaders in whom this confidence was placed – Generals Botha and Smuts – ever betrayed the trust reposed in them. But a large section of the Afrikaner people have been utterly unable to see the history of South Africa since Union in this light and have done much to destroy the confidence that gave birth to the Act of Union.

No English-speaking South African has become Prime Minister in the fifty years since Union and, except for a short spell during the Second World War, all Cabinets have been dominated by Afrikaners. In fact, for more than half this period the ruling groups have actually been Afrikaners, who for most of their period of office were in bitter conflict with those Boer leaders in whom the English-speaking section had placed their trust.

What the majority of English-speaking South Africans, and many moderate Afrikaners, failed to appreciate at the time of Union was the depth of colour prejudice that clouded the view of the rural Afrikaner population. At the time it was believed by enlightened opinion both in the Union and in England that, with education and culture, the strong Afrikaner prejudice against non-Whites would mellow and that ultimately the attitude to colour prevalent at the Cape would prevail in the Union as a whole. Unfortunately, this belief has so far proved unfounded.

The Nationalist Party

For some years after Union the colour issue did not figure prominently in politics of the day. The first major split in the political ranks occurred only two years after Union, when General Hertzog was forced to retire from the Cabinet on the language issue. In his view, the Government was not proceeding fast enough with the recognition of Dutch as an official language. His retirement was followed by the establishment of the Nationalist Party to which the more militant and extreme sections of the Afrikaners became attached, but which also included numbers of moderates who felt strongly on the language question.

The First World War

Hardly had the Party been formed than the First World War broke out. General Botha, the Prime Minister of the day, found himself in an extremely difficult position, because, under the constitution at the time, the Union was automatically at war as soon as Great Britain became involved. Botha accepted the situation and proceeded to render the British what aid the Union was able to give. This attitude was resented by many of the former republicans, who staged a rebellion in the belief that their opportunity had now arrived to re-establish the independence of the republics with German aid. Botha suppressed the rebellion but forfeited a great deal of support among the Afrikaners, who now flocked to join the newly-established Nationalist Party under General Hertzog.

Looking back, it is difficult to avoid a measure of sympathy with the rebels, who a mere twelve years previously had been locked in a fierce struggle against the British, whose cause they were now expected to support. On the other hand, Botha's step was a courageous one, and his vision was fully justified since the British won the war.

Unfortunately, Botha died soon after the return of peace and his successor, General Smuts, was not given the Afrikaner support that Botha had enjoyed. Smuts took office, but his short term was plagued by a post-war depression and also by strikes in which blood was shed. This brought him considerable unpopularity among the Labour movement of the day, and in 1924 he was ousted from office by a coalition of the Nationalist and Labour Parties.

Fortune favoured the coalition for a number of years, for the depression lifted soon after it took office and the country enjoyed a term of prosperity. Then, after five years of coalition, the nation again faced a general election. Meanwhile, the Labour Party had disintegrated and the Nationalists decided to face the election purely on their own merits. While they had antagonized the majority of the English-speaking Labourites, they had to a certain extent watered down the Coloured vote, which is usually held against them, by extending the franchise to White women but not to Coloured. Having enjoyed a period of prosperity, the Nationalists had a fairly good case to put before the electorate. But, instead of doing so, they resorted to an election cry which revived the century-old difference between Boer and British about the treatment of non-Whites.

*

The 'Black Menace'

The Afrikaner colour prejudice is really rooted in fear – fear not only of competition from low-paid Black labour, but also fear that, being in the minority, the white man will in the long run be assimilated by the black. The Nationalist leaders played upon these innate fears which had become an obsession with most Afrikaners. This cry of 'Black menace' proved highly successful in gaining votes for the Nationalist Party, which accordingly won the election by a substantial margin. But, it naturally brought about a hatred for Whites on the part of the non-Whites, which has been growing ever since.

The United Party

The victorious Nationalists were unable to see their five-year term of office through, however, for hardly had they taken office after the 1929 election than the world depression of the early 1930s struck its devastating blows. The United Kingdom, after some years of depression, suspended the gold standard, but the Union Government, by not following suit, intensified the effects of the depression in South Africa. Farmers whose products had to be exported were facing ruin, and the country in general was in a shocking state. As a result, the Nationalist Party split and part merged with the official Opposition. In the ensuing election this United Party gained an overwhelming victory and governed the country for the next seven years. They were some of the most fruitful years for the country since Union. The price of gold was doubled and new goldfields were opened up, with the result that the country soon emerged from the depression and began to prosper at an unprecedented rate.

The Second World War

In Europe the depression had brought Hitler into power in Germany and soon that country, armed in defiance of international agreements, was again threatening the peace of the world. All efforts to avoid war failed, and in August 1939, the armies of Europe were on the march again. Britain became involved, and most of the Commonwealth countries immediately sided with her in the struggle.

South Africa hung in the balance; the Government Party was rent from top to bottom, so the question was referred to Parliament. General Smuts led those who felt obliged to enter the war on the side of Britain, but General Hertzog and the official Opposition led by Dr Malan sought neutrality. General Smuts won the day, and South Africa was once more in the field on the side of Britain against Germany. Thus ended the period of co-operation between General Smuts and General Hertzog, which had yielded much for the benefit of South Africa.

As the Germans had stolen a march upon Britain and France in armaments, they went from victory to victory, during which period the Opposition openly sided with Nazi Germany in the struggle. This made matters doubly difficult for General Smuts and his Cabinet; but by exercising patience and tolerance South Africa emerged from the war without an internal upheaval. Again the vision of the Boer General Smuts, who with Botha steered South Africa through the First World War, brought the country safely through the struggle on the side of the victors. His courage and wisdom, which the world recognized, proved a priceless asset to his country during these stormy years. But a prophet is hardly ever honoured in his own country; so, like Winston Churchill in Britain, Smuts was defeated in the first general election after the return of peace.

The Nationalist Government

At this election the 'Black Menace' was once again resorted to by the Nationalist Party in order to gain Afrikaner votes. This time the Party assured the electorate that it had a ready-made solution which would lay the 'Black Menace' for ever: apartheid – a word which since then has been heard all over the world and probably included in the vocabulary of many languages. The promise of apartheid did the trick for the Nationalist Party in the 1948 election, but whether the remedy can achieve what the Party promised is very much open to doubt. Indeed, throughout the world and among many South Africans it is strongly felt that apartheid, far from solving the racial problem, can only aggravate it.

In the first place, apartheid has never been clearly defined by the Party: to some it means the complete separation of the races in separate territories, but to others it merely means official discrimination between the races in every walk of life, although living within a common boundary. Various other shades of interpretation have been advanced, but no one can say definitely what it really means.

Be that as it may, the Nationalists, after gaining power, began introducing relatively mild measures in implementation of their policy. These measures only served to exacerbate feelings among the Coloureds in the Cape towards the White population without achieving very much new in the direction of apartheid. It must be explained that traditionally South Africa, even at the Cape, observed a form of separation among the races in that there was very little social mixing of Whites and non-Whites and, as far as practicable, the non-Whites lived in areas separated from the Whites. This was more or less a voluntary code of behaviour, but the Nationalists sought to give it official sanction.

The people who suffered most under these laws were the Coloureds at the Cape, who were traditionally regarded as an appendage of the Whites and accordingly, under the benign code which characterized the Cape, enjoyed greater consideration and amenities than the Africans. But, as clamour from rank and file Nationalists for the implementation of the apartheid promise became more insistent, more and more measures were introduced in Parliament which purported to be part of a plan for the gradual achievement of apartheid. These measures touched various phases of life among the non-Whites – residential and trading separation, pass-bearing, education, job reservation, trade unionism, freedom of movement, attendance at meetings, and even church attendance. While these measures may or may not conform to a master plan for apartheid, it is very difficult to see in them anything constructive that can lead to complete separation, on the one hand, or satisfied co-existence between White and non-White on the other. On the surface, they are nothing but restrictions on the liberties and meagre amenities formerly enjoyed by the non-Whites.

From the political point of view, the most drastic step taken by the Nationalists has been the removal of the Coloured voters from the common voters' roll and the substitution for it of a severely-restricted separate roll and representation for the Coloureds. This measure required a two-thirds majority of both Houses of Parliament sitting together, which the Nationalists did not enjoy under the constitution. The measure was bitterly opposed by the Opposition, but neither this nor the two-thirds majority under the constitution deterred the Nationalists. After trying various means to circumvent the constitution they ultimately resorted to packing the Senate with their supporters to achieve the whittling-down of the enfranchisement of Coloured voters – a right which these people had enjoyed for a hundred years.

More will be said later about the policy of apartheid, but although the Nationalists have now been in power for about twelve years, the only outcome of their measures, from the historical point of view, is a greater concentration of non-Whites in the economic life of the nation and consequently a greater dependence of the Whites upon the non-White labour force. History will also record that the years of Nationalist rule have brought about a very serious deterioration in race relationships in the country, the outcome of which no one can clearly foresee in this age of emancipation of non-White races throughout the world.

3

RACES AND RACE RELATIONSHIPS

In order to become nations, most countries at one time or another have had to face the problem of accommodating and assimilating different nationalities or races. Even where the races were of the same colour, merging into a people with a distinct national sentiment was in most cases a gradual process involving hardship and friction – the best cement usually being common suffering in a common cause. Where the races are of different colours and at different stages of development, such a blending of peoples is doubly difficult and may indeed be impossible until the more backward of the races succeeded in bridging the gap between the civilizations.

South Africa, as the home of several races of varying colours and civilizations, is confronted with the most perplexing and formidable of tasks in trying to create a nation. The very concept of a people with one national sentiment within the borders of the Union is frowned upon by many – particularly by the ruling races. As a consequence, the major groups into which the population of the Union is divided live side by side, each claiming the country as its homeland, but some refusing to acknowledge the rights of others in this their common country.

To add to the problem, the different races and nationalities are each prone to fan the embers of their distinctive brands of nationalism to the exclusion of the others. This accentuates suspicions and prejudices and dims the chance of the emergence of a South African outlook acceptable to all. Foreigners will no doubt see the folly of this attitude, for it seems that the people of South Africa are building a nation divided against itself; but only those living in the country can appreciate the stresses that give rise to it. The merging of different peoples into nations is a process which has been going on in history since the earliest

77

times, and one tends to believe that this process is an inseparable part of the evolutionary forces moulding the future of men and nations. A primary function of evolution, it would seem, is the advancement of the more backward civilizations; and as this takes place the path of assimilation between different peoples should become smoother. Time, therefore, is an essential feature of this process.

In South Africa, however, deep-rooted convictions and prejudices are thwarting the process of evolution: the privileged are seeking to retain their privileges indefinitely, and many of the underprivileged are determined not only to remove the privileges, but to banish the privileged class from the country. Nevertheless, it seems that policies in South Africa which are opposed to evolution must in the long run be ground under, for evolution cannot for long be deflected. Opposition to it will not only lead to humiliation and defeat, but may also result in much hardship and suffering.

This is the predicament facing South Africa – perhaps not in the immediate future, but inevitably sooner or later, if the country does not adjust its course in line with evolutionary trends. The attainment of a common national consciousness in South Africa is something that appears almost impossible in the near future, and it is as well that those who live in countries outside the melting-pot should appreciate how unpleasant and dangerous our future is likely to be. South Africans need the sympathy of the outside world, not uninformed criticism.

To understand the toughness of the problem, it is necessary to know something about the races and nationalities that live within the Union. In the outline of the country's history, mention has been made of the differences which have plagued the Afrikaans- and English-speaking South Africans over the past one hundred and fifty years. The antagonisms between the White peoples have been staged in an arena where the majority of those present have been non-Whites – Africans, Coloureds and Indians. The spectators have hitherto played a subordinate role. But can this state of affairs continue indefinitely? Can the Whites afford the luxury of bitter recrimination among themselves, and expect the non-Whites to respect them in this atmosphere and be content to live their lives in subservience? The obvious answer is, No.

Before attempting to forecast the future trend of events, let us examine the character and outlook of the different peoples who populate the Union. These fall into five main groups, according to numbers, the Africans, the Afrikaners, the English-speaking South Africans, the Coloureds, and the Indians. None of these is a truly homogeneous group, although the Afrikaners may appear to be. The Africans can be split into four main ethnic groups, but in fact are made up of many more tribes subject to different loyalties. The Afrikaners are linked by a common language, but in their formative years had roots in two distinctive soils. The English-speaking, besides those descended from the peoples of the British Isles, include a considerable proportion of Jews from all over Europe. The Cape Coloureds are a mixed race, not all followers of the Christian faith, as the Cape Malays are included in this group. The Indians include both Hindu and Moslem.

The Africans

The Africans are the most numerous but also the most primitive of the peoples inhabiting the country. Except for a relatively small number who entered domestic and farm service, the Africans did not leave their native kraals in any numbers until the present century. Detribalization can be said to have started then, yet today over two million adult males are employed on the farms of the Whites and in mining, manufacturing, commerce, transport and other services.

While a considerable proportion have progressed in the skills of these activities, most of the Africans are still regarded as unskilled labourers, although this term means something very different from what it did even thirty years ago. The progress would have been considerably greater had the advancement of the African not been thwarted by a colour bar or by the fact that the migratory system does not lend itself to efficient labour in industry. At first the African, as far as practicable, avoided entering the service of the white man and had to be forced to leave the kraal through the imposition of hut taxes, but for some time now the economic pressure of poverty in the Reserves has forced him to seek this employment.

In his primitive state the African male was not a worker, but a warrior; he did not tend the cattle, nor sow and reap the land – this was left to the women. His adaptation to modern industrial conditions has thus meant a major upheaval in his mode of life. To the African reared in the kraal, the demands and complications of modern city life are bewildering in the extreme, and in some ways the negation of all he learned from his elders. On top of this, he has been subjected to a mass of restrictive legislation which the legislators themselves would be hard-pressed to interpret. As a result, he often finds himself in jail for offences of which he is unaware or does not understand, and which are in many cases no credit to the South African statute book.

This transition from kraal to modern industrial centre has been going on for many years and is still in full flood. It has created major problems both for the native and for the community into which he has been sucked by the advance of industrialization. Successive governments have failed to face the problems, with the result that inadequate amenities, e.g. housing, have been provided for the detribalized African. Because they are herded together in ghastly slums, with virtually no outlet for the exuberant spirits of the younger generation, crime has become rampant in these Black locations, and protection is inadequate for the vast majority of the law-abiding in these places. Belated efforts are now being made to catch up with the backlog in African housing, but the problem has not yet been tackled on an adequate scale.

The uprooting of the African from the primitive, indolent life of the kraal and his transplantation to the modern industrialized city is a major operation, accompanied by many perplexing physical and human problems. Its successful implementation could have been achieved only at considerable cost by a humane and sympathetic administration. Unfortunately, such an administration has not as yet made its appearance in South Africa, largely because the majority of the privileged Whites – those who exercise power – have been unsympathetic and even negligent, generally indifferent to the perplexities and sufferings of the uprooted people, and not prepared to spend the sums that successful transplantation would have required.

Beside the neglected problem of the detribalized African's transplantation, another pernicious development affecting the African has been taking place: the system of migrant labour. Under this, the African works for varying periods of up to two years at a stretch in the industrial centres or on the farms of the Whites, and then returns home to his family in the kraal for shorter periods before taking up work again in the White centres. During most of his working life, therefore, the African lives away from his wife and family and is housed in a form of barracks where men are herded four to eight in a room. This system was initiated by the large mining companies in the early days of mining development, and no doubt could be justified as a temporary measure, but it has now persisted for more than seventy years and is even encouraged by the present Administration as preferable to the settlement of African families in the large industrial centres.

The system is thoroughly bad and can never become a permanent feature of the economic life of a highly-industrialized country. Besides being inhuman, thus resulting in many social evils, it is extremely wasteful of working time and of skill. The long periods of absence from work in the kraals are sheer waste of working time and highly detrimental to the acquisition of skill in industrial employment. In a competitive world, industry based on this system of labour must in the long run succumb to that based upon the more efficient use of the worker. In South Africa this system has unquestionably lowered the level of African earnings, particularly as migrant workers have been brought into the country in large numbers from neighbouring territories; and seems bound to undermine South African industry.

In the education of the African, the record of South Africa is not bad compared with that of education in the backward countries of Asia and Africa, and even parts of Europe. Illiteracy among the Africans is still high, but considerable progress is being made towards its reduction. For this improvement a debt of gratitude is due, in the first place, to missionary effort in South Africa, and in the second to the late Mr J. H. Hofmeyr, who was Minister of Finance and also of Education when the finances available for education were placed on a more liberal basis. It cannot be said, however, that the African community in the Union has made much progress on the road to civilization. Numbers of individuals have acquired academic degrees and the African generally has proved his ability to master semi-skilled jobs in industry, but there is as yet little evidence that he has initiative, business acumen, or ability to organize or manage. His emergence from tribalism has been too recent to have given him much opportunity to display these qualities, which come not with book-learning but with background and experience.

The African is in the throes of a dangerous transition from primitive tribalism to modern industrial civilization. It is unthinkable, therefore, that at this stage all Africans should be enfranchised without reasonable qualifications to establish their level of civilization. Universal suffrage is hardly justifiable under the best of conditions, but in a country such as the Union, where half the population have no idea of the meaning of democracy, let alone its implications, it can only result in the sabotage of all that has been created by the civilized elements.

The white races have unquestionably pioneered the Western standards of physical achievement, culture, and individual liberty in South Africa, and in the interests of all concerned, White, Brown or Black, they should retain control of government for the foreseeable future. This does not mean that the non-Whites should have no say in the affairs of the state. On the contrary, they should be given adequate representation, should be fully consulted on matters directly affecting them, and should be given full scope to take part in the development

and administration of the country; but until they are qualified
in the more advanced requirements of Western civilization and
can satisfy the white races in the country that impartial justice
can be expected from them, there will be little sense in the
Whites surrendering their leadership – for without such satisfaction this would amount to suicide.

People outside Africa must realize that there is a vast difference between the Union of South Africa and countries like
Ghana or Nigeria. In those the white populations are negligible,
being largely government officials or big merchants who spend
only part of their lives in the territory, so that independence
brings very little hardship for the Whites. In the Union, on the
other hand, there are over three million Whites who have made
the country their home and who have played the principal role
in developing it into a modern, industrialized state. Nowhere
yet is the African in a position to provide the quality of government necessary to administer a modern state such as the Union.
But it is understandable that Africans want to rule themselves
in accordance with the principle 'Better to reign in Hell than
serve in Heaven', and in countries like Ghana and Nigeria this
is possible without much hurt to others. In the Union this is not
so, for inexperienced and bad government can bring ruin to
three million Whites and disaster to the country as a whole. It
is imperative, therefore, that the Whites should hold the reins
in the Union for many years to come.

A question of the utmost importance to the Union on this
issue is whether the Africans have it in them to follow in the
footsteps of the Whites. This is largely a matter of the quality
of the races. There are those who feel that the African is thousands
of years behind the European in development and that it must
take him thousands of years to catch up. While it is true that
it has taken the European thousands of years to create the
civilization we know today, it does not follow that the African
is going to take thousands of years to reach the European's
level because he is only now emerging from barbarism.

Creation and assimilation are two very different processes:
as a rule, it takes very much longer to create than to assimilate

and it may well be that, under the stimulus of modern knowledge and education, the African will be able to assimilate
Western civilization and culture in a relatively short time, if
encouraged and not thwarted. Anthropologists tell us that the
brain of the African is no different from that of the European
and that there is no reason to believe that he cannot reach the
same heights of achievement and culture. Many who have
practical experience of the various races doubt this, however,
and are convinced that, intrinsically, the African races are not
the equal of the European in intelligence potential and creative
ability. In support of this they point out that among individuals
in any group there is a wide range of intellect – among Europeans from the genius to the half-wit. They feel that if an
average intelligence for all humanity could be determined, a
large proportion of Europeans would rank above average in
intelligence, while an even larger proportion of Africans would
rank below average. This would make the European races as a
whole vastly superior in intelligence to the Africans, although
there would still be a material overlap in which a considerable
percentage of Africans (the upper layer in intelligence) would be
superior to a fair percentage of Europeans (the lower layer).

Personally, I am very much inclined to support this theory,
although it is possible that, with better opportunities of education and higher living standards, the average intelligence among
Africans could show a material improvement. This, however,
would take many generations. History seems to support this
theory, for in almost every walk of life the record of the European over the past two thousand years has been infinitely
superior to that of the African. Excuses, such as climate and
disease, have been made in defence of the African's poor record,
but they are by no means convincing.

None the less, the existence of the overlap already mentioned
is fact, and failure on the part of the Whites to recognize it can
only mean trouble in the long run. The Portuguese, the French,
and Belgians recognize this fact, hence the superior status
given by them to the *assimilados* and *évolués* among their African
populations.

In my own mind, I am so convinced of the inherently superior intellect of the European that if, in fairness to the African, a system of franchise could be devised dependent upon a relatively high standard of education and achievement, irrespective of colour, I believe the European would retain the majority vote in this country for many generations to come. The African possesses many admirable qualities – particularly in his natural state in the kraal: he has respect for authority, a sense of humour, almost unlimited patience, and, in the case of many tribes such as the Zulus, an exceedingly high code of honour. With these qualities go the superstitions and practices, often cruelties, of a primitive people.

In the white man's efforts to bring civilization to the African he has unfortunately concentrated too much on the negative side of the process: he has passed laws to suppress the superstitions and practices, but has done very little to encourage and fortify the African's excellent natural attributes. In fact, through indifference to and neglect of the human aspects in the life of the Africans, especially during the process of adaptation to the modern industrialized state, many of the excellent qualities have deteriorated and decayed.

In bringing a primitive people to work in highly industrialized centres, special legislation to protect both Whites and Africans is necessary. Hence there are a number of laws on the statute book of the Union in which provision is made for such protection, and these laws are fully justified – particularly if they are regarded as temporary measures until the Africans have acquired the elements of modern civilization and adapted themselves to industrial conditions. Unfortunately, in addition to these measures, many laws have been passed – particularly in the past twelve years of Nationalist rule in the Union – which are wholly restrictive and discriminatory against the African. They were passed solely for the benefit of the Whites, largely to protect the privileges enjoyed by them as part of the policies of apartheid and White supremacy. Frustrating in the extreme, they are bitterly resented by the Africans.

In consequence, these laws and the indifference and neglect

referred to are undermining the good qualities inherent in the African and bringing to the surface a hatred of the Whites, the outcome of which it is impossible to foretell. Until recently the Africans in the Union were loyal only to their respective tribes, but today a Black nationalism is lifting its head. This development is, of course, not the result of conditions within the Union only; it is spreading throughout the African continent, fanned at times by the emancipation and rise of the non-White peoples throughout the world, and to some extent exploited by Communism. Essentially it is a process of evolution; yet here in the Union every effort is being made to stamp it out, regardless of the fact that the movement is world-wide.

Any realist sees in these acts the futile efforts of a King Canute. Unfortunately, the restrictive legislation and the active opposition to the rise of Black nationalism can only intensify the hatred of the Africans for the Whites and inflame the very nationalism that the authorities seek to suppress. Without a far-reaching change and a more human approach in the attitude of the authorities to the non-Whites in the Union, it is difficult to see how a head-on collision between the Black and White nationalisms can be avoided.

The Afrikaners

The second largest group in the Union are the Afrikaners. They are the descendants mainly of the Dutch and French settlers who came to the Cape in the latter half of the seventeenth century. Their numbers have, however, been augmented from time to time by small additions of people of Dutch, German and even British descent. The language of the group is called Afrikaans, which is derived principally from the Dutch of Holland. While the vocabulary is very similar to that of Dutch, the speech has taken on the character of a distinct language because of the long separation of the early Cape colonists from, and their lack of contact with, the Dutch in Holland.

Today approximately sixty per cent of the White population of the Union falls within this group. They number about

1,750,000, and are probably the most homogeneous group in the country, although not as homogeneous as many of them are wont to believe, because for more than one hundred and fifty years there was a sharp division in outlook, customs, temper and culture between those who remained in the Western Province or Boland and those who continually trekked in search of pastures new. In fact, two distinct growths had been produced by the end of the nineteenth century – one with firm roots in the older districts of the Cape and the other with roots frequently uprooted and replanted over the northern expanses of the country.

With the conquest of the Transvaal and Orange Free State by the British, the growth in wealth of the north as a result of the development of gold-mining, and the coming of Union, this difference began to blur as more and more of the southern Afrikaners moved north in search of better opportunities which the gold industry had brought. Moreover, as the administrative capital of the Union was at Pretoria, this contributed too to attracting many southerners to the north.

Then, as industrialization spread and more and more Afrikaners left the land to take up employment in industry, a sprinkling of the northerners moved south to the industrial centres of the Cape. So, after nearly one hundred and fifty years of separate development, the twentieth century has seen considerable integration of the earlier separate growths. Despite this mingling, however, there are still strong traces in the Afrikaner people of their separate roots, although they can hardly be demarcated by geographical boundaries. Many Afrikaners still draw their inspiration from and conform to the codes practised by their forebears from the older districts of the Cape. Others are attracted by and imbued with the outlook and concepts of the earlier frontiersmen and their descendants in the former republics. While at one time it appeared that the more tolerant attitude of the Cape would prevail, prosperity in the north and persistent propaganda have greatly strengthened the more extremist wing of Afrikanerdom.

In the eighteenth and nineteenth centuries, which were the

formative years of the Afrikaner people, those who were constantly on the move northwards were augmented from time to time by small numbers of southerners, but those who sank their roots in the older parts of the Cape were the more influential and affluent sections of this community. They were mainly agriculturalists, although there was a fair sprinkling of merchants, industrialists (wagon-builders), and professional men among them.

The agriculturalists produced wheat, fruit and wine, reared horses, and ran livestock for meat, milk and butter production. They were a substantial people who owned large farms, lived in most attractive houses, and possessed distinctive and attractive furniture. Until the abolition of slavery they were virtually an aristocracy of estate owners, for all their hard work was done by slaves, who in many instances formed a substantial part of their wealth. In the earlier years they received little school education, but they were a cultured and alert people with a strong religious background. On the whole, their treatment of the slaves was humane and considerate.

Very different were those who were constantly on the trek northwards; they included a fair sprinkling of young men looking for adventure, but mainly they were drawn from the less affluent and influential sections, virtually unable to find employment in the older districts of the Cape because of the use of slave labour. They trekked northwards with few possessions to settle in areas previously unoccupied by the Whites, there to run livestock and to hunt.

The form of tenancy and the right to the farms occupied by these frontiersmen, as authorized by the Dutch East India Company, have already been described. The process of occupying more and more land by the growing numbers of frontiersmen went on throughout the eighteenth century. But the lands occupied were previously the hunting grounds and pasture lands of the Hottentots and Bushmen who, when the frontiersmen took occupation, had either to flee to more remote areas or enter the service of the Whites.

The frontiersmen in the main were not agriculturalists, but

pastoralists and hunters. The land they occupied was on the whole poorly developed and little of their produce entered the trade of the country. As farmers, they produced principally for their home needs and not for the market. Consequently their standard of living was primitive; their homes were rough-and-ready structures with very few comforts and only the bare necessities for furniture; their food was coarse and lacked variety; their clothing scanty and home-made.

Many even lived in covered wagons, trekking from one part of the country to the other in search of adequate pasture for their stock. Their children received very little schooling and for a number of generations their only contact with the written word was through the Bible. This being their life, it stands to reason that their level of civilization deteriorated seriously compared with that of their countrymen in the south. Culture almost faded from their lives. The redeeming feature of their existence was, perhaps, their strong attachment to the Bible. This probably saved them from an unhappy fate, but it nurtured in them a narrow, austere, fundamentalist concept of religious conduct and principle which often laid greater stress upon the outward observance of religious rites than upon the development of character or the exercise of brotherly love.

This simple, crude life, isolated from friends and relations and virtually out of range of authority, was bound to leave its impression on the character of these people. They developed resourcefulness, self-reliance and bravery in the face of physical danger, but they also became undisciplined, intolerant and extremely self-righteous (possibly the result of their concept of religion). As the principal obstacle to peaceful existence on their newly-acquired farmlands was the presence of displaced Hottentots and Bushmen, who, in resentment and in order to survive, thieved wherever possible, the frontiersmen developed an extremely harsh attitude towards them, which ultimately became a phobia against all men of colour.

The tragic fact about these people is that during those formative years they were being conditioned to an unrealistic form of life, which could not endure but which had to end when the land available for further trekking gave out, and when evolution and industrialization demanded recognition of the rights of the non-White, underprivileged peoples. To this day a large proportion of Afrikaner opinion has failed to grasp the implications of the century and a half spent in isolated and virtually undisciplined life on the veld.

When the British took over the administration of the country in the first decade of the nineteenth century, the two sections of the Afrikaner people were in striking contrast: in the older districts lived the aristocrats, on the whole cultured and well off, but on the frontier an increasing number of the pastoralists and hunters were eager to trek farther north and eastwards to occupy and settle new lands in accordance with their custom. But at this stage the farms they sought were not the pasture lands occupied by Hottentots or Bushmen, but those already in use by the African tribes in the process of trekking southwards. This head-on clash between frontiersmen and Africans opened a new chapter in the history of South Africa. The British administration sought to introduce a measure of control over the activities of the frontiersmen in this respect and introduced measures to regulate the relationship between frontiersmen and displaced Hottentots, which was getting out of hand.

Many Afrikaners will dispute the sharp distinction I have drawn in this chapter between the descendants of the former frontiersmen and those whose forebears were nurtured in the older districts of the Cape. The difference has been blurred since Union because of the intermingling of the sections since that date, and also because of the general and rapid improvement in conditions in the Transvaal and Orange Free State that resulted from the mining of gold and the prosperity that this brought. Nevertheless, by the close of the nineteenth century a marked difference did exist between what might be termed the colonial Afrikaners and the republicans.

At that stage the colonials were clearly the more enlightened, cultured and advanced of the two sections. For this, some credit must surely go to the British colonial system under which Afrikaners were given the same rights, protection and opportunities as were extended to the colonials of British descent. Some Afrikaners will, however, deny that this was so, because Dutch was not accepted as an official language at that time. This is true, but it should be remembered that when the British took over the colonial administration of the Cape the White population numbered barely twenty thousand, of whom large proportions were virtually illiterate. In the circumstances, the Colony hardly warranted two official languages. While attempts were made, off and on, to anglicize the colonists, it cannot be said that the Administration deliberately discouraged the use of Dutch in social and religious spheres. On the contrary, the Scots who were imported into the Colony as ministers of religion and teachers rather encouraged the use of Dutch, for they realized that they were more likely to succeed in their professions through the medium of that tongue, and the Afrikaans language first took root and made headway in the Cape – a British colony – and not in the republics to the north.

On the whole, the colonial Afrikaners prospered, and not until the Anglo-Boer War did there appear to be any deep-seated dissatisfaction among them with the gradually-evolving developments under British rule. This was not the case with the republican elements, who were constantly at loggerheads with the colonial administration. They were an unfortunate people, who throughout the nineteenth century believed that they were being deliberately persecuted by the British. For this reason more than any other they trekked from the Colony to escape British rule. Yet if the facts and occurrences of those days could be judged dispassionately and in perspective – particularly in the light of current sentiments and beliefs the world over – it would be hard to escape the truth that many of their hardships and frustrations were not so much due to injustice on the part of British administrations as to their own unfortunate circumstances and misconceived beliefs.

The early frontiersmen were a neglected and virtually disowned people. As a result, they were prone to take the law into their own hands and resented any form of discipline. They came to regard their practice of taking possession of more and more land, first from the territory occupied by the Hottentots and then from that occupied by different African tribes, as an inalienable right. In this process they paid scant regard to the traditional interests of the dispossessed tribes, whom they evicted without much compunction.

While this procedure was not uncommon in earlier colonial days, by the nineteenth century the prevailing sentiment in civilized countries was disapproval of the alienation of individual or communal possessions or rights of a conquered people without some form of compensation. This concept had no place in the code of the frontiersmen. As far as the fertile plains of the Cape, and later of the Transvaal and Orange Free State, were concerned, these passed by conquest to the victors with little or no compensation to the victims. Instead, the dispossessed tribes had either to seek refuge in the mountains and deserts or to accept service with the conquerors on rather one-sided terms. In the minds of the frontiersmen, the Hottentot or Bantu tribesmen were humans of an inferior species who had no right to occupy pasture lands required by a superior species. To them, this was the inalienable right of the superior and not merely a privilege due to their possession of better weapons.

In the nineteenth century, however, this doctrine of the right of possession had already given way to a more humane one: superior force, wealth or brainpower had come to be regarded as a privilege and not a right; and the continued enjoyment of these privileges received approval only so long as the superior force actually existed and the privileged exercised their superiority in a humane manner towards the underprivileged. In the circumstances, no conscientious administration worthy of the name in the early days of the nineteenth century could have condoned the practices of the frontiersmen. Consequently the policies of the early British colonial administration were not without merit, and in broad outline, although not in all their details, deserve a greater measure of approval than hitherto given them.

This interpretation of privilege as a right exists to this day among a section of the Afrikaners. It had its origin in the formative years of the people when they were continually trekking to new pastures without the necessary curb of law or discipline. This cult of privilege, as I have chosen to describe it, instead of diminishing with the years as enlightenment spread, became strongly entrenched in that section of Afrikanerdom whose spiritual ancestors were the voortrekkers. This has been so partly because of the interpretation placed upon certain episodes in South African history and partly because of fundamentalism in religious beliefs.

In the teaching of history in this country undue prominence has been given to the voortrekker movement. It is true that the people were courageous, and experienced hardships, but to represent all of them as heroes and saints who were persecuted, suppressed and harassed by an unjust British administration is not a true picture of this episode. In the clash between the trekkers and the British, the latter were certainly not bent on victimization, but merely tried to hold the scales of justice fairly between the different populations in the country. They may have been tactless and short-sighted at times, but they did not deny the frontiersmen any fundamental rights.

What they sought to do was to put some curb on the privileges these people had exercised in the past in alienating by superior force lands previously used by Hottentot and Bantu tribesmen, and to protect the latter against what appeared to them to be rather harsh treatment. Indeed, under present-day concepts of colonialism the British would be open to criticism for not having done enough in this direction. Yet most Afrikaner versions of history to this day picture the voortrekkers as a persecuted people escaping from the clutches of a tyrannical administration. It is this slant on South African history – the deification of the voortrekkers – that has contributed largely to the firm conviction among a section of the Afrikaners that certain types of privilege are inalienable rights. While the voortrekkers themselves can be exonerated for having held such beliefs, their perpetuation in successive generations of Afrikaners is unwarranted and can only have unfortunate consequences for the country as a whole. Indeed it is a travesty of history that the colonial Afrikaners, who were the most advanced and cultured, receive scant recognition, while the republicans are exalted, for it is from the colonial Afrikaners that the leaders in most walks of life have been drawn.

The other contributory factor to this cult of privilege is the fundamentalist teaching of the Scriptures. Ministers of religion have indoctrinated a section of the people with the belief that Afrikaners are a God-chosen people placed by Divine Will in the southern tip of Africa in the interests of humanity at large. This belief has ingrained a self-righteousness in many of them and a conviction that certain privileges are absolute rights. It also accounts in no small measure for the Nationalist Party's attitude that its adherents are the only true South Africans and that the Party has an inherent right to govern the country in the interests of its supporters (notwithstanding that these comprise only about ten per cent of the population), and that it is entitled to govern no matter how it distorts the constitution.

This idea of privilege has been evident in most of the stormy episodes of South African history over the past one hundred and fifty years. It started with the early frontiersmen, culminating in the Great Trek. The history of the Boer republics, in particular that of the South African Republic, provides considerable evidence of this, and Kruger's stand against the demands of the Reform Committee, no matter how sympathetically this may be regarded in other ways, cannot but be judged in this light, if seen in perspective. While Kruger's fears on that occasion were real enough, the fact that all the approaches to the Transvaal were protected by the British and that the backbone of Transvaal economy was provided by British capital, enterprise and, to some extent, labour, cannot be ignored.

A more recent example of this cult of privilege is the political use of the Afrikaans language to eliminate the influence of English-speaking South Africans from the public services of the country. So, too, is the mass of racial legislation and the rather shabby manipulation of the constitution of the Union by successive Nationalist Governments during the past twelve years. Even the system of farm taxation – particularly where it relates to well-to-do farmers – could be cited as an example of extending privilege to Afrikaners, for it is very doubtful whether such favourable taxation provisions would have been extended to farmers if they had been predominantly English-speaking.

The past twelve years will surely be seen by future historians as a period of deprivation of rights of certain sections of the community for the sole purpose of boosting the privileges to be enjoyed by Nationalists. Throughout the mass of racial legislation enacted there are virtually no provisions that could be said to confer benefits on anyone other than the Nationalists, whereas in almost every enactment there has been a curtailment or a diminution of the rights of others. Predominantly this deprivation of rights has been at the expense of the poorest elements of the population, the non-Whites, but in a more subtle way even the English-speaking South Africans have seen many of their sentimental attachments and even some of their rights whittled away in order to satisfy sectional privilege.

The Nationalists always see the Afrikaners as a persecuted race – persecuted mainly by British imperialism. But this at least can be said for the British, that they never discriminated against Afrikaners in the electoral laws. Afrikaners have always had the same rights in British-controlled territories as people of British descent. In the Cape Colony, Afrikaans- and English-speaking peoples were accorded the same political rights, but not so in the South African Republic under Kruger. Moreover, since Union, because of the system of underweighting country constituencies, the Afrikaner voter has been given a measure of privilege. Yet, not satisfied with this, the Nationalist Government has gone out of its way to manipulate the electoral provisions in favour of its supporters.

In the past twelve years the Nationalist Party has not hesitated to govern the country in the interests of its supporters, notwithstanding the fact that it derived its power – a large parliamentary majority – from a minority of voters. The Jameson Raid has always seemed to me a rather shabby attempt on the part of Rhodes to gain control of the Transvaal: but is the Nationalists' device of establishing their power through distorted electoral provisions any less shabby, as the Nationalists themselves seem to think?

The cult of privilege can be said to have paid dividends to the Nationalists. It has so far been successfully exploited, and few would begrudge this success were it not for its ultimate implications. The exercise of privilege is, unfortunately, a form of action that inevitably invites reaction detrimental to the privileged, and sectional Afrikaner privilege seems unlikely to prove an exception. The existing policies of the Nationalist Government towards non-Whites must ultimately lead to an unfortunate, if not disastrous, reaction against the Whites in South Africa. On the economic front alone the reaction is likely to be disastrous if present policies are persisted in.

The English-speaking group

The English-speaking members of the South African community make up the third group. They are not as homogeneous a group as the Afrikaners, for, although the majority are of British stock, included among them are the Jewish people, many of whose ancestors came from countries outside the British Isles. Nevertheless, the English-speaking section has been and still is largely influenced by British standards and outlook, although in speech and habit the English-speaking South African differs markedly from the average Englishman or Scot. Just as the average Australian or Canadian has developed a distinctive personality, so has the South African of British descent. The influence that British traditions and way of life have upon the English-speaking South African is something that the Nationalist Afrikaner tends to resent: he feels that the only true South Africans are those who have shed all sentimental attachments to the countries from which they have come, and he does not hesitate to accuse his countrymen of British descent of not being true South Africans.

To the impartial observer, however, it is strange indeed how little sentiment the Nationalist Afrikaners have for their countries of origin – mainly Holland and France. During the

Second World War most hard-core Nationalists were strongly pro-Nazi, despite the fact that their original homelands were overrun and exploited by the Nazis. To understand this extraordinary attitude of mind one has to go back into the history of these people which shows that the early ancestors of the Afrikaners were virtually fugitives from the parent nations: the French Huguenots because of their religion, and the Dutch colonists because of their opposition to the high-handed methods of the Dutch East India Company. In consequence, they do not feel indebted to the countries of their forefathers.

This has not been the case with the bulk of the immigrants from the British Isles. Apart from early friction between the 1820 Settlers and the British authorities, very little has occurred over the past one hundred and fifty years to alienate the English-speaking sections from the home of their ancestors. On the whole, the South African of British descent has been well treated by his country of origin: as the new country developed, he was given more and more authority in running local affairs, and he always had the rich heritage of the British Isles to draw upon in planning his life in the former South African colonies. Furthermore, during the main period of immigration from Britain, substantial improvements in world communications were gradually taking place, making it possible for the immigrants to keep in fairly close contact with relatives and friends overseas. Why, then, should they break their early ties, which have brought them far more good than harm? Indeed, South Africans in general are heavily indebted to the British Isles in almost every walk of life: in administration, in finance, in mining and industrial know-how, in education and culture generally, and also in sport, the British contribution to South African welfare has been made on a munificent and unselfish scale.

When the British took over the Cape from the Dutch East India Company, they did not regard the country merely as a refreshment station, but set about its colonization in an enlightened manner. Naturally they made mistakes, but after picking up the threads of the earlier administrations, their administration was directed towards the betterment of conditions for all concerned – Afrikaners, British settlers and non-Whites generally. They built roads and bridges, encouraged trade, improved what system of education existed, introduced legal and administrative reforms – all at a critical time when the eastern frontier was in a ferment as a consequence of the clash between the northward-trekking frontiersmen and the Africans moving south.

Many of the reforms introduced, and the abolition of slavery, were fiercely resented by the Afrikaners in the first half of the nineteenth century, but in the light of present-day ideas most of the steps taken were fully justified, although at times they could have been effected with a little more tact and considera-tion for Afrikaner susceptibilities. While many of the reforms were mainly in the interests of the non-White population, and as a consequence strongly opposed by the Afrikaners, it can be claimed for the British servicemen and settlers that they bore the brunt of the fighting in the subjugation of the Africans – certainly more British than Boer heroes were lost in the process, because they consistently had to face the more warlike of the African tribes, the Xhosas and the Zulus.

In addition, when the country faced an economic revolution as a result of the discovery of diamonds and gold, it was again the English-speaking peoples who provided the capital and know-how for this step forward. Unfortunately, many of the new immigrants were unpleasant characters who did more harm than good to British influence. On the other hand, many Cornish miners gave their lives in the early development of the gold industry. They were victims of the deadly phthisis that scourged the first mining endeavours on the Witwatersrand. Workers today are almost immune against this disease, but the underground pioneers suffered torments. Their sacrifices have received little praise or recognition, but the country is deeply indebted to them.

Since the turn of the century, Afrikaners have made rapid and material progress in both the cultural and economic life of the country, but it can hardly be denied that over the past one hundred and fifty years, since the British occupation of the

Cape, economic and cultural development in the country has mainly been pioneered by the English-speaking section. This is in no small measure due to the fact that they had a considerable advantage over the Afrikaners because of their close ties with the culture and enterprise of Great Britain.

Even today the English-speaking section controls the main share of the economic life of the nation, other than farming. It is understandable, therefore, that the English-speaking South African strongly resents the gibe that he is no true South African because he retains sentimental ties with the people from whom he stems. He is rightly proud of the achievements and traditions of his forefathers, and considers it inhuman and ungrateful that he should break those ties of blood and achievement that bind him. He feels that his section of the South African community has made contributions second to none to the welfare of the country, and that, despite his sentimental attachment to Great Britain, he has as deep a love for, and as vital an interest and material a stake in, his homeland in southern Africa as any other section. In fact, he firmly believes that his ties with the Old World have enriched, not impoverished, South Africa, and that the retention of these ties will continue to do so, while their severance can only mean material and spiritual impoverishment through isolation in an unfriendly world.

He is also fully convinced that in general the Nationalist Afrikaner, who insists on a policy of 'South Africa alone', would have been a less self-centred and self-righteous person and a spiritually richer character had he retained some sentiment for, and contact with, the lands from which his forefathers came – Holland and France. This view is shared by many Afrikaners, who also feel that only enrichment can flow from material and spiritual contacts with countries beyond the national horizon.

A point which many Nationalists fail to understand is that the English-speaking South African's attachment is not so much for present-day England, Scotland or Wales, but specifically for the British Commonwealth, which is a living and evolving entity of which he has never ceased to be a member. In this he has been no different from the average Australian, Canadian or New Zealander, and just as these people do not regard their attachment to the Commonwealth as in conflict with their more specific attachments to the lands in which they live and work, so the English-speaking South African regards his. After all, everybody has multiple attachments – to his school, his home village, his province, and to his country. Is the English-speaking South African so much at fault when he takes his loyalties a stage further and embraces the Commonwealth? Is he not, in this, displaying a greater maturity than those whose loyalties end with the countries in which they live? Isolationism on the part of a section of the Afrikaners is one of the major tragedies that have befallen this country over the past century. It has cost us dearly in the past, but instead of abating it has taken on a more virulent form over the past twelve years in that, to preserve a pure Afrikaner culture and species with roots in an impossible way of life, it strives to isolate every section of the country's complex community according to ethnic and cultural origins. That way lies national disintegration and ultimate ruin.

English-speaking South Africans, for all their contribution to the development of the country, have at times displayed weaknesses and suffered failures – more particularly since the advent of Union in 1910. While on the whole the British colonists did not assume an aggressive attitude towards their Afrikaner countrymen during the nineteenth century, they did develop a spirit of jingoism in the last decade of that century. During the period of the Uitlander agitation in the Transvaal, and during and immediately after the Anglo-Boer War, there was a tendency to assertiveness which did not endear them to Afrikaners generally – indeed, it gave rise to considerable suspicion on the part of the Transvalers in particular.

Much of this attitude is attributable to the aggressive leadership of Rhodes and Milner, whom most Afrikaners to this day regard as the worst enemies ever to set foot on South African soil. Yet from an objective standpoint these two probably possessed the most far-seeing and constructive minds of all the Britishers who rose to eminence in this country.

Probably a greater poison to harmonious relationship between English- and Afrikaans-speaking South Africans during this period was the superiority complex displayed by many Englishmen and some English-speaking South Africans. Nobody cares to accept an inferior role, and when people, unconsciously or deliberately, assume a superior attitude, they are disliked. This superior attitude was a rather objectionable trait in a certain class of Englishman in the early years of this century, and when it was used to belittle the Afrikaans language it hurt the Afrikaner badly and made him more determined than ever to enforce his language upon the country. It must be added that, generally, the Scots were never guilty of this attitude.

While throughout the latter half of the nineteenth century it was the desire of the British to bring about a *rapprochement* between Boer and British colonial in South Africa in the form of either a federation or a union (the Anglo-Boer War was largely fought for that purpose), once Union was achieved it was the British and not the Boers who faded out of the political life of the nation. In fact, since Union the English-speaking section, other than the Jews, has played a rather passive role in the affairs of the country. During this period the country has not thrown up, except in business and sport, an English-speaking South African of stature – certainly not in politics. Indeed, in politics the South Africans of British descent have relied almost entirely upon the moderate Afrikaners to express their attitude on major issues.

While a passive role of this kind served a purpose after the Anglo-Boer War as an antidote to the aggressive attitudes of Rhodes and Milner, there are many who believe that it has now gone too far to be in the interests of the country generally. It is at present placing an almost impossible burden on the moderate Afrikaners, who are accused by their kith and kin of being traitors to the Afrikaner cause. It has also contributed in no small measure to the shabby treatment extended to the Coloured people of the Cape since Union, but particularly by the Nationalists during the past twelve years. A stronger and more active attitude on the part of English-speaking South Africans is definitely called for – particularly on the issue of colour, for it is on this issue that the future of the country is being endangered by the purblind, biased and selfish policies adopted by the Nationalists.

It is fully appreciated how warily English-speaking South Africans have to tread when they come up against the fear complex of extreme Nationalism on the issue of colour. On this question, as on the historical role of the British in South Africa, the extremists are devoid of reason and refuse to face facts. On the slightest provocation they will become dogmatic and insulting, making it extremely unpleasant for the average English-speaking parliamentarian to express his views openly and with conviction. This should not, however, deter the English section from active participation in politics. The country is the poorer for the lack of forceful presentation of the English-speaking South African's point of view. And in the long run even the Nationalists would have greater respect for them if they were to come out more forcibly and aggressively with their views, instead of sheltering behind the opinions of the moderate Afrikaners.

It is not only in political life that the English-speaking section has been inclined to coast during the past fifty years. In educational and cultural spheres also, they have not pulled their weight. The Afrikaners have many achievements to their credit during this period, but the English appear to have concentrated mainly on money-making and sport. They have to a considerable extent avoided the nobler but less remunerative professions; and it is certainly to their discredit that for many years they have been unable to provide an adequate number of teachers to staff the English-medium schools.

The trouble is that, generally, the English-speaking South Africans have attained a level of comfort and leisure in the Union virtually unparalleled in any other part of the world, and this has done them a considerable amount of harm. They do very little physical work, which is mainly in the hands of the non-Whites, and the lower-paid professions, including the public service, are filled principally by Afrikaners. So long as their business interests or their sport are not disturbed, they appear to be quite content to accept life as it comes their way. Yet this is no time for such complacency. Apart from the fact that citizenship demands a spirit of service, time is running out for the white man in South Africa. While many may enjoy their creature comforts to the end of their lives, it is not at all certain that when their children grow up, they will be as fortunate. South Africa needs its English-speaking citizens as much as it does the moderate and level-headed Afrikaners; the country will have to look to them more than to any others to build the bridges that can lead to racial peace and understanding in this complex, multi-racial country. Certainly, the non-Whites will not indefinitely accept the role of a voteless and underprivileged proletariat; they may allow themselves to be led for years to come, but they will undoubtedly refuse to be *driven* any longer. Let us hope that English-speaking South Africa will not be found wanting when that day arrives.

The Coloureds

The fourth group is the Coloured population – a heterogeneous mixture derived from the slave population brought to the Cape from parts of Africa and Asia by the Dutch East India Company, the indigenous Hottentots, and the Whites of both nationalities. The traditional home of this group is in the Cape Province, where miscegenation among the races began in the early days of the Cape and has continued throughout the three hundred years of its occupation by Whites. Mixed marriages between Whites and non-Whites were, however, infrequent, the infusion of White blood into the group resulting mainly from illicit relations.

The population of the group today exceeds one and a quarter million, but in colour and appearance its members differ widely – from near-White to pure Hottentot. Of all the sections in the Union, it has the highest birth- and death-rates, and since with better medical attention the latter is tending to fall, its rate of increase is also the highest in the Union. As a mixed race, these people have no firm roots or traditions and their background is somewhat tragic. With the exception of a small section called the Cape Malays, who have tenaciously clung to the Mohammedan religion of their ancestors, most of the Coloureds have adopted Christianity and the customs and outlook of the West. Hitherto those with White blood in their veins have taken considerable pride in it, but this attitude is rapidly changing. Where the degree of whiteness exceeded fifty per cent it has always been the endeavour of the people concerned to pass as White. Recent laws, however, have made it much more difficult to transcend the racial barrier. This may in the long run be a blessing in disguise to the Coloured population, in that it may force them to take greater pride in their community and so knit themselves into a more homogeneous group with greater powers of self-help. Until now they have been victims of the cruel colour and race prejudice in South Africa. Because they are descended from slaves and displaced Hottentots, they have been looked down upon by the Whites; and those with strong traces of White blood – the half-castes – have been ostracized and have become outcasts.

Besides suffering from the stigma attached to colour in South Africa, this community has also been the victim of strong liquor. The early Hottentots, like the Indians of America, sold their birthright for a few gallons of liquor, and this craving for strong drink appears to have been inherited by the majority of the Coloureds. Also, as in America, the Whites, instead of helping the Coloureds to resist its abuse, actually exploited their weakness for personal gain. Not only were the Hottentots deprived of their cattle and grazing grounds through their weakness for strong drink, but for over two hundred years the Western Cape has been producing wines and spirits, the bulk of which has been and still is being disposed of to the Coloured community almost without restriction.

The havoc that this has wrought upon the health, moral fibre and living standards of these people is shocking, and an ugly blot on the record of White stewardship in the Union. As a result, misery and abject poverty have been the lot of the majority of these unfortunate people. This curse, together with the blight of having been born Coloured in a country where colour is a mark of inferiority, has deprived many of them of self-respect and ambition. In the rural areas the majority are cowed, submissive and servile, yet these are the traits that are regarded by their masters as the hallmarks of good Coloured folk. Where they display independence of spirit, and assertiveness, and stand up to any injustice on the part of their masters – traits usually praised in white men – they are regarded as disrespectful and bad Coloured folk. Their existence has been tragic indeed in these parts. In the cities and large towns, however, a fair proportion have been able to rise above the handicaps and succeed in maintaining human dignity and being sober, hard-working and thrifty.

As a people they are often criticized in South Africa for their improvidence, promiscuity, lack of cleanliness and moral fibre generally. Their poverty and drunkenness are ascribed to these weaknesses in their character; but there is some confusion here between cause and effect. Many who know them and appreciate the cruel handicaps under which they have lived during the past century and more are fully convinced that, given opportunities and an existence in an atmosphere where the colour of their skins is not a sign of inferiority, a number of them could become first-class citizens and the average would not fall far below the average of any community anywhere. They are not a people just emerging from tribalism like a large proportion of the Africans; they have been living for the past two hundred years within a civilized community, but unfortunately in its shadows and not its sunlight.

As most of the Coloureds live in the Cape Province and their education falls under the Cape administration, they have been relatively well treated in this respect in recent years. Large numbers are passing the departmental senior certificate examination (matriculation) annually, and their standard of education is increasing steadily. The children display a keenness to learn, and there is a considerable measure of latent talent among them. In the past lack of opportunity and education has stifled the expression of this talent, but slowly, under the guidance of sympathetic Whites, it is now being brought to the surface. In spite of their handicaps, they have displayed some excellent qualities over the years: they have shone as craftsmen; they have shown considerable bravery in face of danger; and they possess an excellent sense of humour. Without doubt, the material is capable of being turned to good account.

Because of their being a mixed race, with little tradition and background on which to build racial pride, they lack cohesion and self-assurance as a people. Consequently they have in the past tended to lean too heavily on White guidance and leadership. Their reward for past loyalty to the Whites has been virtual betrayal by the Nationalists, who unfortunately act for the Whites at present. This has given rise to disillusion and bitterness towards the Whites in general. This disillusion, however, is likely to instil in them a race-consciousness and a determination to seek their own solutions to the problems which beset them. If it leads to greater cohesion among them as a national group, the Nationalist rejection of their loyalty to the Whites may be a blessing in disguise. It will make their life harder and less pleasant in the immediate future, but if they can emerge a united people imbued with self-respect and self-reliance, they will have achieved something that no Whites will be able to ignore. The hope is that they will seize their opportunity and not succumb to Communist and other propaganda which can only bring them into further conflict with the present ruling race and further suffering and disillusion. No purpose will be served if they adopt a sullen, negative, anti-White attitude; instead, it will pay them handsomely if they face up to their past weaknesses by adopting a positive attitude towards group improvement. There is much scope for them in this direction. They must fight drunkenness and improvidence with all their resources, and concentrate on developing their talents through education and otherwise so that they can make their contribution to the literature and arts of the country.

They have it in them. For leisure, let them enter whole-heartedly into sport, for which they have considerable liking and aptitude. By these means they will achieve full citizenship in South Africa much sooner than they believe. It will pay quicker and higher dividends than recourse to sullen discontent and political agitation. In the adoption of a positive and constructive policy towards group improvement they will have the assistance and sympathy of a large body of Whites in the country, and industrialization and evolution are definitely on their side.

The Indians

Lastly there is the Indian community, resident mainly in the province of Natal. Its number is approximately 450,000, comprising largely Hindus but including also a proportion of Mohammedans. The bulk of them are descendants of the indentured labourers brought to the country about the middle of last century to work on the sugar plantations in the then colony of Natal. Today this section of the population is subject to much criticism within the Union. Not being indigenous, and keeping largely to themselves, they have become the most unwanted people in the country. White South Africans tend to resent them because they add to the total of non-Whites in the country, and the Africans at times have been none too happy about their presence.

They have not fused with Africans, and continue to live a life rather alien to conditions in the Union, largely because of their religion – the rest of the population, Whites and non-Whites, being mainly under the influence of Christianity. The Indians are therefore regarded as a community apart – a bit of Asia transplanted into an African setting where European culture and standards dominate. They are, however, an industrious and intelligent people, and as such the most advanced and affluent of the non-Whites in the country. Along with the other sections of the non-Whites, they are subject to restrictive legislation, and in fact have no political representation whatever in the councils of the country, being in this respect worse off than the Africans and the Coloureds.

In recent years antagonism towards the Indians on the part of the Whites has become intensified because, as a result of their appeal to their mother country, India, the latter has spotlighted the complaints of the South African Indians in the Assembly of the United Nations.

The problem of civic rights for these people is a vexed one, and there is much to be said for both sides in the dispute. Under normal standards there can be no gainsaying the claim of the South African Indian to political and economic rights, for these people have now been in the country for nearly a hundred years and have certainly given their labour and energies freely in the development of the Union. Generally speaking, those who employ Indian labour will agree that for the price paid it is the most profitable in the country. But the Indian does not blend satisfactorily with the rest of the community: his outlook and philosophy are alien to the country, and despite all the years he has been in Natal, he is still basically an Indian and an Asiatic. Ethically he conforms to different standards in his business dealings, and is prepared to accept living conditions which, in open competition, will undermine the European standard of life recognized in the country.

This attitude is in direct conflict with Western concepts of industrialization, which seek and thrive upon ever-higher living standards for the workers. The Indian has probably inherited this willingness to accept lower wage-scales from the over-populated conditions prevailing in his mother country. To become a true South African, he must outlive his attachment to an Indian outlook and to Indian conditions, but this will be a slow process because of his religion and Indian affiliations. While one can sympathize with his aspirations for full citizenship in the land of his adoption, he must recognize that, on the whole, he is far better off economically in South Africa than are his relations at home. In one respect, however, he has been an example to those Whites who are fearful that their particular race or nationality will be swamped by the Blacks among whom they live and work, for the Indian has kept his race pure for over a hundred years, despite the fact that he has been surrounded by Africans in far greater numbers.

Nations normally evolve out of a fusion of different peoples living within defined borders, but fusion implies a common interest for all concerned and presupposes equal opportunities and, in the end, equal rights for the various groups, irrespective of race or creed. The achievement of all this may take centuries, and in the meantime the people affected may have to pass through many phases before attaining that common national consciousness which is the hallmark of a nation.

In the formation of the older nations there was almost invariably a phase where a master race lived side by side with a subservient one, and the outcome of this phase has inevitably been ultimate fusion and a common cause. Nevertheless, at the present stage of her development, it is hard to visualize a fusion of the groups that now populate the Union. The Whites of both nationalities are determined that it shall not come about, and what makes the problem in South Africa particularly tough is the fact that the Whites, the most advanced section, are outnumbered four to one by the non-Whites, most of whom are not only backward but primitive, and in many cases just emerging from tribalism.

What, then, is the future of South Africa? Can the country thrive and exist as an entity through all the vicissitudes that an average nation is called upon to face, and yet deliberately keep the races within it divided and bitterly antagonistic, one against the other? Or will evolution ultimately make the country conform to pattern in the formation of nations? In the following chapters we shall examine future possibilities in the light of current facts and knowledge.

4

POLITICS AND POLITICAL PARTIES

THE long-term outcome of the co-existence of different races in the Union is not the issue examined in this book. It is almost impossible for anyone to foresee the state of the world or of any country in the distant future. Conditions are changing so rapidly that concepts and viewpoints long accepted and cherished may be jettisoned in a relatively short time. The intense nationalisms and racial differences which today plague the international scene may be things of the past within a hundred years. It is quite likely that national boundaries may not have the same significance, or that racial prejudices will not be so universal and insistent as they are today.

Co-existence and racial admixture

Evolution appears to be moving in that direction; its prime objective in the economic sphere seems to be the advancement of the underprivileged and hence the narrowing of the gap between rich and poor, between one race and another. This it is achieving through the spreading of industrialization which brings in its wake improved communications, better education and more extensive travel, resulting in enlightenment and the breaking-down of the barriers of misunderstanding and prejudice. In the circumstances, a dogmatic outlook is out of place under present conditions, for what is most detested and feared today may well have vanished in the world of tomorrow. Our emphatic dislikes and fears concerning racial integration may well mellow in the more enlightened and less troubled atmosphere of a tomorrow where evolution has done its job of ironing out inequalities of privilege and wealth.

In South Africa such a development would make possible a common national consciousness among the diverse elements making up the community, which alone could mould us into a nation. There is even the possibility that such a consciousness could be acquired without much loss of racial purity on the part of the distinctive groups in the community, for there is no evidence that a literal blending of the races of the world is an essential part of the process of evolution. The clearly discernible objective of evolution in the social sphere too is the ironing-out of inequalities among men and nations through advancement of the underprivileged – not the intermixing of the races. This is incidental and the result of human frailties. In fact, there is a natural tendency, also essentially human, for like to seek like, and it may be possible voluntarily to strengthen this tendency, so that miscegenation among different species of the human race could be reduced to a minimum.

It is true that, in the formation of the older nations known to us, there has been a high degree of blending of the different peoples comprising them, but there are also instances of groups which have maintained their separate identity throughout the centuries. And in the modern world, with its massive achievements in science and its growing knowledge of eugenics, we should be able far better than our ancestors to keep the races pure, if it is desirable. If, however, evolutionary progress should result in a blending of the races of the world, the process should hold no terrors for us here in South Africa, for our development would then merely be in line with that of the rest of the world. While admixture of races is still taking place in some parts of the world, there is little evidence to show that it is an essential phase of evolutionary progress, and any conscious effort to keep a race pure seems both legitimate and laudable, provided that in doing so the rights and aspirations of other races are not withheld, nor their progress thwarted.

★

Baasskap

This brief reference to the question of racial admixture has been made merely to illustrate that the ultimate outcome of racial differences in South Africa is largely in the hands of Providence, although evolution does not appear to dictate an inevitable blending where races live side by side. Generally speaking, the different races in the Union, with the possible exception of the Coloureds, earnestly desire to maintain racial purity, and even the Coloureds are growing more and more conscious that they constitute a distinct group. If, therefore, the hypothesis is right that evolution postulates the elimination of economic and social inequalities but not interracial admixture, it should be possible to integrate the different groups to achieve a national consciousness common to all and yet retain a fair measure of racial purity. Obviously this will be no easy task and will demand much self-denial and possibly suffering. On the other hand, a common national consciousness can never be achieved by keeping alive the inequalities of the past. We can never become a nation in the true sense of the word so long as we maintain the attitude of *baasskap*. Baasskap is the belief, firmly held by most Afrikaners, that in everyday life the White man should never accept a situation where a non-White, however enlightened, exercises authority over a White, however depraved. In other words, in every walk of life the Whites should always be the masters and the non-Whites the servants. Baasskap must sooner rather than later end in conflict and disaster, for it flagrantly opposes the course of evolution. As an alternative, apartheid has been advanced, but whether it is possible at this stage of the history of South Africa will be examined later.

Politics and Privilege

We in South Africa cannot escape the fact that we are a multi-racial society, and no party policy that does not take this fully into account can hope to succeed for any length of time.

With the progress of science and the spread of education, every section of our community will be striving for improved living conditions and will also be seeking, as an indisputable right, an effective say in the formulation of those conditions. While people are backward, weak and divided, they will for a time accept domination by a more enlightened and better-equipped group – but not lightly, and then only if they can be persuaded that they will stand to gain through submission.

Human nature being what it is, however, no people, whether White or non-White, will indefinitely accept a position of inferiority. As they become educated and have access to the universal pool of knowledge, they will inevitably claim the benefits of such knowledge. Any denial of those benefits will be fiercely resisted, to the death, if necessary, for they are gifts bestowed on mankind as a whole, and not merely on those who happen to discover the keys that unlock Nature's secrets. The acceptance of these facts is universal, and as a result the collective urge of emancipated humanity for better living conditions and the abolition of privilege manifests itself in the relentless drive which is identified with evolution. Yet, while the demand of peoples throughout the world for the abolition of privilege becomes daily more insistent, a large section of the White population in South Africa openly seeks to entrench the privileges they have hitherto enjoyed by denying rights to and retarding advancement by non-Whites.

Disproportionate representation

Politics in South Africa are somewhat removed from the world of reality. Being human, we are really only able to legislate for the foreseeable future, yet our governing politicians, instead of pursuing policies that aim at providing stable conditions for that future, persist in passing laws and administering the country for the benefit mainly of one section of the community.

It stands to reason that such policies result in bitter resentments and hatreds, the ingredients that stir up defiance and revolt within national borders and open warfare between nations.

The professed aim and justification of such a policy is the maintenance of White supremacy, on the grounds that the country has been civilized and developed largely through the efforts of the Whites. Unfortunately four-fifths of the population of South Africa are non-White, so that justification for a policy of discrimination against the four-fifths would appear to rest on a poor foundation.

To most people abroad this policy of discrimination is shortsighted, for to them the shape of things to come in South Africa will ultimately be determined not by the many discriminatory and restrictive laws passed in recent years, which have as their avowed objective the protection of the White races, but by the relentless march of events springing from forces beyond human control. In explanation it must be admitted that, of all institutions in the Union, Parliament is surely the most unrealistic. Its atmosphere is extraordinarily foreign to South African conditions generally. While South Africa purports to be a democracy, its Parliament is by no stretch of the imagination representative of the people who live in, work in and mould the country. Furthermore, much of the legislation enacted during the past decade has been provocative in the extreme and manifestly disruptive of harmonious conditions among the people who should make up the nation.

That such a state of affairs can exist in a well-developed country in the second half of the twentieth century is a phenomenon that requires some explanation. Before that, for the benefit of those who do not know conditions in the country, it would be as well to give some of the facts which make Parliament so foreign to South African conditions. The people over whom Parliament exercises power comprise the populations of the Union and of South West Africa. Together they are at present roughly: 10,000,000 Africans, 3,000,000 Whites (of whom about 1,750,000 are Afrikaans-speaking and 1,250,000 English-speaking), 1,400,000 Coloureds and 450,000 South Africans of Indian origin. These people, since the 1958 elections, are represented in Parliament, made up of a General Assembly and a Senate, as follows:

PARLIAMENTARY REPRESENTATION

Party or Group	Number of Members: Assembly	Senate[2]	Total	Approximate Numbers represented	Ratio of Members to People represented
Nationalists	103	77	180	1,500,000 Afrikaans	1 : 8,400
Opposition Parties	53	8	61 {	1,250,000 Eng. sp. 250,000 Afrikaans }	1 : 24,500
Coloureds	4	1	5	1,400,000 Coloured	1 : 280,000
Africans[1]	3	4	7	10,010,000 Africans	1 : 1,430,000
South African Indians	Nil	Nil	Nil	450,000 Indians	: 450,000

[1] The African representatives were abolished during the 1959 Parliamentary Session.

[2] Legislation is now being formulated to reduce the number of senators and to alter the basis of their election.

No matter how these figures are analysed, it is impossible to find any underlying logic that justifies such a representation of South African opinion. Indeed, the whole thing is fantastic and proves beyond doubt that Parliament in South Africa is an unrealistic body unrelated to the true conditions that exist in the country. As far as the non-Whites are concerned, their actual representation is even worse than that disclosed in the table, for among the 253 members there are no non-Whites. This is because the electoral laws provide that they can only be represented in Parliament by Whites, who in some cases are unfortunately not wholly acceptable to the majority of the people they actually represent.

While representation bears little relation to the populations of the various groups, there are indisputably sound grounds for not extending such representation proportionately to numbers in the case of the non-Whites for the simple reason that many of them – particularly Africans – are as yet ignorant and un-civilized and without the faintest appreciation of the principles of democracy. On the other hand, actual conditions in the country warrant far greater representation by the non-White groups than previously extended to them, particularly when account is taken of the contribution these groups make to the economic life of the country as a whole. In this respect it should be remembered that the Indians and the majority of the Coloureds are neither ignorant nor uncivilized, and that a large and growing number of the Africans are today operating modern industrial tools and performing tasks the exact equivalent of those performed by people in Western countries who have full civil rights. Many among these groups are enlightened and cultured people, and they can only regard the fact that no non-White may represent his group in Parliament as a reflection upon the colour of their skins, and a cause for bitter resentment.

Not only do the electoral laws differentiate between White and non-White, but, as the table shows, there is discrimination against English-speaking people also. This is largely, but not entirely, accidental. The grounds for any such discrimination cannot be ignorance or backwardness, for the English-speaking people, together with those Afrikaners who support the United Party, include among them the major share of the business acumen, industrial know-how and professional skill to be found in the country. Furthermore, this group contributes far more in taxation to the revenues of the country than do the Nationalist supporters. While the upper levels of the latter are highly educated, well-to-do and cultured people, the lower strata include a large number only recently rescued from poor-Whiteism, and below the White average in the country in intelligence, culture and achievement.

Much of this differentiation in White representation is accidental and due to the tendency of the better-off English-speaking South Africans to congregate in the more prosperous suburbs of the cities, while the majority of the Nationalist supporters are distributed over the country districts and in the less affluent city areas. This distribution of the White population has had the effect of giving the United Party large majorities in a small number of city constituencies and the Nationalists smaller majorities in a very much larger number of constituencies throughout the country, consequently giving the latter more members in the Assembly.

Another contributory factor in the uneven distribution of members is the system of loading urban constituencies, where

most United Party supporters live, with approximately thirty
per cent more votes than are included in the rural ones, where
the majority of voters are Nationalists. This practice was introduced at the time of Union to offset the sparseness of the rural
population and the greater effort required of the rural voter in
registering his vote. At that time there was a considerable
English-speaking labour vote in the cities, so that this system of
loading can be interpreted as a measure designed to protect the
Afrikaner voter – predominantly rural – against the English-
speaking voter – mainly urban.

The system was actually sponsored by the leaders of the
former South African Party – the predecessor of the present
United Party, with the result that their plan to protect their
Party has actually recoiled against it. While there may have
been legitimate grounds for such a system of loading at the time
of Union, there can be none at present. Conditions have altered
radically since those days, for the motor-car and the construction of excellent roads have removed any disadvantage previously suffered by the farming community in recording votes.
Today the system is just plain discrimination against the city
voter.

Nationalist aggravation

While the Nationalists cannot be blamed for these fortuitous
circumstances favouring their Party under the existing electoral
system, they might well have recognized their advantages
and been content to let the matter rest there. The Nationalist
Party, however, does not see the fortuitous advantages in this
light; to its members they are merely incentives to gain further
advantages under the electoral system. In consequence, they
have exploited these advantages as grounds for weighting the
elections still more in their favour: they have altered the laws
relating to the election of the Senate and have *packed* that
Chamber to a ludicrous extent with their supporters; they have
removed the Coloured voters (traditionally United Party
supporters) from the common electoral roll – a right enjoyed

by these people for over a hundred years; they have extended seats in Parliament to representatives in South West Africa, where the substantial German vote is cast against the United Party because of its war record (incidentally giving three times the weight to the votes of the Germans, most of whom were Nazi supporters during the war, compared with those of English- and Afrikaans-speaking South Africans, whose fathers, sons or husbands gave their lives in that war); they have altered the immigration laws against immigrants from the Commonwealth and have adjusted the demarcation of constituencies in a manner disadvantageous to their opponents.

The effect of all this has been the distortion of Parliament into a hopelessly unrepresentative body, so that it is today almost an un-South African institution controlled by people who have the interests of only a small section of the population at heart. This is largely because the hard core of the Nationalists lack perspective on the achievements and merits of those sections of the population (ninety per cent in all) which do not subscribe to their tenets, but which are nevertheless truly South African; and the Party itself dances to that tune.

That the Nationalist Party should lend itself to dealings of this description is accounted for by the fact that it is openly a racial Party, appealing to Afrikaner sentiment only. The cement that binds its members is made up of Afrikaner blood, Afrikaner aspirations and Afrikaner fears; and their leaders make no bones about it. Accordingly, its efforts are circumscribed by Afrikaner interests to the exclusion of all other interests in the country, despite the fact that the Afrikaners number less than twelve per cent of the population. The rank and file of the Party see little wrong in the doubtful expedients resorted to, for they have been openly adopted to safeguard what they regard as Afrikaner interests and way of life, which to the Nationalists generally are sacrosanct.

While such an attitude is understandable and may in some circumstances be forgivable, it is extremely dangerous in a multi-racial country, where peace and relative contentment can survive only in an atmosphere of justice and fair play to all sections of the community. Many Nationalists doubtless realize the consequences of such an attitude, but allow any such convictions to be submerged by their intense loyalty to what they regard as an Afrikaner cause. Unfortunately, a section of the Afrikaners has had a chequered and frustrating history and this has bred certain complexes and prejudices in a large number of them – particularly among those who have not been favoured by fortune in the common struggle for better living conditions.

These prejudices and complexes have proved fertile soil for political exploitation and the Nationalist leaders have never hesitated to dig deeply into it. Their exploitation has in turn produced a self-centred and dangerous mentality which the Nationalist leaders are no longer able to ignore, and to which they have to pander in order to retain its support. This mentality is, unfortunately, fairly common among the lower strata of Afrikaners who today comprise the hard core of the Nationalist Party. And whether the upper levels among the Nationalist supporters – for the Nationalists have their full share of enlightened and cultured people – are aware of it or not, this hard core is dragging the Party along an extremely dangerous path. As a consequence, the Party's statements and behaviour, while they may give satisfaction to its rank and file, have tended to exasperate the non-Nationalist groups, both White and non-White, to an extent that can only lead to bitterness and harm.

In recent years the Nationalists have passed numerous laws to curtail the movements, rights and scope of non-Whites. They have naturally given rise to a solidarity among these people and have fanned an anti-White sentiment in them, which is growing in intensity and at times comes perilously near open hatred for the Whites in general – whether Nationalists or not. This feeling among the non-Whites is intensified by the knowledge that in every other country emancipation of the coloured peoples is proceeding at an ever-increasing pace as a consequence of the spread of education, knowledge and industrialization – the tools of evolutionary progress in the economic sphere.

Much of the recent legislation has been passed for the benefit of the lower strata of Nationalists – the hard core – since they are the most exposed to competition from non-Whites, and hence those most likely to fall victim to any race admixture. Loyalty to this section, which comprises probably over forty per cent of the Nationalists, and the knowledge that without its support the Nationalist Party cannot rule the country, have induced the leaders of the Party to pass restrictive legislation of a kind unparalleled in any free country. In this the Party has had the support of many of its more enlightened and affluent members, but not of all; some of its intellectuals have clearly indicated that they are not happy about the course chosen by the Party in recent years. So far this uneasiness has not led to an open break because blood ties and a sincere regard for Afrikaner interests and aspirations in general have proved too strong.

While loyalty to one's people and support for one's weaker brethren are on the whole admirable qualities, they can at times be extremely dangerous – particularly where loyalty and support are given to a large body of people who have complexes and are prejudice-ridden as a consequence of a frustrated past. Such support, if given without qualification, only strengthens the complexes and prejudices and makes the recipients intolerant and self-righteous. This, to a large extent, is what has happened to the hard core of the Nationalist Party. The result is that they, and many others who are blinded by Nationalist propaganda, live in a world of their own, where – they think – they are the only true South Africans.

Their historical background has given rise among many Afrikaners to a particularly harsh view on the question of colour. While, in the physical sense, the Afrikaner has never been brutal in his treatment of the non-Whites, the Nationalists in general cling grimly to the idea of baasskap, and, in fact, although not generally admitted, baasskap is the policy of the Nationalist Party on the question of Coloured peoples. While among the educated Whites this relationship of master and servant is more or less the natural state of affairs, among the less enlightened Whites – particularly those of Afrikaans extraction – the relationship has a rather precarious footing and is defended with a measure of aggression which on occasions comes near to hysteria. The policy of the Nationalists, at times somewhat camouflaged by nebulous propaganda, naturally has a strong appeal to the less affluent sections of the White population – Afrikaans- and English-speaking alike, because they are most exposed to competition from the non-Whites.

Much has been heard during the past decade about the policy of apartheid, which implies a policy of keeping the races apart, but at bed-rock the Nationalist policy has been baasskap rather than apartheid. The policy of apartheid has never been clearly defined and to this day has different meanings for different people – even among the Nationalists themselves. The concept nevertheless gives scope for policies acceptable to the enlightened members of the Nationalist Party who on moral grounds are unable to accept baasskap as a long-term policy.

The impracticability of apartheid is the stumbling-block, however, with the result that the more closely one examines its application over the past ten years, the more clearly emerges the pattern of baasskap. Many Nationalist leaders have openly admitted that, in fact, the Nationalist policy is baasskap. Some go even further and insist that the Nationalist Afrikaners have been divinely inspired to see that this policy is carried out. To the less enlightened section of the Afrikaners the policy has an irresistible appeal – linked as it is with race and religion. To these people it has become more than a policy: it has become a crusade to keep the country safe for the White man. In such circumstances, scruples take a back seat, however unjust or hurtful the application of the policy to those who stand in its way.

The danger about Afrikaner Nationalism lies in the fact that its policies are at present hardly compatible with democratic government. Democracy presupposes differences of opinion, and hence different parties, but for it to be workable, the parties must be open to reason, to conviction, to differing opinions, and never immune to them through prejudice, fear or hatred. Moreover, democracy is only effective where the opposing parties subscribe to the rules of the game and where differences are not treated as life-and-death struggles between bitter enemies.

With the Nationalists, however, politics amount to a religion, with the result that they arrogate to themselves the role of a chosen people and regard the rest as infidels or nonentities, thus creating an atmosphere in which democracy cannot function. In the circumstances, democratic government is virtually out of reach of ninety per cent of the people of South Africa. If the remaining ten per cent were representative of all the peoples in the Union, a good case could be made out for its control of the government, for South Africa is certainly not yet ripe for universal suffrage. But as the ten per cent is representative of only one group out of five – and in certain respects an immature and biased group at that – government by such a party can never be acceptable to the people of the country as a whole.

Apartheid

The only ray of hope on the Nationalist front at present comes from a growing number of intellectuals who have hitherto supported that Party. They realize the dangers inherent in a policy of baasskap and seek a solution of the racial problem in what is known as total or territorial apartheid. This policy envisages the complete separation of the Whites from the Africans – the latter to be established in distinct parts of the country, where they could develop their own industries and other economic activities and enjoy a measure of autonomy. If this section of the Party could gain in strength sufficiently to influence the leaders to adopt a more humane course, much could be achieved.

What these people preach would be an aim worthy of pursuit, if only it were capable of being put into practice. Unfortunately, their previous ideas have been inconsistent with the world of reality and the course of events which evolution in its present phase has pretty clearly mapped out. The Nationalist Government at one stage appeared to be toying with similar ideas, but it is evident that they have now been dropped because of the impracticability of their application. Apartheid as a policy remains a nebulous concept; although it was heralded with a great flourish as *the* solution of the racial problem in South Africa about ten years ago and the country was led to believe that the ultimate objective was complete territorial apartheid, in recent years Government policy on this issue has been diluted to apartheid *where practicable*. This, as the past ten years have shown, means no more than discrimination against colour wherever possible, or in other words baasskap.

In the circumstances, it can at least be said for the Government that its policy is realistic while that of the Nationalist intellectuals is only a dream. But the Nationalist intellectuals do shed some ray of hope upon the South African scene. In future they will be compelled more and more to examine their proposals in relation to the world of practical affairs, and, in attempting to reconcile the two, which in defence of their theories they must do, they will come up against the hard facts of economic life in South Africa. At this stage they will be confronted with the choice between blood and conscience. It is to be hoped that they will choose the latter, for it could mean a reorientation of party loyalties in the Union.

This may give the impression that only Nationalist Afrikaners subscribe to the policy of baasskap. This is certainly not so, for the policy has great attraction for a considerable proportion of English-speaking South Africans. Only a few of these have previously supported the Nationalist Party, but, were it not for the historical antagonism which a section of the Afrikaners has displayed towards the British, a very much larger proportion of the English-speaking people would have openly supported such a policy. The history of race relationships between Whites and Blacks the world over establishes beyond dispute that, when peoples of different colour live side by side, prejudice and antagonisms come into the open, and what is more, the intensity of these feelings increases among the Whites, who are

invariably the more advanced. The less prosperous and enlightened they are, the more bitter and intolerant they become.

It will not need much imagination, therefore, to appreciate
that a policy that promises permanent mastership to Whites,
however low they may have sunk in the scale of civilization, has
a strong appeal to the weaker elements of this population –
whether Afrikaans- or English-speaking. It is precisely because of
this sinister appeal that the policy is so dangerous – dangerous
because it feeds the ever-hungry baser instincts of the White
races. The higher qualities of the human race, such as reason,
enlightenment and toleration, are not so easily reached by the
political propagandist.

Nevertheless, the hard core of the Nationalist Party – that
section which insists on baasskap – comprises Afrikaners. It
may well be asked how it comes about that so many of the
Afrikaners believe in baasskap. In the first place, a larger
proportion of the Afrikaners are in the lower income and less
enlightened groups, where they are particularly exposed to
non-White competition. This situation, in turn, has its roots in
the history of a section of these people – a section made up of
those who could be described as the problem children of
southern Africa. Many Afrikaners will resent any such reference
to this section of their people – people whose ancestors have been
almost deified in legend and history books. It is not with any
disrespect that these people are so described, but rather in
order that their present station in life may enlist sympathetic
understanding and less uninformed criticism – especially from
abroad.

The Problem-child mentality

The parallel with the problem child is very clear, if the
history and development of these people is seen in the light of
the concepts of human relationships universally accepted today.
The children in question were born of parents – the Dutch
East India Company – in the early years of the eighteenth
century. As infants they were neglected, more or less disowned

by their parents, so that they wandered over the untamed veld doing very much as they pleased: they took what land they wanted, shot what game they pleased, and forced into their service the displaced aborigines, who were unable to fend for themselves. This was not an unusual pattern of colonization in the seventeenth and eighteenth centuries, although by the nineteenth century a better-disciplined form of colonization and a more humane outlook towards native races had emerged.

The Afrikaner frontiersmen, however, as a result of their isolation, gradually retrogressed and virtually lost a century in the rising scale of civilization, so that when their foster-parents – the British – took over their homeland and tried to introduce a measure of discipline and a code of life in accordance with up-to-date concepts of civilization, the frontiersmen misunderstood and strongly resented their actions. The British, too, were at times rather impatient and tactless, and this aggravated the tension between children and foster-parents. As in the case of any child who suffers from parental neglect, the disciplinary measures were regarded as frustrations, awakening in the frontiersmen a firm conviction that their ideas of life were the true ones, and all others false.

This attitude bred the self-righteousness which characterizes a section of the Afrikaners to this day. In fact, this trait became more firmly ingrained as the frontiersmen trekked on to new land, only to find the ubiquitous British everywhere demanding a code of life foreign and distasteful to them. These demands were not only regarded as frustrations, but were construed as ample evidence of British ill-will and of British designs to deprive them of their birthright. In consequence, the Afrikaners came to regard themselves as persecuted – also a characteristic of the problem child.

The tragedy about all this is that these developments took place in the formative years of Afrikaner consciousness, cutting deeply into the Afrikaner character and making a lasting impression. Yet what came to be regarded as ill-will towards the frontiersmen and their descendants on the part of the British was really not so. The fact was that the way of life of the frontiersmen held no hope for their descendants, who sooner or later would have had to face the stern realities of life. Land was not inexhaustible to enable them to continue their trekking habits, nor would the indigenous population always enter their service on unfair terms. In fact, the continuous trekking of the Boers gave rise to a great deal of uneasiness on the part of the African races in many parts of the country, and it fell to the British on several occasions to make some attempt to allay those feelings.

While the Boers were merely looking after their own interests, the British on many occasions were confronted with the onerous task of keeping the peace and dispensing justice among the many conflicting interests. It cannot be said that the British ignored the interests of the Boers; on the contrary, on certain occasions British decisions were distinctly unfavourable to African interests, where they conflicted with those of the Boers.

At the time, the trekkers had little regard for the interests of others and did not realize that their way of life could only lead to frustration, and that many British actions merely sought to correct or curb a code of living which, if persisted in, could only have led to worse frustration, if not disaster. The wrong turning in the life of the frontiersmen was not when the British took over the Cape; it happened more than a hundred years before that, when the Dutch East India Company introduced slavery into the country, thus curtailing the opportunities for the early settlers in the Cape to make a livelihood, unless they were in possession of land.

When the British put on the brake in the interests of the country as a whole, they immediately became the scapegoats for the thwarted aspirations of the frontiersmen. The idea that the British were the arch-enemies of the Afrikaners gained currency as a result, and has now been kept alive for more than a century. Over the past hundred years South African history has been interpreted in this light by many Afrikaans parents, teachers and even ministers of religion, with the result that children in their impressionable years have imbibed tales of British misdeeds and ill-will.

In the circumstances, a considerable proportion of the Afrikaners have nurtured anti-British sentiments and have tended to ascribe most of their frustrations and misfortunes to British interference. Even to this day many have not as yet recognized that the cause of much of their frustration lies in the fact that in their formative years they were an unfortunate and neglected people, who had adopted an impossible way of life which sooner or later would catch up with them. In fact, the emergence of poor-Whiteism in the latter half of the nineteenth and the first quarter of the twentieth century was a direct consequence of the way of life into which they had been moulded and which became impossible to sustain as available land for further settlement was exhausted. As this and other misfortunes overtook a proportion of the trekkers and their descendants, they came to believe that they were deliberately being persecuted by the British.

To this day, the theme that the Afrikaners are a people persecuted by the British persists. The facts, however, are very different, for, under present-day conditions it would be hard to conceive of any people in the world who are more privileged than South Africans generally, and rural Afrikaners in particular. From the point of view of South Africans in general, the country has been extremely fortunate since Union: precious minerals have been discovered and mined on an extensive scale, lifting the standard of life of the average White South Africans to a level higher than that of any other country in the world, with the possible exception of the United States of America; the country has been spared devastation by war, and, although it participated in two world wars, it gained vastly more than it lost; the White population have a much easier existence, and more leisure, than any other population in the world, because all unpleasant and physically heavy work in the country is performed by the non-Whites; taxation is light and cost of living relatively low because the country does not bear such a heavy cost of defence as other Western countries, and because non-White labour is inadequately paid.

From the point of view of the Afrikaners, the country has

been governed predominantly by their section since Union – by Nationalists for more than half that period. Such governments have been the outcome of the rural vote – mainly Nationalist – having a higher value than the city vote – primarily English-speaking. Government services are predominantly Afrikaans-speaking – to an extent that English-speaking South Africans are shy of joining such services, because they feel that in the upper ranks the dice are loaded against them. Lastly, because of the disproportionate weight of farming interests in successive Union governments, the farmers – largely Afrikaners and Nationalists – have received considerable concessions in taxation and enjoy specific consideration under the insolvency laws of the country.

Taking all these facts into consideration, it would be hard to find a people anywhere in the world who have been more pampered than the rural Afrikaner during the past fifty years. Nor have these people particularly merited such favourable conditions, for in the economic development of the country the capital and know-how, except in agriculture, have in the main been provided by the English-speaking population, and the heavy labour by the non-Whites. Yet in spite of all this, the Nationalist Party continues to campaign as if its adherents are an underprivileged and persecuted people striving for rights hitherto denied them.

The cancer of privilege

The fact of the matter is that this mentality – the problem-child mentality – has become a cancerous growth in the hard core of the Nationalists. It is understandable and excusable that the voortrekkers succumbed to it, for they were the victims of harsh circumstances. But to keep alive and actively to foster the belief that the voortrekkers and their descendants were all saints and martyrs, as do many of the Nationalists, is indefensible; such action merely feeds and stimulates the cancer which unfortunately took root among a section of the early Dutch colonists in the opening years of the nineteenth century.

Continuous pandering to these beliefs is certainly not in the interests of the Afrikaners, it will not build a healthy Afrikaans community but a diseased one which, sooner rather than later, will undermine not only the Afrikaners themselves but also the White man's position in the country.

The disease is a mental cancer: it induces those afflicted to believe that they are persecuted, and that they are divinely inspired. Unfortunately, the section afflicted is quite substantial, for its growth has been stimulated for the best part of a century and a half. No political party which seeks an Afrikaner majority in Parliament can afford to ignore it. But, as most Afrikaners have a natural desire to keep alive distinctive Afrikaner characteristics – in itself no bad thing – they are more or less compelled to seek the co-operation of the afflicted section, in order to satisfy this desire, rather than to co-operate with the English-speaking people. To do this they have to descend to the level of the diseased mentality and to feed it with the very poison that stimulates its growth – the constant assurance that the afflicted are persecuted and God's chosen race. In this way the cancer spreads, whereas in the interests of all it should be rooted out.

The strength and implications of this malignant growth have manifested themselves clearly in the treatment meted out to successive prime ministers who, since Union, have all been of Afrikaner stock. No sooner were these leaders elevated to the high office of Premier than they became suspect. In accepting this responsibility, they naturally had to recognize the rights of others – particularly those of the English-speaking section; but in doing so they gradually forfeited the respect and support of that section of the Afrikaner people which regards itself as God's chosen and hence entitled to privilege in the South African community. One by one Afrikaner first ministers have had to give way to leaders of the people who, initially, were more willing to pander to the diseased beliefs, until they in their turn were cast out. By this process, every change has meant a surrender to extremism with resultant spread of the cancer.

With the rising tide of colour throughout the world, more and

more is heard of the necessity for Afrikaners and English-speaking South Africans to come closer together. It would indeed be a
blessing for the country if its politics could be run upon non-
racial lines. But how can the Nationalists expect the co-operation of English-speaking South Africans so long as they identify
themselves with and play up to this diseased mentality? To
offer such co-operation the English-speaking South Africans
would have to hate themselves and all they stand for, because
one of the fundamental manifestations of the disease is dislike
of everything British, which springs from the belief that the
British are traditional enemies and consistent persecutors. The
English-speaking people could only do this if they themselves
also suffered from disease – softening of the brain.

There is only one way in which co-operation can be achieved,
and that is by elimination of the cancerous growth. In doing this
the Nationalists will be doing White South Africa an outstanding service, for if it is not uprooted it will inevitably destroy
White leadership in the country much sooner than even our
most extreme pessimists believe.

Some Afrikaners will ask: how can we possibly eliminate this
cancer without letting these people down? For over a hundred
years they have been led to believe that God was ever on their
side; that the actions of their forefathers throughout history
were always inspired by the purest of motives; that as a people
they were wilfully persecuted by the British; and that non-
Whites had no place in society except as servants. To deny their
beliefs would be to destroy their faith in us as well as in themselves.

Unfortunately, the breaking-down of these illusions can only
be the most unpleasant of tasks. But in the interests of the
country they will have to be broken before long. The way of
truth, even if accompanied by disappointments and tears, is
ultimately the only possible way. It will make a far better
people than false beliefs and unearned privileges. Nor does it
necessarily follow that the afflicted people will be let down or
suffer hardship as a result. Theoretically, a reversal of the
Nationalists' policy of privilege entrenchment will expose the

less affluent among the White population to corroding competition from the non-Whites. In reality this need not be so, if
the Whites would reorientate their understanding of labour
and its reward by bringing it into line with the modern concept
of the dynamism of industrial development.

Unfortunately, one cannot escape the conclusion that the
policy of the Nationalist Government since it took office in
1948 has been (and still is): first, the gradual and systematic
elimination of all traces of British traditions and influence from
the country as far as White relationships are concerned; and
secondly, as far as non-Whites are concerned, the maintenance
of both Blacks and Coloureds as subject races in conformity
with the ideas of two hundred years ago. To these ends, the
constitution of the country is being distorted and the statutes
loaded with discriminatory legislation of the most shabby and
reactionary character. But in pursuing this policy, which the
world is watching with growing concern, the Nationalists are
unwittingly vindicating in the eyes of humanity everywhere the
nineteenth-century policy of the British in South Africa towards
the voortrekkers and the Boer republics – and this at a time
when the British themselves had accepted a measure of responsibility and guilt for the actions ascribed by liberal opinion in
England to over-zealous imperialism. Less than sixty years ago,
at the time of the Anglo-Boer War, the Boers gained the sympathy and admiration of the world; today this has been dissi-
pated and the name of South Africa is suspect because of
Nationalist policy and deeds.

Partition

Apart from what is termed integration in the parlance of
the country's politicians, but which in reality is the process of
evolution, there is only one other problematical course which
the country could pursue. This is the partition of South Africa
along the lines adopted in India, Ireland, Israel and Korea.
But in none of these has partition been a conspicuous success.
If it is to survive for any length of time in southern Africa,

partition will have to be just and will have to entail a division of the country on a scale which no White section of the population has previously advocated, or could advocate. In fact, it is unlikely that partition on the necessary scale will be acceptable to any part of any section of the country's population. The existing nebulous concept of apartheid is nothing more than an illusion, and is likely to land the country in an even greater disaster than baasskap. The Nationalists will, therefore, have to do some hard thinking in the next few years if the country is to be saved from the consequences of the problem-child mentality of its hard core.

The United Party

Besides the Nationalists, there are three other parties in the Union[1] – the United, the Labour, and the Liberal Parties. Of these, only the United Party has sufficient support seriously to contest the Nationalists. This Party draws its support largely from English-speaking South Africans, but its Afrikaner support is by no means negligible – probably from fifteen to twenty per cent of the Afrikaner voters. In fact, the Party has always been, and still is, led by Afrikaners, who are its most active members, English-speaking South Africans having played a somewhat passive role in politics since Union. The principal reason for this is the fact that English-speaking South Africans have been insufficiently bilingual to make any impression on Afrikaans-speaking audiences, who are rather insistent that Afrikaans only be spoken at political meetings. This is the penalty paid by the English-speaking South African for his unwillingness to become proficient in Afrikaans.

Be that as it may, Afrikaners have always headed the Party – and its predecessor, the South African Party – and among them were General Botha, General Smuts and Mr J. H. Hofmeyr, who must rank among the most outstanding men that South Africa has yet produced. The Afrikaner support comes in the main from the more enlightened and affluent members of this group – some outstanding Afrikaners in the educational and

[1] See Postscript.

cultural spheres have supported and still support this Party. It has taken a great deal of courage on the part of these Afrikaners to continue in support of the Party, because they have been subject to considerable abuse by the Nationalists, who openly accuse them of being traitors to the Afrikaner cause.

The first leaders of the Party virtually dedicated their lives to the healing of the breach between Afrikaners and English-speaking citizens which came into existence soon after the British took over the administration of the Cape and widened considerably as a consequence of the Anglo-Boer War. In the early years of Union, hopes ran high that this breach would be healed, but the advent of two world wars, in which all members of the British Commonwealth supported the mother country in her struggle, made the task of the leaders of the Party doubly difficult.

In both these wars the leaders chose to throw in the lot of South Africa against the Germans. This was incomprehensible to many Afrikaners and strongly resented by the hard core of the Nationalist Party, which openly sympathized with Germany in the conflict. But as South Africa in both wars was on the side of the victors, and as the country gained much economically (and even territorially in its acquisition of South West Africa), history will undoubtedly justify the decisions of the leaders. Unfortunately, while South Africa gained immensely in the material sense because of the vision and efforts of its leaders at the time, the ideal to which these leaders dedicated their lives suffered a grievous set-back, and seems more remote now than at any time since Union. This is a tragic reflection on the lives and work of those men who, in the opinion of the world, surpassed in greatness any others born in South Africa.

Instead of co-operation, trust and harmony between the White races living in the Union, the prejudices, fears and complexes that have distorted the outlook of the hard core of Nationalist Afrikanerdom are in control of the country, so that the lives of these great men would almost seem to have been in vain. But the spirits of these leaders may live again and with greater success in the years to come.

In the past the United Party, or its predecessor, was called upon to govern mainly during years of stress and strain: the uncertain years after Union, the years when the strength of the country was committed in war, the years of reconstruction after wars, and the years when the country struggled against deep depression. To its credit, it brought the country through to safety and prosperity on every occasion, and its leaders displayed courage and vision. The Nationalist Party, on the other hand, has governed successfully only in times of prosperity, surrendering office when the storms gathered. This points to the fact that a party that is founded on self-righteousness, fear, and a persecution complex has no innate strength, and cannot in consequence survive adversity.

That the United Party had to spend its time and energy in mastering situations imposed from abroad, such as world wars and depressions, is singularly unfortunate, because as a result it was never given an opportunity to tackle purely local problems with the thoroughness they deserved. Racial relationships between the White and non-White populations suffered because of these preoccupations. The problem of adjusting the African to developing industrialization was accordingly allowed to drift. In fact, until its defeat in 1948 the leaders of the Party were so engrossed in their wartime problems and in their efforts to reconcile the Afrikaans- and English-speaking sections that they did not fully appreciate the magnitude of the problem of African adjustment to industrialization.

This, however, cannot be said of Mr J. H. Hofmeyr, who was always ahead of other South African leaders in matters relating to African development and African problems generally. For this he was accused of being a negrophile by the then Opposition, and was even criticized by members of his own Party for his advanced and liberal views. That he was more than right on these questions subsequent events are proving more and more clearly, but when he lived he was ahead of opinion in South Africa, and even to this day few politicians in South Africa appreciate the accelerating tempo of world changes in this respect.

The United Party itself is as yet by no means abreast of world developments on these questions, and as a consequence its policy concerning the non-Whites appears to the outside world strangely unsuited to the requirements of the developing situation in Africa, and a mere pale reflection of the policy of the Nationalists. This view does not do the Party justice, for at bed-rock it is vastly different from the Nationalists: its hard core is made up of enlightened and fairly affluent elements who have much at stake in the Union, and who are capable of seeing South Africa's problems in their true perspective. In consequence, it is guided in fundamentals by reason, whereas the Nationalist Party panders to a hard core which is hidebound by prejudices and emotions, which in turn strait-jacket the Party itself.

Most of the leaders and many of the followers of the United Party must be fully aware that its policy on racial issues is not yet attuned to the rapid changes that are taking place in the non-White continents of Asia and Africa, but as so large a proportion of the rank and file among South Africa's White population is still firmly tied to customs and concepts which today are anachronisms, the Party is faced with an extraordinarily delicate task. It has to appeal to a public which for the most part is not yet ready to accept the changes in racial relations that the present situation in Africa demands. To counter the dangerous policies of the Nationalists, the Party must enlist sufficient support in the country, and at the present time it can only obtain this by making haste slowly on racial problems, until education and general enlightenment eliminate prejudices and modify opinions.

There is no denying that the policies of baasskap and apartheid have a strong appeal to many – both English- and Afrikaans-speaking – who for other reasons support the United Party. This is because those policies – especially baasskap – promise the people conditions very much to their liking. To people with limited vision and strong prejudices, a policy which purports to give what they desire naturally has a strong appeal – and there are many such people who normally support the

United Party. Indeed, it is virtually impossible to live in a multi-racial community without being tainted by racial prejudices. But the rub lies in the feasibility of such policies in the years ahead, and in this respect voters should be guided by what is best for the country and all its people in the long run, and not by immediate gains or personal likes.

Reason v. prejudice

Unfortunately, that which would be best for the country in years to come is something intangible, and any appeal to the public along those lines is as a rule unpopular and often misunderstood. This is the problem that confronts United Party leaders. The Nationalist Party openly appeals to those prejudices and fears of Whites which are normally to be found in multiracial countries, and offers popular policies that, on the surface, purport to ensure their existing privileges, regardless of the practicability of such policies. In contrast, the policy of the United Party has to date been nebulous and its outcome hard to visualize. It is virtually impossible to formulate a practicable policy in South Africa that would satisfy its enlightened supporters and at the same time overcome the prejudices and fears of the man in the street. And it is in this respect that the task of the United Party is so much more difficult than that of the Nationalists, for the hard core of the United Party consists of its enlightened supporters who are in the majority and would be alienated by an impracticable and manifestly unjust policy, whereas the hard core of the Nationalists is made up of the self-righteous and complex-ridden sections who demand privilege, no matter how impracticable or unjust to others. In essence, the policy of the Nationalists appeals to hot emotions, while that of the United Party cannot deviate much from reasoned practicability.

But, with all its faults and its somewhat equivocal appeal, the backbone of the United Party is men and women of both English and Afrikaans extraction courageous enough to subscribe to a policy of broad South Africanism. In terms of this policy, all who live in South Africa – whether White or non-White – make up the nation, and should enjoy rights and bear obligations in accordance with their civilized standards. In contrast, the Nationalists seek to pursue a policy in terms of which the nation should be made up of only Afrikaners and those Whites prepared to swallow completely the Nationalist tenets. Non-Whites would be tolerated in the South Africa of Nationalist hopes only as servants or in segregated spheres where they would be given severely-curtailed rights – always subject to the discretion of Parliament, which is to be an almost exclusively White body and in which only minor and ineffectual representation would be given to non-Whites.

United Party policy

The United Party advocates residential and social segregation, and this to many people beyond the borders of the Union would seem indefensible. However, enlightened people who live in multi-racial countries and who have to rub shoulders daily with members of other races, would not regard it as such – provided this segregation is not enforced by restrictive legislation. In fact, voluntary segregation in South Africa would meet the wishes of the majority of the different races in the country. This is because there is a natural tendency for like to attract like and for members of the particular groups in the community to stick together.

Residential and social segregation has been the traditional policy of the country since the white man set foot in South Africa, and on the whole has not given rise to undue friction. What has caused resentment, however, is the enforcement of separation by the restrictive and discriminatory legislation which is essentially the policy of the Nationalist Party. Much can be said for an enlightened policy of residential and social segregation if carried out constructively and generously – without recourse to restrictive laws. The emphasis in such a policy should be inducement and not restriction. It would entail the setting aside of adequate and suitable areas for the respective groups and the provision of liberal finance to attract them to the areas set aside for them without resorting to compulsion.

Unquestionably such a policy would give rise to some overlap among the races, but this has always existed in South Africa and would be a small price to pay for the resultant goodwill. In so far as this is the policy of the United Party – and there is no reason to believe that it is any other – it is surely defensible and worth while for the foreseeable future. With the progress of evolution, other ideas may prevail, but it would be folly at this stage of the country's development to enforce integration, as is being done in the United States of America, with so much resentment and hard feeling on the part of many Whites.

In one respect the United Party has exposed itself to considerable and justified criticism in recent years: in its election campaigns since 1948 it has been guilty of making far too many promises which it could never have carried out. In doing this, it has actually embarrassed its hard core, without whose support the Party could not survive. In the past far too much damage has been done by the White population of the Union through neglect of and indifference to the living conditions and rights of the non-Whites to warrant any highly optimistic view of the country's future. Later it will be shown that, generally, the Whites in the country have not given the non-Whites a square deal, and as a result are in some measure living in a fool's paradise.

South Africa has been a fortunate country during the past twenty-five years and more, but she should not expect this good fortune to continue indefinitely. The future is going to demand considerable sacrifices from White South Africa. It would, therefore, have been wiser for the United Party to have warned the electorate of sweat and possible tears, rather than to have promised never-ending prosperity – prosperity which the country has had the good fortune to enjoy, not because of the intrinsic merit of its people, but because of new gold-fields, uranium deposits and world prosperity generally. Greatness and success are not built on prosperity, but on sacrifice and hard work.

Another weakness of the United Party is that it is made up of diverse elements with varying viewpoints. It is not nearly as homogeneous as are the Nationalists, who are bound by common roots, a common language and common fears. As a consequence, leadership is of far greater importance to the United Party than it is to the Nationalists, who will follow any leader who plays up to narrow Afrikaner sentiment.

For all its faults and shortcomings, the United Party has in the past rendered invaluable service to the country. Despite its small representation in Parliament, it still has powerful backing, although this backing is inadequately represented because of the weaknesses of the constitution. Furthermore, the Party includes the lion's share of the best commercial, industrial and financial brains in the country, and the material interests of its members far outweigh those of the Nationalists. In outlook and balance it is also much better suited to the requirements of the country: it is broadly based and embodies a tolerant and co-operative spirit; it is not anchored to the past or inhibited by prejudices and fears as the Nationalists are; it is forward-looking and expansionist, and is prepared to face the future with courage and confidence despite the emergence and rise of the large non-White population of the country.

To it and the spirit that imbues it, we in South Africa owe the advent of Union and the acquisition of South West Africa, while because of the inhibitions and fears of Nationalist Afrikanerdom, we have lost the Rhodesias and are likely to lose the Protectorates. In contrast to the Nationalists, the United Party believes in integration – the process of building up. The Nationalists practise differentiation – the process of breaking down.

The Labour Party

There is also a Labour Party in South Africa. At one time, particularly after the First World War, it had a considerable following in the larger cities. Large proportions of the miners and artisan classes in the country were at that time English-speaking, and they followed the pattern of the Labour movement in England. Subsequently the Union's White labour force has been drawn predominantly from the Afrikaners, who have been subject to heavy pressure from Nationalist propaganda to support that Party instead of linking up with the Labour movement.

This propaganda has been particularly successful. The appeal to these Afrikaners has been on frankly racial lines, in which the persecution complex has been exploited to the full. Blood ties have consequently proved stronger than labour solidarity. As a reaction to this successful appeal to Afrikaner sentiment, the English-speaking workers have tended to move away from the Labour Party to the United Party. As a result, the Labour Party has fallen between two stools, to the extent that at the last General Election it returned no candidates to Parliament. Whether this means the extinction of the Party only time can tell. In this connection it should be remembered that the Labour Party at present really represents only White workers, for the bulk of the unskilled and semi-skilled workers in the country are non-Whites who have no place on the common electoral roll.

The Liberal Party

A fourth party has come into existence in recent years, the Liberal Party. It is really an offshoot of the United Party, comprising those members who became dissatisfied with the Party because of its apparently ambiguous attitude on the treatment of the non-White population of the country. It is the only multi-racial party in the Union, open to and including members of all races. Its racial policy is, therefore, much more sympathetic towards non-Whites than that of the United Party: it aims at full citizenship for non-Whites by gradual degrees as the latter rise in the scale of civilization. For the present, it seeks the breaking-down of discrimination against colour in all walks of life – particularly in the economic and political spheres. While it would remove the colour bar almost immediately, it does not sponsor universal suffrage at this stage, but proposes a fairly low electoral qualifying standard for all peoples. Its support among the White community comes mainly from English-speaking South Africans, but a number of liberal-minded Afrikaners have also given it their blessing. It is also essentially a party of intellectuals, who sincerely believe that the only possible policy for the country in the long run is acceptance that the nation is made up of people of different races and colour, and that in the circumstances there should be no discrimination on the basis of colour. Its ideals in certain respects find considerable unofficial support among a section of the United Party. On the other hand, its policy and attitude on racial issues are anathema to the Nationalists, who regard it as being as dangerous to the future of the country as they do the Communists.

To date the Party has but a small number of official adherents, as the recent General Election disclosed. While many in the United Party would subscribe to Liberal ideals, they feel that the Liberal Party itself does not yet face up to the practical difficulties with which the country is faced – any more than the Nationalists do from the other extreme. They consider that the time is not ripe for such a party and that its existence embarrasses rather than helps the United Party in its fight against Afrikaner nationalism. On the other hand, many people, including leading Nationalists, believe that the Party is destined to fill the role of official Opposition in the not-too-distant future. In their view, the United Party is likely to fall between two stools in advocating a middle-of-the-road policy coupled with 'go slow' schemes for non-White progress.

The Liberal Party is certainly the only true protagonist in South Africa of Western ideals and democratic concepts. But at this frightening stage in world affairs it might well be asked whether the present Western concepts of democracy are really all that they are cracked up to be, and whether they provide the most suitable system with which to meet the challenge of

Communism, which by all appearances is gaining ground daily.

Those who live in Africa are particularly concerned about this progress, because this continent is a prominent target for Communism. We in South Africa must be pardoned, therefore, if we question the efficacy of present democratic methods in times like the present. Since the Second World War, under the leadership of the United States of America, democracy seems to have taken on a new emphasis. Much is heard today about individual liberty and the right of self-determination, as if these were the be-all and end-all of human existence, but all too little is mentioned about the responsibilities attached to democratic government or about the discipline and co-operative effort necessary to make it work. The result is that we are witnessing abuses of freedom and the right of self-determination.

Every ethnic group, however small or backward, demands self-government. And this at a time when Communism encroaches more and more into lands which were formerly governed – and well governed – by enlightened and experienced nations. In Russia and her satellites this very Communism denies to millions the barest elements of individual freedom, let alone freedom to decide who shall govern. We in South Africa should not be blamed, therefore, if we question the new emphasis on democratic principles. We see few victories to its credit and too many defeats. Under the impact of this emphasis the prestige of the great Western democracies appears to be sinking, while that of Communism rises.

So much for international developments; in the democracies themselves we see unstable governments, mounting crime, and the spread of juvenile delinquency. We yield to none in our belief that democracy is the best form of government yet devised, but we feel that a sensible and balanced view of its rights and responsibilities should be taken. Much more emphasis should be placed upon the responsibilities attached to it; upon the discipline that it demands; and upon the sacrifices inherent in it. After all, democracy is a form of government that can only succeed in a civilized community where its responsibilities are appreciated and where self-discipline is practised.

To give it to people who do not understand its first principles is courting disaster. We are convinced that the implement used to confer power upon the ruling authorities in democracies – the franchise – should be extended only to those who fully understand its implications and who have earned the right to use it. It should be regarded more as an obligation than a right, and should not be given automatically to all who become of age – let alone to immature youngsters of eighteen years. In other words, a fairly high qualification should be set for the right (or obligation) to exercise the franchise.

It is largely because of opinions such as these that many in the country at present refrain from supporting the Liberal Party. While the ideals of the Liberals are admired, the time is too out of joint to support a policy of laissez-faire – the traditional philosophy of the Liberal creed. With militant nationalisms, both White and Black, determined on sectional gains, on the one hand, and with Communism on the other, stirring up mud and awaiting its opportunity to take advantage of the troubled waters, a negative creed such as that of Liberalism is more than likely to be 'taken for a ride'. If ever there was a time for enlightenment and strong leadership in South Africa, it is now – leadership that only visionaries like Smuts or Rhodes would be capable of giving. In calmer waters intelligent and benign Liberalism may yet play its part in South Africa.

At the present juncture in the history of South Africa, Afrikaner nationalism is firmly in the saddle – not because it is supported by the majority under an effective democratic system, but because it has been chosen by an electorate by no means representative of the people of South Africa, and, moreover, by one that has been deliberately exploited in the interests of Afrikaner nationalism. But below the privileged White upper class which exercises the vote, a Black and Coloured mass of humanity, outnumbering the Whites by four to one, is beginning to stir. This mass is not yet represented in Parliament by its own people and in some respects is still deprived of even elementary rights of citizenship. These people, however, are daily becoming more conscious of the latent power which one day they expect to wield.

Daily contact with modern civilization is gradually awakening in them an understanding of the implications of this era of mechanization, especially of the implications of industrialization and its corollary – the necessary advancement of the underprivileged. How long, therefore, will it be possible for a White aristocracy to deny the steadily awakening non-White proletariat full title to those awards that are an inevitable part of industrialization? This is the burning question which at present confronts White South Africa.

The Republican idea

A great deal is heard in and out of Parliament about this question, but so far very little has been done to meet the developing situation. Instead, the Afrikaner Nationalists are now planning the establishment of a republic in South Africa, for, according to them, only under a republic will a truly South African spirit develop among the English-speaking section, thereby enabling White South Africa as a whole to meet the 'menace' of a rising Black nationalism.

Whether a republic in South Africa will have this effect upon the English-speaking section is open to question, and will doubtless depend largely on the form taken by the republic and how it is established. It can be said without hesitation that, if the republic is to be foisted upon the English-speaking section (who have a traditional feeling for the present monarchist form of government) by means of doubtful electoral expedients such as have previously been employed (and which the extension of the vote to eighteen-year-olds would be), its effect upon them will be the exact opposite of what the Nationalists expect. A large section of English-speaking South Africa will not lightly be party to any move having as its objective the further holding down or frustration of the non-White population, whether by baasskap or by camouflaged and impossible proposals such as the territorial apartheid at present envisaged.

Instead, any such ideas will either awaken in them an even stronger feeling for their hereditary ties, or cause them to turn away in disgust from future interest in South Africa, since any such action and policy on the part of the Nationalists can, in their opinion, lead only to an inevitable clash between Afrikaner and African nationalisms in which they would not care to be embroiled. Reaction such as this would indeed be unfortunate for South Africa, for no other section in the country is better equipped to bridge the antagonisms between White and non-White.

For the republic to succeed, it will be necessary for the Nationalists to approach the question in an unbiased manner, without any preconceived ideas of an Afrikaner-dominated state. All sections of the population will have to be fully consulted and a constitution provided under which no section is especially privileged merely because of a white skin or because of Afrikaner sentiment. Naturally the stage reached in civilization by the non-Whites will have to be taken into consideration, but the franchise otherwise should not be weighted against any particular group or interest. In addition, as the non-Whites are with us in South Africa whether we like it or not, just and fair representation should be given them, and it should be progressively adaptable, with safeguards, to the level of civilization reached by them.

If, however, the proposed republic merely envisages a constitutional change to satisfy Nationalist Afrikaner sentiment, and if it perpetuates all the anomalies and unfair discriminations at present practised by the Nationalist Party, it will have been built upon a false foundation and consequently will never endure. In fact, it will die far sooner than seems possible at present. What will take its place cannot yet be clearly foreseen, but in the shadows lurks the Communist monster, ready to pounce where conditions favour a kill.

5

THE AFRIKAANS LANGUAGE

No survey of conditions in South Africa would be complete without some reference to the rise of the Afrikaans language. The development of this language must be regarded as one of the major achievements of the Afrikaners, for it is doubtful whether such an achievement has been paralleled anywhere else under modern conditions. There are still those who regard Afrikaans as a patois or just another dialect of the Dutch of Holland. This, however, is not true, and Afrikaners have the right to claim that they have a language of their own. It goes without saying that they are exceedingly proud of this achievement, and rightly so. The language is very dear to their hearts, and Afrikaners of all shades of opinion treasure it as a mother does her child. They are therefore sensitive to any adverse criticism of the language which now and then is expressed in the country. Generally speaking, the language has been accepted by all sections of the South African community, and the criticism that does come to the surface is not of much consequence.

The feeling for the language among Afrikaners is sharpened by the fact that it has become identified with their struggle to establish their identity as a separate people – or nation, as they regard themselves. Whether, in the long run, this struggle to achieve a distinct identity as a people has been a wise one is another question, to which only the future has the answer. However, since they have chosen this course rather than merge with their English-speaking colleagues, the latter have really no choice but to respect the strong desire of the Afrikaners to remain a separate people and to accept the development of Afrikaans as a signal achievement on their part.

*

Colonial Dutch

Over the past one hundred and fifty years the people who today are accepted as Afrikaners have displayed a truly tenacious urge to establish themselves as a separate entity. In earlier years, when the language of the people was still seventeenth-century Dutch or a slight corruption of it, it manifested itself in the nomadic way of life ingrained in the people by their constant trekking to new pastures, irrespective of the rights and wrongs towards the indigenous inhabitants at the time.

Every attempt to curb those habits, or their attitude towards the indigenous peoples, was strongly resented and hotly contested. Moreover, slave ownership by their ancestors and relations in the south had to a certain extent already conditioned their attitude towards non-White peoples in general. The urge to occupy new pasture lands during that period became the dominating impulse of these people towards separation. The break with British rule and the establishment of the Boer republics sprang in the main from this urge. But throughout this period the language of the people was still officially Dutch. Even in the Boer republics up to the time of their dissolution the official language was Dutch.

'Kitchen Dutch'

The first stirrings in favour of Afrikaans did not occur in the republics but among the Cape Afrikaners of the Western Province, that is, among the colonial Afrikaners, who did not at that time have the same strong desire for independent development. The movement took root slowly at first. There was considerable opposition among the people themselves because at the time they regarded the speech as a corruption of Dutch originating mainly from the Coloured people, who by that time had already adopted a form of Dutch as their lingua franca.

The early pioneers of Afrikaans had thus to overcome opposition from their own people, who held strong prejudices against anything that savoured of Coloured origins. This opposition actually proved tougher in the northern parts of the country, which included the Boer republics, than in the south, where colour prejudice was milder. In the early days of Afrikaans it was actually branded by many as 'kitchen Dutch', implying that it was the language spoken by the servants in the kitchen.

Development of Afrikaans

Rapid progress in the development of the language did not materialize until after the union of the four provinces which at present make up South Africa. In the intervening years a few staunch supporters of the ideal of a separate language were laying the foundation of an Afrikaans literature. Their efforts yielded a few surprisingly good works, which were published about that time. These stalwarts demonstrated the merits of the language, which very appropriately expressed the thoughts and feelings of a people who were attached to the land and the wide open spaces of the veld. Opposition to its general adoption persisted for a considerable time, and it was only towards the middle of the 1920s that Afrikaans replaced Dutch as one of the two official languages of the country.

The Dual Language Provision

Until Union, English naturally was the official language of the two British colonies, while Dutch was that of the republics up to the Boer War. Under the Act of Union both these languages became official and the teaching of both obligatory in Government schools. In the mid-1920s Afrikaans superseded Dutch. In the Cape Colony Dutch was taught before Union as an optional or second language.

Unfortunately, English-speaking South Africans did not take readily to learning Dutch in the pre-Union years. In this, they displayed the reluctance of all English-speaking peoples to acquire languages other than their own. On the other hand, the colonial Afrikaners, having been forced to learn English, became reasonably proficient in it, at the same time acquiring a sound grasp of Dutch. With the advent of Union and the adoption of two official languages, the colonial Afrikaners immediately enjoyed an advantage over their English-speaking colleagues in their knowledge of both languages.

At first, the application in official circles of the dual language provision was not rigidly enforced. In fact, this provision of the South African Act came to be interpreted more as conferring optional usage of either language rather than compulsory usage of both. Subsequently, however, when the Nationalists gained power in 1924, this interpretation was altered and compulsory usage gradually enforced. This step proved something of a hardship for many English-speaking public servants, whose knowledge of Dutch was scanty and of Afrikaans even less.

Viewed in retrospect, however, there can be no doubt that, in the years immediately after Union, Dutch was not given the usage in official circles that the spirit of the South Africa Act envisaged. The medium of correspondence and record remained predominantly English. Furthermore, it can hardly be denied that the interpretation of optional usage was overdone by English-speaking South Africans, and that at that stage steps were necessary to see that the other official language, Dutch, gained its rightful place in official quarters. In pressing for this, the Nationalist Government of the late 1920s had much right on its side. English-speaking South Africans, nevertheless, had in some instances to pay dearly for their earlier reluctance to acquire a knowledge of Dutch. Promotion was forfeited because of this, and the public service as a career began to lose much of its attraction for them. In later years political bias, unfortunately, added to the earlier language handicap of the English-speaking South Africans, with the result that they are today inclined to shun public service careers altogether.

As a South African whose home language was predominantly English, who attended school in the Cape during the changing conditions described above, and who, in addition, spent some of the best years of his life in the public services of the Union, I feel justified in expressing some of my feelings and thoughts on this issue. Fortunately, my knowledge of Dutch, and subsequently of Afrikaans, was always sufficient to satisfy the bilingual standards required. In spite of this, I have always felt that in the public services of the country, since the advent of the Nationalists in 1924, the dice were somewhat loaded against English-speaking South Africans, and for two reasons. The first can best be illustrated by my own experience: in my school years, while accustomed to English at home, I was taught Dutch in the classroom, but in the playgrounds spoke the budding Afrikaans of those days to my playmates.

This difference between the spoken and the written form of my second language did not, at the time, endear either to me. As a consequence, my interest in this second language lacked stimulation; and this unfortunately was the experience of many other South Africans of my age group whose home language was English. The second reason arises from the fact that, on the whole, Afrikaners do not appreciate the unequal benefits that flow from learning English as a second language, on the one hand, and Afrikaans as a second language on the other. The Afrikaans youth, in acquiring English, immediately obtains the key to a vast store of wealth. The language he acquires enables him to be understood in almost every corner of the globe, opens up to him the finest and most comprehensive literature the world has to offer, and makes available to him complete ranges of textbooks on any conceivable subject. Against this, the English-speaking youth, in learning Afrikaans, acquires a vernacular just recently raised to the status of language, with but a slender literature, of limited use as a medium of higher education, and of relatively little value outside the Union itself. This disparity in the incentive to learn the respective second language is profound, and so long as men are swayed by incentives, the Afrikaans youth is unduly favoured. Conditions are not so bad today as they were in my youth, but the disparity will obviously continue for a long time.

*

Ascendancy of Afrikaans

However, the younger generations of English-speaking South Africans are taking more readily to the study of Afrikaans – particularly as there is no longer the confusion with Dutch. There is even the possibility of the English-speaking section drawing parallel with the Afrikaners in bilingualism – especially in the country districts where the Afrikaner's knowledge of English has deteriorated considerably. Despite that, the members of the English section have only themselves to blame for the disadvantageous position in which they find themselves. Having agreed to the dual language provision of the South Africa Act, they should have applied themselves much more diligently to the learning of Afrikaans and the implementation of this provision of the Act. Their grounds for complaint, where it rests upon their bilingual shortcomings, are therefore weak. Where their advancement is being thwarted by political bias, however, which unfortunately has crept into the public services of the country, the loser in the long run will be the country as a whole.

One cannot but admire the fight the Afrikaners put up for the recognition of their language. Not only had they to meet the formidable challenge of English, which at one stage appeared to be well on its way towards becoming the sole official language of the country, but in addition they had to overcome the division in their own ranks as to whether Dutch or Afrikaans was to be the final choice. I can well remember in my youth the bitter arguments on this issue, for the advocates of Dutch often stigmatized Afrikaans as the language of the Hottentots – a term of opprobrium used by some to describe the Coloured peoples of the Cape.

In this fight for the recognition of Afrikaans, General Hertzog and his associates played a leading part, and it is a reflection on Afrikaner generosity that so little has as yet been done to commemorate his services in this respect. While English-speaking South Africa could not approve of much of the General's policy, I do believe that, on the whole, the English-speaking section today has a great admiration for the tenacious fight he put up for what he sincerely believed to be the rights of the Afrikaner people.

This feeling was greatly enhanced by his resolute refusal to jettison the principle of equal rights for both sections in the Union, when confronted with a demand for this from a section of the Afrikaners during the tragic phases of the Second World War, when victory appeared to be in Hitler's grasp. Although this stand meant his obliteration as a political force in the Union, it did highlight the character and sincerity of the man, proving to the English section that in him they had a friend in adversity.

Afrikaans and the future

I believe that, when the history of the rise of the Afrikaner people comes to be seen in perspective, the struggle and ultimate victory for the recognition of Afrikaans will be seen as one of their outstanding achievements. During this period their strivings were constructive and creative, and gave their leaders direction and a clear and worth-while objective. So much of the Afrikaner's struggle before this was basically a quest for privilege or the entrenchment of existing privilege – in particular, privilege over the non-White peoples of the country.

Unfortunately, with the victory for Afrikaans and its final establishment, the drive of some of these people in seeking new outlets is once again manifesting itself in the traditional urge towards separation. This section is convinced that in every walk of life the Afrikaners must move and act as a distinct entity, as a pure racial group, as if commanded to do so from Heaven.

Despite the freedom and massive privileges enjoyed by Afrikaners in general, many believe that they have not yet reaped all the fruits that should be theirs. In consequence, they seek larger freedoms and greater privileges. Among the more extreme Nationalists, the republican aim and the policy of apartheid are supported with fervour in the belief that that will sever Commonwealth ties, and confirm the privileges of baasskap. Somehow, membership of the Commonwealth is linked in the minds of those people with the dominant position exercised by the English-speaking section in the economic life of the country. Therefore, they feel, the severing of this link is imperative and should speedily lead to the Afrikaner gaining what he believes to be his rightful share in the industry and trade of the Union. There is, however, no such connection. The relative backwardness of the Afrikaners in the trade and industry of the country is due to the fact that, until the turn of the century, they were essentially pastoralists and hardly interested themselves in commerce and industry. Since then they have been making considerable headway in these spheres.

At bed-rock the extreme Nationalist wants Afrikaner domination of the economic life of the nation, or economic independence as he calls it, and for this a republic becomes essential. But the republic in itself will not end the extremist's ambitions. If economic domination does not speedily follow it, he will employ subterfuge and political devices, no matter how shady, to achieve this end. He will have no scruples.

To the extent that the more level-headed Nationalists are prepared to allow their Party to be used for such purposes, the country will be led along an extremely perilous path. Objectives which merely seek entrenchment and extension of privilege are spurious and are bound to result in turmoil and loss – loss of prestige and of hard-won achievements, even loss to the language. It should not be forgotten that the language of the Coloured peoples is also predominantly Afrikaans. And it cannot be disputed that those people played an important part in the moulding of its idiom and expressiveness in its cradle days. Leaders among them claim that the Afrikaans language is as much (if not more) theirs as it is that of the Afrikaners. Enforced apartheid or baasskap could therefore conceivably turn these people away from Afrikaans, making it the poorer for such loss. As it is, in the development of Afrikaans little regard has been paid to the wishes and feelings of these people.

The propensity for Afrikaner distinctiveness on the part of a section of the people has also to some extent resulted in the stimulation of the language by what one might term hot-house methods. A language, like a plant, should, after its infant nursing, be allowed to blossom in its natural environment, to acquire vigour and adapt itself to the conditions around it. Excessive pampering often leads to weakness and early decay. In this respect there is a growing feeling that perhaps too much stress is being laid upon what is regarded as the purity of the language. As a result, there is a tendency to formulate new and cumbersome words, instead of adopting appropriate foreign words extensively used by Afrikaners in everyday discussions – especially English words derived from peculiarly British or American developments. It would almost seem that the Afrikaners are going out of their way to make the language difficult for the English-speaking person in the country, let alone for the average Coloured or African. The Dutch are not nearly so fussy about the adoption of foreign words, and the English language is riddled with them. Surely in a multi-racial country it would be an advantage if the respective languages could be drawn closer together rather than driven apart. It is to be hoped that this excessive zeal for Afrikaner distinctiveness will pass in the course of time, for it is likely to retard rather than encourage the use of the language, and so detract from the merit of this significant Afrikaner achievement.

PART TWO

The economics of race differentiation in South Africa

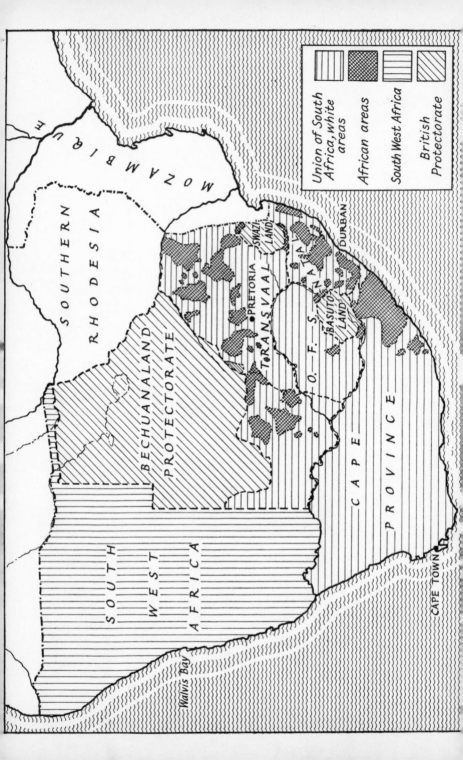

6

PROSPERITY DURING THE PAST
TWENTY-FIVE YEARS

ECONOMICALLY, South Africa has been one of the most fortunate countries during the past quarter of a century. In the early 1930s the country faced an economic crisis of the first magnitude, for at that time the gold-mining industry appeared to be on the decline, and the severe world depression very nearly ruined the farming community. During that period the United Kingdom was forced off the gold standard, but the Union, fearing for the future of the gold industry, decided to cling to the standard. This merely intensified the crisis to such an extent that, after a year of deepening gloom, the Union was forced to follow the British precedent. Despite the earlier fears, this step actually proved to be the turning-point in the material welfare of the country. Since then South Africa has not looked back, as events favourable to the economic fortunes of the Union followed in quick succession.

The fortunate years

The link with sterling at that stage resulted in an increase in the price of gold in terms of South African currency. This in turn revived the flagging profitability of the low-grade mines on the Witwatersrand and provided the necessary incentive for the opening of new mines. As world prices at that time were subject to severe deflationary pressure, the increased gold price was not overtaken by rising costs for some years. South Africa reaped an enormous benefit from this rise in the price of gold. But as if this were not enough, President Roosevelt, in his desperate efforts to defeat the depression in the United States, raised the dollar price of gold from 20·5 dollars to 35 dollars per ounce soon after; and this greatly increased the stimulus given to the gold-mining industry. Money poured into the country, not only to develop the gold-mines, but also for the general expansion of trade and industry that followed.

After some six years of boom conditions in the Union, the Second World War intervened. The effect of the war on the country's economy was very different from that experienced in Europe. Instead of industry being disorganized the Union was given an opportunity to develop secondary industries without having to meet world competition. Supplies of many manufactures having been cut off, the country was thrown upon its own resources, and made good use of this opportunity. Fortunately for South Africa, the production of gold during those years was maintained, despite the considerable pressure brought to bear upon the authorities to close the mines so that the plant and manpower could be directed towards increasing the country's war effort. All this enabled the Union to forge ahead economically – in no small measure at the expense of the older industrial countries of Europe and America, which were actively engaged in the war.

On top of this came the discovery of the rich goldfields in the Orange Free State. These were opened up after the end of the war, when hundreds of millions were invested in them. Capital continued to pour into the country on an unprecedented scale, the influx being substantially augmented by the transfer of British funds from India after independence was extended to that country. But fortune still smiled on the Union: yet another rich goldfield was opened up, this time in the Klerksdorp district of the Transvaal. And to crown it all, the development of nuclear power overseas and the urgent demand for uranium enabled the gold industry to earn vast sums through the extraction of the oxide of this metal from certain gold ores. The equipping of the industry for the extraction of uranium was financed by overseas agencies to the extent of over £70 million, virtually without recourse to South African capital resources. There seemed to be no end to the good fortune of South Africa during those twenty-five years.

Yet the average South African does not see the amazing development and prosperity of the country in this light. He tends to take the good fortune for granted, as if it has been his due. The dangers of this attitude will be shown later. There have nevertheless been cases of outstanding merit during these years, for a balanced picture of the country's progress could not be given without recognition of the immense financial courage displayed by some of the mining groups (principally the Anglo-American group) in opening up the Free State goldfields, where particularly difficult mining problems were encountered.

But all too frequently our political leaders boast of the nation's progress as if it were the result of purely South African endeavour. At this stage in the life of the Union we dare not overlook the good fortune of the country over the past twenty-five years. To do so would be to court disaster; nor can we leave out of the reckoning the far-reaching post-war world developments on whose currents we have drifted.

Increasing urbanization

In step with the rapid economic progress, profound changes have been taking place in the population of the country. During the past twenty-five years the White population has increased by more than one million and the non-Whites by over four million. The economic progress has been industrial rather than agricultural, with the result that the major increases in the population have been in the cities and towns, away from the essentially rural areas. In fact, there has been an actual drainage of Whites from the farming areas of about 150,000 during the quarter of a century under review, so that the White population increase in the urban areas actually exceeded the total for the country as a whole.

This pattern has not been followed entirely by the non-Whites, for although the larger increase has taken place in the cities and towns, the rural areas have absorbed an increase of about one and a half million. This means that over the past quarter of a century the non-White urban population has increased by something like two and a half million – an increase considerably greater than the number of non-White urban dwellers at the beginning of the period. In fact, this population has grown by about 130 per cent in the short span of twenty-five years.

These large increases in the urban areas have brought major problems in their train. Although in the early 1930s the African population in the cities did not appear to present a particularly serious problem, in the second half of the 1950s it has become the country's biggest headache. Industrialization everywhere is accompanied by problems of housing, transport and amenities generally, but in the Union, where African labour is paid a sub-economic wage, the problems become doubly difficult. Only in recent years have these obligations come forcibly to the fore, and it is not easy to escape the conclusion that White South Africa has slipped up badly in its obligations to non-White labour during the past quarter of a century of rapid industrialization. Even to this day I very much doubt whether the authorities have fully grasped the implications and magnitude of the problem.

The truth of the matter appears to be that the industrialization of the past twenty-five years has been much too rapid for the public conscience to keep pace. In our anxiety to develop industry, we have failed to appreciate the effects of such development on the non-Whites, and the Africans in particular. Hitherto White South Africans have been prone to regard the African, because of the colour of his skin and his primitive life of yesterday, as a raw, unskilled worker of an almost sub-human species, caring very little where and under what conditions he lives, and only being concerned that he turns up to work in our factories and other places of business regularly and on time. We wanted his labour, but did not want to know his human problems. Gradually it is coming home to most of us that he is a human being with feelings and opinions of his own, primitive though they are, and also that he is capable of developing skills and anxious to improve his lot and that of his family by education and other means.

We find that he responds to incentives and reacts to industrial employment very much as the white man does. In fact, where he is engaged in industry it is slowly dawning upon us that such industry can be efficient and thrive only if he is properly looked after, given peace of mind and the wherewithal to acquire those necessities of life that have come to be associated with industrial conditions the world over. Unfortunately we have lost a generation in our obligations to the African worker, and it is going to take many millions in money and much sympathy and understanding on the part of the Whites to recover this loss and retrieve the situation in the interests of all concerned – White and non-White alike.

It is unfortunate that the authorities see this question in a totally different and rather selfish light. Their outlook is clouded by fear for the future of the white man in South Africa. True, there are grounds for this fear, but the methods they are employing to safeguard the future do scant justice to the rights and aspirations of the non-Whites, and, if persisted in, will undermine the very foundations and standards the Whites seek to preserve and upon which in the final analysis White leadership rests. In the following chapters facts and figures will be given which cast some light upon the present prosperity of the country and which in some measure reveal the foundations upon which this prosperity rests. These will in large measure support the generalizations already expressed.

Economic uncertainties

Although apartheid or separate development of Whites and non-Whites has been the professed policy of the Nationalist Government for the past eleven years, to date very few statistics have been compiled to support or justify it. One would have thought that, before embarking upon so radical a policy, an effort would have been made to obtain facts about the respective contributions to and the benefits derived from the national economy by the Whites and the non-Whites. So far virtually no government publication has appeared in which such an analysis

has been attempted. Admittedly it would necessarily be somewhat empirical in the initial stages, but it could be improved,
and any publication would be better than none at all, for without facts and figures about the respective contributions and
benefits, the application of a policy of true apartheid would
be a mighty and dangerous step in the dark.

Professor Tomlinson, in the report of the Commission which
he headed, has given a considerable amount of information in
statistical form to illustrate the position of the Africans in the
Reserves. Although somewhat disjointed, much of this could
prove valuable. In fact, the statistics in the report are, to my
mind, the most valuable contributions made by the Commission
to the subject under investigation, for much of the report itself
is frankly tendentious. Apart from this, however, there is very
little published statistical information on the relative positions of
Whites and non-Whites in the economy of the country.

Under present conditions, no enlightened body would under-
take any vast scheme or put into practice any far-reaching
policy without adequate information from which the implications could be assessed. In this respect we might well follow the
United States of America and Soviet Russia, for both go to
endless pains to collect and tabulate information in statistical
form before embarking on any major project. Yet the present
South African Government, and the Nationalist Party in particular, is prepared to plunge the Union into the most revolutionary of projects, entailing the dismemberment of the
country's existing economic structure and its reconstruction
according to ideological concepts which have never as yet been
put into practice and whose outcome is·as yet problematical.
They have no blue-print whatsoever from which to construct
the country's future.

While it would be no easy matter for the private investigator
to compile comprehensive information on the multi-racial
aspects of the country's economy because he has no access to
many government records nor any statistical Act to back his
inquiries, yet intelligent analyses could be made from existing
published figures to illustrate the implications and consequences

of the policy of differentiation (baasskap) on the one hand, and separate development (apartheid) on the other. In the following chapters certain official facts have been presented in a form that should shed some light upon the relative contributions made and benefits received by the different racial groups that make up the population of the Union.

From these figures many revealing deductions can be made, giving an insight into the probable consequences of the policies of baasskap and apartheid. While it cannot be claimed that the picture given is a hundred per cent accurate (no worth-while statistical presentation ever is), it is believed to be sufficiently so to give a reliable indication of the Union's economic trends and the consequences of their being harnessed to a policy of separate development of the races.

There will doubtless be those who will question the reliability of the data given. Others will contend that figures can be manipulated to prove any pet theory or viewpoint. To the latter I quote the adage: 'While liars figure, figures do not lie', and to satisfy the statisticians, I have given in an appendix to this book fairly comprehensive details of the computations from which many of my deductions have been made.

This, under the title 'Statistical Survey of Earnings, Living Costs and Living Standards in South Africa', is included as an addendum rather than in the book itself because it is felt that many readers would not be interested in the detailed computations, which are somewhat technical and make rather tedious reading for those not versed in statistical methods. The survey nevertheless furnishes much information which should prove of value to students of economic conditions in South Africa. It is hoped that some government or public body will pursue the study initiated in the addendum, improve upon it in the light of more accurate and detailed information, and extend it as further information becomes available.

7

EARNINGS AND LIVING CONDITIONS OF THE DIFFERENT RACE GROUPS

I N the survey given in the appendix a study has been made of the changes that have taken place in the earnings and living conditions of the different racial groups in the country over the fifteen-year period from 1938/9 to 1953/4; it is unfortunate that the study could not be taken up to a more recent date, but this is mainly due to gaps in the information available. While the Union has a pretty good statistical service, the value of the information is often reduced by the fact that it is published only after far too long a delay. However, sufficient information about succeeding years has now become available to satisfy me that the trends shown over the fifteen years under review have continued over the later period also.

Another weakness is the grouping of the Coloured and Indian communities. While the living conditions of those communities vary considerably, they can both be regarded, from the point of view of living standards, as intermediate groups, between the Whites on the one hand and the Africans on the other. Subject to these qualifications, the survey supplies interesting and valuable information about the changes that have taken place in the living conditions of the different peoples in the Union over fifteen of its most significant years. The years cover the period of the Second World War, when much of Europe was destroyed and her economy ruined; the immediate post-war years with their amazing recovery from wartime dislocation; and, finally, the years of unprecedented progress up to what has come to be known as the atomic era.

*

164

The cost of living

During those years South Africa was singularly fortunate. Fortuitous developments, together with general world prosperity, lifted the economy of the Union to unprecedented heights of well-being. The appendix shows that the net national income of the country rose from £363·9 million in the year 1938/9 to £1,402·7 million in the year 1953/4 – an increase of 285 per cent over the relatively short period of fifteen years. However, much of this increase is accounted for by the general increase in price-levels.

The official cost-of-living index for the Union reflected a rise over this period of 94 per cent. This percentage I regard as an understatement of the true increase, and therefore, for reasons given in the survey, I have used a figure of 108 per cent. On this basis, the real increase in the national income is reduced from 285 per cent to 85 per cent. By real increase is meant that increase that remains after eliminating the portion accounted for by the higher price-levels. During this period of fifteen years the total population of the country rose from 10·07 to 13·3 million – an increase of approximately 32 per cent. Per head of population, therefore, the real increase in income amounted to approximately 40 per cent, which means that, on the average, the standard of living of the population (White and non-White taken together) improved by 40 per cent over the fifteen years under review.

Living costs and racial groups

When we come to examine the changes that have taken place in the different racial groups we see a totally different picture. Before giving the findings of the survey on this, I must call attention to a most serious misconception in the country – one for which the authorities must carry the major share of the blame. It is generally supposed that living costs have risen by the same percentage in the different racial groups. Nothing could be farther from the truth. But because of this supposition only one cost-of-living index has previously been compiled; and this on the basis of the living expenses of the average *White* middle-class family.

In the circumstances, this index has been used indiscriminately to register changes in living costs for all the groups. While the percentage of error, where such an index is used for the measurement of rising costs among the Coloured and Indian communities (the intermediate group), may not be excessive, it is totally false where it is made to apply to Africans – more especially to those whose families live in the Reserves or on the farms of Whites. And even when applied to a considerable section of the rural Coloureds and Indians the index is inadequate.

I have gone to considerable trouble in the survey to build up an index number which could, with a fair measure of justification, be applied to the living conditions of the Africans. I have not attempted to compile corresponding indices for the Coloureds and Indians, mainly because of the lack of the requisite information. Because they are intermediate groups, their respective index numbers would fall somewhere between those for the Whites and those for the Africans. In computing the living conditions of these groups I have used the official index (as adjusted in the survey), but in doing so am conscious of the fact that such application would not be fair to large numbers of families falling within these communities.

African living costs

The index (compiled by me) covering African conditions, registered an increase in living costs over the fifteen years ended 1953/4 of 152 per cent against that of 108 per cent in respect of Whites. Those who would dispute this increase need only examine the increases that have taken place in the major items of food consumed by the Africans, and in native blankets. For the period under review these are:

Maize meal	..	..	155 per cent increase
Meat	..	..	..	200	,,	,,
Milk	..	..	..	100	,,	,,
Sugar	..	..	..	56	,,	,,
Blankets ..	..	..	400	,,	,,

The straight average of these increases is 182 per cent against the 152 per cent reflected in the index number given in the survey. Africans working in the cities, of course, eat other products, such as bread, beans, etc., and wear cheap European-style clothing. They also incur house rental and transport costs. These have been taken into account in the index I have compiled. When comparing an African index number with that officially compiled for Whites, it should be borne in mind that in the latter such items as rents (increase 53 per cent), bread (increase 25 per cent) and power (increase 30 per cent) form a substantial portion of the budget of the average White family. In the case of Africans living on farms or in the Reserves (the bulk of the African population) these items are negligible. The increases in the items I mentioned have been kept within limits by either subsidy or legislation and, accordingly, have kept down the increases in living costs for Whites, but not for most Africans.

The substantially larger increase in the cost of living of Africans compared with that of Whites, which to all intents and purposes has escaped official recognition, has had disastrous consequences for the bulk of Africans. This is clearly demonstrated by the relative figures for the different racial groups given in the appended survey. According to these figures, the standard of living of the average White family improved by something like 46 per cent over the fifteen years under review, while that of the average African family, excluding some 260,000 families whose living conditions underwent a fundamental change during those years, actually deteriorated to the extent of approximately 6·5 per cent. The 260,000 families excluded from this computation are those who removed themselves permanently from the Reserves and farms to the cities and towns during this period. Their living standards in 1953/4 were hardly comparable with those in 1938/9, for in the former year they lived in huts of their own making, incurred no transport costs, clothed themselves only in blankets and lived largely on un-processed foods, while in the latter they were compelled by city life to pay rent and transport, wear European clothes and eat processed foods. Of this small proportion of the total African population more will be said later. Against it, nearly, 1,600,000 families are included in the group which suffered a deterioration in real income of approximately 6·5 per cent. On the other hand, the Coloured and Indian group appear to have enjoyed an improvement in their standard of some 11 per cent, but this is in all probability an overstatement because of the application to their position of an inappropriate cost-of-living index number.

Decline in African real income

To the average African family this decrease in real income has meant privation and hardship, for its earnings have at best been sub-economic. There are, of course, cases where African real incomes have shown a substantial improvement over the years in question, but these are balanced by other African families whose standards have deteriorated by more than the 6·5 per cent average. A contributory cause of this deterioration springs from the fact that an ever-increasing population of Africans is confined to the limited Reserves, whose agricultural output continues to decrease as a consequence of soil erosion – the result of over-population by man and beast. Then, too, the rural African has been accustomed to supplementing his food supply from wild life available in the Reserves and on the farms. But while the African population in these areas steadily in-creases, the supply of wild life steadily dwindles.

Nevertheless, the predominant cause of the deterioration in African living standards arises from the absence of official recognition of the materially larger increase in the living costs of Africans compared with those of Whites. This has resulted in inadequate compensation to meet the higher costs of living – particularly in that proportion of the African wage which is payable in cash. The responsibility for this grave injustice to the African community must therefore fall primarily upon the Government and in particular the Department of Bantu Affairs, the obvious function of which is to care for the welfare of the Africans.

The magnitude of this offence against the African community can be gauged by the fact that, had the Africans been allowed to advance their living standards at the same rate as the Whites, their racial group would now be receiving annually an additional £80 million or more. This is a colossal sum for so poor a community as the African section in the Union, yet instead a good proportion of this sum must be finding its way annually into the pockets of the Whites.

There will, of course, be those who will contend that this bit of maladministration has been deliberately conceived in the interests of the Whites. This is definitely *not* the case, but this blunder of omission does reveal the unfortunate attitude of mind of a large section of the White population of the Union – an attitude of sheer indifference to the true welfare of the non-Whites. Moreover, it shows up the country in a singularly poor light as regards overseas critics in that the Africans have no representation by their own people in Parliament and are debarred from forming unions to protect their interests. Additionally, the disparity in the index numbers of progress recorded for the different race groups over the period in question can only be regarded as a complete refutation of the Government's interpretations of its apartheid policy. It reveals this policy not as one of just, separate development of the races, but of harsh discrimination against the Union's non-White population. In conjunction with the mass of discriminatory legislation enacted in recent years against people of colour, it casts a shadow over the sincerity of the white man in South Africa.

In the one instance where apartheid should have been for the benefit of Africans – in the use of a separate cost-of-living index for this group – it is ignored, but in every instance where the Whites stand to gain, the policy is vigorously enforced. This is most unfortunate and disconcerting to South Africans like myself, who sincerely believe in the superiority of White leadership.

The indifference of White South Africans to the true welfare of the Africans, as revealed by the fall in the living standards of the latter over the past fifteen to twenty years, is something that deserves the strongest censure. It can at best be branded as negligence, which will surely not go unpunished in the years ahead. The fall in the African's real earnings is a particularly nasty blot on White South Africa, for this deterioration has taken place during a period of unparalleled good fortune in the Union and unparalleled progress throughout the world. In every country standards have been rising and even in European countries, which fifteen years ago were crippled by war, the workmen today are enjoying materially improved conditions. In Great Britain today, for instance, the real income of the average wage-earner is 35 per cent higher than it was in the year immediately preceding the outbreak of the last war.

There are people who contend that the African does not deserve a higher real income because his labour is not worth more. While I do not believe that most White South Africans would subscribe to such a view, it has been expressed – both in and out of Parliament – by prominent members of the Nationalist Party. To arrive at any convincing conclusion on this issue, one would have to examine the causes which have given rise to the considerable improvement in living standards throughout the world since the Second World War.

Increased mechanization

Predominant among these is the increased application of mechanization to industry and economic effort generally. At no time in recorded history has there been a comparable increase in the application of power. And the function of power in mechanization (horse power, as it is termed) is to augment human power, so that greater quantities of goods and services can be produced by a given quantity of human power. In this way the earnings and living standards of the workers are consistently raised. Indeed, the real earnings of the workers are a function of (that is, directly proportional to) the amount of power used in industry. Under present-day industrial conditions it is the lower income groups that gain most by the application of power for, by so distributing the resulting benefits, the markets for the products of industry enjoy the optimum boost. This is actually what has been taking place the world over – except in South Africa, where the benefits of power have been appropriated exclusively in the interests of the Whites.

In the Union the increase in the use of power has been impressive. A fairly reliable record can be obtained from this table:

INDEX OF INCREASE IN POWER CONSUMPTION BETWEEN 1938/9 AND 1953/4

	1938/9	1953/4	Increase
Electric power	5,453 million units	9,676 million units	77 per cent
Oil	240 „ gallons	504 „ gallons	130 „
Coal	18 „ tons	31 „ tons	73 „
Agricultural tractors	6,500 units	75,000 units	1,050 „

Against these increases, the population of the Union (White and non-White taken together) rose by no more than 30 per cent over the same period. So that in the year 1953/4 the power used per head of every worker must have been at least 40 per cent higher than in the year 1938/9. Yet the bulk of the workers – the Africans – reaped no benefit whatever from this impressive increase in the use of power. Nor could it be argued that the African did not earn a higher living standard because he did not operate power tools.

To the older generation of South Africans there has been nothing more significant about the labour force of the country than the extent to which the African and the non-White generally have taken to the operation of power tools. Everywhere they are to be seen in control of them: in factories they feed or tend power-driven plant; in the mines they operate rock drills and other mechanized implements; and on the farms they drive tractors and lorries, feed threshing machines, and manage a wide range of farm implements. In fact, there are not many mechanical aids to production which the non-Whites do not operate. There can, in consequence, be no possible grounds for denying these people the monetary benefits that should inevitably flow from the use of power tools. This denial of the benefits of mechanization is not only an unfortunate development on moral grounds, but even more so on economic grounds, for the Whites in the Union are actually defeating the objects of mechanization by thwarting the dynamic process which sponsors the growth of industry.

White and non-White family incomes

Not only has the African been denied any benefits from the increased use of mechanical power, but there are grave doubts whether his level of earnings, even were he to be compensated to the full for his rise in living costs, is adequate remuneration for the work he performs. The statistical analysis in the appendix furnishes some enlightening data about this too. According to this analysis, the average income per White family for the year 1953/4 amounted to £1,616, against average family incomes of £308 and £145 respectively for the intermediate and African groups. In arriving at these figures the earnings of all members of the average family have been taken into account, and in the case of the Whites the family income has been considerably augmented by receipts from investments in the form of dividends, interest and rentals.

These figures suggest that the average White family is more than five times better off than the average Coloured or Indian family, and nearly twelve times so compared with the average African family. Whether such disparity in relative incomes is warranted by existing facts is open to the gravest doubts. There will be those who would challenge these figures – especially the level of White incomes. But if they will take the trouble to study the appended survey they will find that the figures are borne out by the details given, which in the aggregate reach the high level of the country's national income which is often quoted in support of the economic progress made in recent years. The following table reflects the position:

NATIONAL AND FAMILY INCOMES BY RACE GROUPS – 1953/4

	No. of Families (in thousands)	Total Income (in £ millions)	Income per Family £
Whites	646	1,044·03	1,616
Coloureds and Indians	287	88·25	308
Africans	1,858	269·79	145
All races	2,791	1,402·07	503

However, for the purpose of perspective, the figures of family incomes require further elaboration. In the case of Whites, many families do not receive anything like the £1,616 shown. In particular this applies to young couples who have small children to care for and depend solely on the salary or wage of the head of the family. In other families where there are no small children or where these are grown up, the family income is usually augmented by the earnings of the wife or the grown-up children, and in most cases also by income from investments. In the circumstances, the young White couples with small children find it exceedingly difficult to make ends meet if they attempt to live at the standard set by the better-placed families.

Unfortunately, in the Union the living standards of the Whites generally are set by the better-situated families, who regard a motor-car, a domestic servant, an annual holiday at the seaside and a wide range of modern domestic appliances as essential. In this respect the average White family in the Union lives at a standard equal to that of its counterpart in the United States of America, but in addition enjoys a great deal more leisure because the latter has to do without domestic help. Compared with the average family income of £1,616, the average male salary or wage for the year 1953/4 was only £715. These figures give some indication of the disadvantages experienced by the young couples who are forced to rely on the earnings of the male head only. In a better-regulated society such families would undoubtedly have received some form of aid during this phase of their married life.

While in the case of Africans the average family income was £145 in the year 1953/4, this figure was the average of three distinct groups who live under very different conditions and received different levels of income. The three groups are (i) those whose families live in the Reserves, (ii) those whose families live on the farms of Whites, and (iii) those whose families live in the cities and larger towns. According to the survey, the average family incomes of the respective groups for the year 1953/4 were approximately: Reserves £97, Farms £120, and Cities £213.

This does not mean that the African city-dwellers are living at a standard more than twice as high as that of Africans who live in the Reserves, for – as already outlined – conditions are vastly different for the respective families. It is therefore extraordinarily difficult to measure their relative living standards. While the one group *in part* still adheres to the hereditary tribal customs, the other has of necessity adopted Western industrial conditions.

In referring to the former group I have said 'in part', because of almost every family living in the Reserves one or more of its members is absent, for part of the year at least, for the purpose of augmenting the family income in the cities or the mines. The survey shows that, of the average income of £97, at least £67 is derived from sources outside the Reserves and only some £30, mainly in kind, from the Reserves themselves.

Racial discrimination and wage rates

Coming back to our comparisons of White and non-White earnings for the year 1953/4 we find that, whereas the average salary or wage of the head of the White group was £715, that of the intermediate group was £210 and of the African group £100 approximately. Using these figures, the average earnings of the Whites were 3·4 times that of the Coloureds and Indians and 7·1 times that of the Africans. These figures, of course, ignore investment income, which to all intents and purposes is confined to the Whites because the incomes of the non-Whites, the Africans in particular, are too inadequate to permit of saving.

Of course the level of earnings of the Whites should in fact be higher than that of the non-Whites, because the former are mainly skilled while a large proportion of the latter are unskilled. But were all the former group skilled (which is not the case) and all the latter unskilled (which is nowhere near the truth), a ratio of seven to one in favour of the former would be insupportable in any modern industrial country. Only in backward countries, where industrialization has not yet taken root and where abundant human labour is extensively used without the aid of power tools, will such a ratio be found.

However, race discrimination is the official policy of the country and the low rates paid to Africans are justified by the low levels of wages in other African territories and in Asia. Critics of this policy are told that the African has really no grounds for complaint, because the Union has hitherto been a magnet for African workers from many neighbouring territories where wage levels are considerably lower than in the Union. This reasoning springs from an attitude customary among the White population of the Union, but is one that has dangerous implications for the future of the country, as later chapters will show. All too frequently the non-Whites, principally the Africans, are regarded as an inferior species, not entitled, even for the same work, to wage levels and living standards comparable with those enjoyed by Whites. Moreover, certain employers of labour still cling to the outmoded concept of the employer-employee relationship characteristic of the capitalist system of the nineteenth century, when labour was regarded as a commodity to be bought on the open market at the lowest possible price, and as African labour could be obtained extra-territorially at low rates, there was no obligation to raise these rates for Africans resident in the country. The argument based on non-White inferiority was once widely held, but is rapidly losing its cogency as non-Whites everywhere show their aptitude in many skills and walks of life. In the Union, however, the viewpoint dies hard among a section of the Whites.

The second argument, which rests upon low wage-rates in other territories, can be answered by reference to conditions in highly-developed countries: what, for instance, would the American, Australian or, for that matter, the White South African workman say if he were told to be satisfied with wage levels earned by his counterparts in, say, Italy or Greece, where wages are of necessity low? Such a suggestion would no doubt be regarded as the height of absurdity, and in fact no enlightened employer would dare to mention such an argument in any labour dispute with those workers. The reason why it is still resorted to where Africans are concerned, rests on the flimsy grounds that the non-Whites are not yet regarded as fully-fledged citizens of the country and are therefore not entitled, among other rights, to share in the national income according to the full value of the work performed by them. In modern industrial countries the workers are now regarded as partners in the equity of the nation, and the trade unions take good care to see that they get their legitimate share of the national product. Non-White workers have not yet reached this status in the Union and are still regarded very much as chattels to be acquired in the cheapest markets.

Under present conditions the earnings of workers bear a definite relationship to the welfare of the community: in countries which have rich resources or are highly industrialized, wage-rates are higher than in those less well endowed or not so highly developed. This relationship is, in fact, fundamental to the continued prosperity of the relatively rich and well-developed countries. But in the Union, owing to the policy and practice of discrimination on the basis of colour, this essential requirement of an industrial society is lacking where the non-Whites are concerned. In the long run, this state of affairs is bound to react to the material disadvantage of the Union.

Underpayment of Africans

It is by no means easy to demonstrate by statistics the extent of the alleged underpayment of non-White labour in the Union. International comparisons of wage-rates and living standards are often misleading, and the relative statistics frequently require qualification if they are to be used as reliable guides. However, if it were possible to relate average earnings per head of population on the one hand, with the degree of industrialization on the other, for a number of countries including the Union, some indication could be obtained of the adequacy or otherwise of the rates of pay in South Africa.

With this object, an index of industrial development has been compiled based upon power consumed per head of population in a number of countries. In the following table these figures are related to the incomes per head of population in the corresponding countries. The power index is given in composite units derived from electric current, liquid fuels and coal consumed. The comparison is for the year 1954. (*See following page.*)

Unfortunately the figures of income per head do not give a very accurate index of the relative living standards in the countries in question. The figures are in sterling and have been converted at the rates of exchange then current. It is common knowledge, however, that the internal purchasing power of most currencies differs greatly from the external worth. This is particularly true of the South African currency, which has a relatively high internal buying power compared with its external equivalent in other countries. For instance, 2·80 dollars (the official exchange rate) in the United States of America buy very much less of the ordinary household requirements than does the South African pound within the Union.

A true comparison of the buying powers of the various currencies within their respective countries is not easy to

RELATIONSHIP OF POWER CONSUMED TO INCOME PER
HEAD OF POPULATION

Country	Power Consumed per Head (Composite Units)	Income per Head £
United States of America	15·2	696
Canada	14·3	485
Great Britain	9·3	326
Sweden	8·9	370
Australia	8·6	344
New Zealand	7·9	375
Union of South Africa		
Total population	5·7	105
White population	(27·0)	376
African population	—	27
France	5·3	293
Italy	2·6	100
Japan	2·6	60
India	·25	25

determine. However, from actual experience it has been found
that the living standard of the average White South African
middle-class family is not far short of that of its opposite number
in the United States of America, and is definitely above that in
any European country and probably higher than that in
Canada. Irrespective of this defect in the table, it is clear that,
in relation to the figure for power consumed, the income per
head of total population is inordinately low, while that per head
of White population is exceedingly high.

Earlier it was demonstrated that, over the fifteen-year period
ended 1953/4, the White population appropriated the entire
benefit in income that flowed from the large increase in the
use of power over those years. This is largely borne out by a
comparison with Indian conditions, where a low power consumption per head of population meant a low income per head
– approximately equal to that of Africans in the Union. The

incongruity of this appropriation is strikingly demonstrated if power consumed in the Union is equated to the White population only. On this basis the power consumption shows a figure of 27 units – virtually double that applicable to the United States of America.

This would suggest that the degree of industrialization among South African Whites is virtually twice that of the United States of America. This, of course, is sheer nonsense, for the average White worker in the Union is not nearly as heavily engaged in industry as are the Americans in general.

Another means of demonstrating the underpayment of non-White workers in the Union would be by a comparison of piece-work rates. For instance, in the Union a wool shearer (often coloured) is paid from 35s. to 40s. per 100 sheep, while in Australia the rate of pay is 160s. per 100 sheep. Converting this to South African currency, the rate becomes 120s. or approximately three times the scale paid in the Union. Yet another significant comparison is the percentage that salaries and wages represent of total national income in different countries. In the Union this percentage is approximately 55, while in other similarly industrialized countries the percentages range from 65 to 70. These percentages suggest that salary- and wage-rates in the Union are low in comparison with those of other countries. But as the incomes of the Whites in the Union rank among the highest in the world, the low rates could apply only to the non-Whites. An extra 10 per cent of the national income in salaries and wages would mean an additional £150 million to £170 million per annum for the non-Whites.

Not only from the point of view of the work performed are the present non-White wage levels inadequate – those of Africans in particular – but also in relation to the minimum food and other requirements essential to efficient and healthy industrial conditions. A study of African family budgets, given in the survey attached, discloses the scantiness and absence of variety of, the diet of these families. In quantity, quality and variety the food standards are insufficient to provide the health and stamina necessary for heavy and exacting industrial labour.

The average sum available for food per male worker in the cities is given in the survey as something like £35 per annum. In the gold-mines, where a close study has been made of the necessary balanced diet to sustain a mine worker, the cost of feeding workers averaged about £40 per annum in 1954. The food items making up this cost were, however, estimated at cost to the mining companies, who buy in bulk at the keenest of rates. At retail prices – the only prices available to city workers – the cost of such items would have been nearer £60 than the £40 paid by the companies. Therefore to feed the average family of man, wife and 2·8 children on an adequate and balanced diet would have cost the city-dwellers about £185 a year. Over and above this, housing, transport, clothes and other necessaries must cost well over £100 per annum if a reasonable standard of respectability is to be maintained. So an income of at least £300 a year would seem to be necessary to maintain an African family in the cities under reasonable conditions of health and comfort.

This does not mean that the head of the family should have earned as much as that, but that the entire family earnings should have approached that figure. Against this sum, according to the survey, the average family earnings of African city residents amounted to £212 in the year 1953/4, so that from the point of view of a minimum standard of health and comfort, this figure should have been approximately 50 per cent higher.

From yet another aspect, wage levels of Africans are much too low. On present wage-scales the average African cannot possibly save, for their family incomes, as shown, are inadequate to maintain even the minimum standards of health and comfort. In the circumstances, the only people who are actually in a position to save are the Whites. The result is that, as the country progresses, all the savings accrue to them. This means that the income gap between Whites and non-Whites continually widens in favour of the former because of the incomes derived from investments.

The country as a whole is, therefore, sustaining a form of capitalism by which the rich grow richer and the poor relatively poorer. This is a serious cancer – the product of racial discrimination – which is made doubly dangerous by the fact that those who grow richer are Whites and those who grow poorer are non-Whites. History offers numerous instances of this type of social system; and inevitably it has ended in revolution. Yet at present, because of the tight control exercised over Africans in the country, we are inclined to believe that any revolution on the part of the Blacks cannot succeed. But, revolution or no, the cancer will inevitably spread unless efforts are made to root it out; and if this is not done, the cancer will in the end, by evolutionary process and economic laws, completely undermine the dominant position of the Whites in the Union.

It would appear, therefore, that from every conceivable point of view – the ethical, the value of the work performed, the minimum consumption requirements, and the future economic stability of the country – the income levels of the non-Whites in the Union are inadequate and call for substantial and urgent increases.

The extent of the underpayment of the African in the Union cannot be determined accurately, but underpayment is an economic fact. On the basis of comparative power consumption in different countries, given in the table on page 178, it appears that the average income per head in the Union is unduly low at £105 per annum. The table suggests that an annual income of about £200 would be more in conformity with the average income-to-power ratios in other lands. As Whites' real earnings are extraordinarily high in the Union, the depressed figure of £105 can only be accounted for by the underpayment of or the lack of efficiency on the part of the non-Whites.

Unfortunately, African labour *is* materially less efficient than White in the Union. This is due to various causes – less knowledge, training, experience and initiative on the one hand, and African traditions and customs on the other. But with the growth of industrialization the gap in the efficiencies is gradually narrowing while that in earnings is widening. It may well be that, after making allowance for African inefficiency, an average income per head of population of approximately £150 would be a fair level for the Union, having regard to the level of power consumption. This would be a compromise based upon recognition that the low figure of earnings per head in the Union was accounted for by 50 per cent for African inefficiency, and the other 50 per cent by underpayment for African services. This figure would permit a trebling of African earnings without any material diminution of White earnings. Such a rise would, however, seriously embarrass individual industries in the country, particularly the all-important gold-mining industry and many branches of agriculture. It is therefore not possible to contemplate a threefold increase in African wages at present, and in one fell swoop.

Economic consequences of underpayment

Nevertheless, Africans are seriously underpaid and it is imperative that a substantial increase be given them in the immediate future – even if this should mean some sacrifice by the Whites. It has already been shown that, at present rates of pay, African families generally are undernourished. So, too, are they inadequately housed and clothed. In the case of city-dwellers it has also been shown that minimum requirements of food, housing and clothing for efficient service would necessitate an increase of at least 50 per cent in present African family earnings.

As earnings on farms and of Reserve-dwellers are materially lower than in the cities, it is essential that these earnings also be increased by at least 50 per cent. The country could well afford such an increase in the immediate future without undue embarrassment to particular industries and with very little, if any, sacrifice on the part of the Whites. In fact, many Whites should even benefit by the increase, as the national income of the country is likely to be increased thereby. In round figures, the increase would give the Africans an additional £150 million or so a year, of which approximately £80 million is accounted for by the inadequate compensation, previously mentioned,

for increases in living costs and standards accorded to the
Whites over the past fifteen to twenty years.

Such an increase would appear highly desirable as a first
step, for it would have the effect of reversing the trend whereby
Africans have been becoming poorer and the Whites richer.
But by itself this increase would be insufficient. In the years that
follow annually-increasing sums would have to be set aside for
non-White housing, education and other amenities, gradually
building up the standards of living of these people. We hear a
good deal about the sums expended on African housing in
recent years: £30 million has been spent in this way over the
past ten years on the construction of some 80,000 houses. This
sum, when compared with an annual expenditure of about £50
million on White housing, does not appear particularly impressive. Indeed, the construction of 8,000 houses a year for
Africans living in the towns and cities will soon prove inadequate to meet requirements arising from the natural increase in
the population of the towns and cities alone. Not only should
more houses be built, but the standard of the houses should be
gradually raised as the Africans become more proficient in
their various walks of life. In this way their wants and resultant
buying power will be raised in the interests of local industry.

On this issue of African remuneration the outlook of the
average White South African requires reorientation. All too
frequently we are told by cabinet ministers and others that
African amenities are costing the Whites of the country something like £30 million a year. Seen in this light, the African is
regarded as a burden to the white man. Nothing is farther from
the truth than this concept. In the Union the facts are entirely
the opposite: on the basis of international standards the
Africans are underpaid to the tune of at least five times the
£30 million mentioned. And the Whites have benefited enormously because of this underpayment. It is high time that
White South Africa realized that its non-White population is an
immensely valuable asset – a valuable human resource which it
should develop to the full in the interests of the country and all
its inhabitants. Nor should we try to justify low wage-rates by

pointing to conditions in undeveloped African territories or in the grossly overpopulated lands of Asia. The concept that human labour is a form of commodity to be acquired in the cheapest market belongs to the nineteenth century. Industrialization, as we know it today, has completely altered this.

The concept of the second half of the twentieth century is that the worker is a partner in the business of the nation and should therefore share in its equity. The best use should be made of his labour and talents and he should receive a just and appropriate reward for the work he performs – whether he be White or non-White. Only so far as this concept of its non-White labour is accepted and put into practice can South Africa, as a nation, hope to keep abreast of modern times. Failure to do so will inevitably lead to strife, retrogression and the ultimate overthrow of White leadership – not in two hundred years' time but before the close of the twentieth century.

8

THE VULNERABILITY OF THE
ECONOMY

THE economy of every country can be said to be vulnerable in some respect or other. So why pick on South Africa? The reasons are twofold: first, this book is about South Africa, and a country is very much like a business in that it is prudent to keep in view its weaknesses. The second and more important reason is that the present Union Government has decided to embark upon a revolutionary experiment in the conduct of the country's affairs. This is the experiment of apartheid or separate development of the races, which is being undertaken without any blue-print or clear appreciation of its economic consequences. And in any such experiment the weak links – not the strong – are those likely to snap.

National income

The progress and strength of a country's economy are usually measured by the growth of its national income – duly corrected for price changes. By this standard the Union has developed considerable strength and made material progress since the Second World War. The striking progress was, in fact, begun several years before the outbreak of the war, with the rise in the price of gold that followed the depression of the early 1930s.

A special feature of this development has been the growth of manufacturing industry which today contributes more to the income of the country than either mining or agriculture. Its contribution for the year 1956/7 was not far short of the contribution made by the other two taken together. The following table shows the relative contributions made during that year:

	Income in £ millions	Percentage of Total Geographical Income
Agriculture, Forestry and Fishing	277·1	14·4
Mining	259·7	13·5
Manufacturing (Private)	452·9	23·5
Total Geographical Income	1930·7	100·0

These figures disclose that 51·4 per cent of the geographical income of the country was derived from agriculture, mining and manufacturing – the sources of income which constitute the foundation of the country's economy, the rest being mainly superstructure. Yet, judging by the percentages shown here, most people would conclude that manufacturing industry today is the most important *prime mover* sustaining the country's economy, which is definitely not the case, for a large section of manufacturing industry, while not exactly superstructure, depends vitally upon either agriculture or mining – particularly the latter.

Exports and imports

To illustrate this, I have made an analysis of exports and imports that pertain to the different fields of production. At the time of the analysis, the most recent detailed figures available were for 1955. For the purpose of the analysis I have grouped exports and imports under the following heads: agricultural products, pastoral products, precious minerals, base minerals, manufactures, and 'others'. To do justice to the respective groups I have split certain of the export items given under 'manufactures' so that agricultural products and minerals could be credited with their due proportions of such exports. The principal items affected were sugar, maize meal, canned fruit, wines, vegetable oils and cut diamonds. The analysis of exports gave the following details:

Exports for 1955
in £ millions

Agricultural products	53·0
Pastoral products	80·0
Precious minerals	247·0
Base minerals	41·0
Manufactures	85·0
Others	8·0
Total	£514·0

These items (except 'others') represent the exports of specific industrial groups. All these groups in some measure or other depend upon the importation of raw materials and equipment, and in certain cases are responsible also for invisible imports, such as dividend and interest payments to overseas investors. Accordingly, so far as practicable, I ascertained the cost to the different industrial groups of imports – both visible and invisible. These costs are debited to, or set against, the exports of the respective groups. In this way I obtained a balance-sheet of the exports and imports of the different industrial groups.

BALANCE-SHEET OF EXPORTS AND IMPORTS BY DIFFERENT
INDUSTRIAL GROUPS (1955)

	Debit Balances *£ millions*	*Credit Balances* *£ millions*
1 Agricultural Industry	—	23
2 Pastoral Industry	—	76
3 Precious Mineral Industry	—	215
4 Base Mineral Industry	—	36
5 Manufacturing Industry	175	—
6 Others	—	8
Available for Direct Imports	183	—
	358	358

The table shows that whereas the agricultural, pastoral and mineral industries (both precious and base) have credit balances on the external payments account of the country, manufacturing industry imposes an onerous debit balance on it. This means that groups 1, 2, 3 and 4 earn more than sufficient foreign currency to maintain themselves in the economy of the country, but group 5, manufacturing industry, is totally unable to do so and, in consequence, can exist only with the aid of the credit balances earned by the other groups. It also means that if the credit balances earned by the four self-supporting groups were to decline to any marked extent, manufacturing industry would suffer a set-back. Such a set-back could be cushioned partially upon direct imports, but in all probability to only a small extent because a large proportion of direct imports, such as oils, etc., must be regarded as necessities.

Another significant feature of the balance-sheet is the size of the credit balance derived from the precious mineral industries – gold-mining in particular. In 1955 this group provided 60 per cent of the total credit balance, and since then, as a result of the fall in prices of primary products, and the increase in gold and uranium production, this percentage has crept up to something like 70.

These figures emphasize in no uncertain terms the tremendous importance to the country's economy of the precious mineral industries, and the extent to which manufacturing industry under present conditions is kept alive by the mining of these minerals and their sale overseas. Furthermore, as the production of gold and uranium is really one industry – for much of the latter could not be extracted economically were it not for the income derived from the mining of gold – it will be realized how heavily the country is dependent upon one particular industry – gold mining. A serious set-back in this industry could result in a virtual collapse of the economy of South Africa.

So often one hears of the increased diversification in the country's economy, and the contention that manufacturing industry is gradually replacing primary industry – agriculture and mining – as the backbone of the economic structure of the country. Unfortunately, the foregoing figures tend to refute this viewpoint, for they show all too clearly that to date manufacturing industry has been no substitute for gold mining in the Union's economy.

Development and weakness of manufacturing industry

Manufacturing industry, however, is not a homogeneous group as gold mining is. It includes building and construction and a wide range of manufactures of varying importance to the country. In the circumstances, one should not generalize too lightly in speaking of this group. A section of it is no less economically significant than gold mining. In this section are included those secondary industries which use local raw materials in the making of products for export, such as fruit, vegetable and fish canning, iron and steel, sugar, and other similar industries. On the other hand, there are numerous industries under 'manufactures' that are vitally dependent upon imported materials, in many instances themselves already partially manufactured. These do not contribute to the same extent to the country's welfare and in some cases may be akin to burdensome superstructure.

The weakness in the manufacturing group is that it does not export sufficient of its products to pay for its necessary imports of raw materials, equipment, etc. The exports of the group have been growing steadily, however, and in the opinion of some should be sufficient to balance its necessary imports in the not-too-distant future. In the year 1955 the position of the group was roughly as shown in the table overleaf.

It should be explained, however, that the figure of exports given below is the net amount after deducting that proportion of the value that should rightly be included in the exports of agricultural and mineral products. The gross figure of exports of manufactures for that year was in the vicinity of £95 million. But of this sum approximately £43 million went to the Federation of the Rhodesias under a special treaty, and at least a further £28 million to the British Commonwealth by virtue of

IMPORTS AND EXPORTS OF MANUFACTURING INDUSTRY (1955)

	£ million
Imports of materials	230
Imports of equipment	20
Dividends and interest on external capital	20
	260
Less: Exports	85
External currency deficit	175

Imperial Preference or dollar restrictions in the sterling group of countries. So approximately 75 per cent of the Union's exports of manufactures have been going to the British Commonwealth under favoured conditions. As a consequence, these exports have not been exposed to the full implications of external competition.

Since 1955 exports of manufactures to the Federation of the Rhodesias increased materially to a total in excess of £60 million for the year 1957. While South Africa remains within the Commonwealth, her exports favoured by Imperial Preference would appear to be relatively secure, but benefits gained through dollar restrictions are likely to fall away in the near future. On the other hand, can the Union reasonably expect exports to the Federation to remain at a level approximating to £60 million annually, while the Union in return imports only about £14 million from the Rhodesias? The more one examines this one-sidedness in the external trade of the two countries, the more convinced one becomes that within the next few years drastic changes in this position will take place. Except where one territory is vitally dependent upon raw materials from another, no country will for long tolerate so great a disparity in trade – particularly under special treaty arrangements and under conditions where the invisible items of trade are also against it, as is the case of the Federation and the Union.

The Federation has been expanding economically at a considerably faster rate than the Union, and manufacturing industry is being established there wherever practicable. When once such industry gets into its stride, the Federation will probably be far less dependent on South African manufactures. In fact, one can visualize a future in which the Federation's industries will be supplying most of the products hitherto acquired from the Union. Except for such raw materials as fish and certain fruits, there is very little in the way of materials which the Rhodesias cannot produce in order to compete with South Africa in her own markets.

New industries in the Federation include iron and steel, sugar, fertilizers, chemicals, rubber goods and even motor-cars – the products of all of which are likely to replace imports from the Union. A time may even come, if the Rhodesias continue their past rate of expansion, when that territory will emerge as a serious competitor of the Union in African markets generally. For in many of these markets the Federation will have a geographical advantage and her more liberal policy in utilizing African labour will meet with greater favour in other African territories. However, for some time yet the Union will enjoy the advantages of greater industrial experience and of a larger local market, though with the passage of time these advantages are likely to disappear. In the circumstances, South Africa's market for manufactures in the Federation of £60 million per annum does not appear to be particularly secure, unless the Union is prepared to take a very much larger quantity of the Federation's goods a year.

Outside the British Commonwealth and the African territories to the north of the Union, the prospects of exports of South African manufactures are not particularly bright. And even in these favoured territories there appear to be set-backs in store. So, under existing conditions and in the near future, the chances of South African manufacturers exporting sufficient to pay for their group's necessary imports cannot be regarded too optimistically.

*

The future of the diamond industry

The next consideration of vital consequence to the country's economy is the outlook for precious mineral production in South Africa. As shown in the balance-sheet of exports and imports, the well-being of the Union depends to an almost overwhelming extent on the mining and export of precious minerals. By far the most important of these minerals is gold, but they also include, in order of importance, uranium, diamonds and platinum. The last-mentioned has so far been relatively unimportant and is unlikely in future to measure up to the other minerals under review.

Diamonds, on the other hand, have played a considerable role in the development of the country. For close on a hundred years the sale of gems has figured prominently in the Union's exports and the industry has been no mean contributor to the welfare of the country throughout this period. In the past few years the value of diamonds produced has exceeded £25 million a year for the Union and South West Africa taken together. During the past decade the industry has enjoyed a high level of prosperity, but it is impossible to say to what extent the fields and mines can continue to yield gems at present levels, for the affairs of mining companies are a closed book. Up to the end of the Second World War it was generally accepted that production had to be curtailed in order not to flood markets, but there is now some evidence that the industry in the Union is experiencing difficulty in meeting demand. It seems that the supply of diamonds in the Union is not inexhaustible and that the time may not be too far distant when sources outside the Union will increasingly have to be relied upon to supply world requirements. On the other hand, the industry is sensitive to world conditions and in times of depression the demand for gems can fall off materially. Such a setback could be most embarrassing for the country, for it may happen that at such times hard-pressed owners may be forced to realize their holdings on unwilling markets.

Then, again, there are reports of rich finds in Russia. To

what extent these reports can be believed it is impossible to say, but if true, these discoveries may have an important bearing upon future production in the Union and South West Africa. To date very few of these stones have come on the markets of the West, and it is most unlikely that the U.S.S.R. will dump them at uneconomical prices on these markets. As Russian exports are strictly controlled, and as that country is in need of foreign exchange for purchases in the West, it is more likely that she will seek agreement with the West for a fair share of world markets at satisfactory price-levels.[1] In the event of such an agreement, production in the Union may have to be curtailed and this would to some extent affect the country's economy. While there is very little indication as yet of any falling-off of production or of any need to curtail output in the Union, the future of the industry has its unpredictable aspects.

Problems of the gold-mining industry

Of prime importance to the Union is the gold-mining industry, with which must go the production of uranium – the by-product of the gold industry. The present output of gold and uranium is valued at approximately £300 million a year, virtually all of which is exported. Furthermore, the industry does not draw heavily upon the external currency earnings of the country, so that over 85 per cent of the value of the output is available for the acquisition of foreign exchange so necessary to keep manufacturing industry afloat and to maintain the high living standards of the Whites in South Africa. What, therefore, is the future of this all-important industry? Can we rely upon it indefinitely to carry the burden of our economy? To answer these questions we must examine its prospects with care.

During the past few years the industry has been breaking records annually. Its production of gold and uranium is still rising and in all probability will continue to do so for some time to come. Moreover, there are those who insist that, under present conditions, gold is undervalued and that an increase

[1] Since this was written such an agreement has been concluded.

in its price is long overdue. In that event the industry in the Union will receive a further boost, and stimulate the country's economy to yet higher levels of prosperity. It appears that the industry is in a most healthy condition and that, from the economic point of view, the prospects of the country are bright.

Unfortunately, there are other aspects of the industry that give rise to some misgiving. In the first place, the gold ore is not inexhaustible, although the opening up of new mines in the Orange Free State and western Transvaal has certainly prolonged the life of the industry for many years. Secondly, the insidious inflation that has corroded money values since the outbreak of the Second World War has apparently not yet run its course, and should this continue it could have disturbing consequences for the industry. Moreover, gold has for some time been losing its former dominant influence on the currencies of the world. A further disturbing factor – one of particular relevance to conditions in South Africa – is the fundamental conflict of interests between gold mining and manufacturing industry in the matter of African wage levels. Lastly, there is the question of the future of uranium. If the price-level of the oxide of the metal is to fall after the termination of the present ten-year contracts, the gold-mining industry must suffer in some measure. All these considerations are likely, in varying degrees, to have some bearing upon the future of the gold industry in the Union.

The first consideration is the probable life of the industry based upon existing conditions, i.e. upon the present price of gold and the known reefs and ore reserves. About thirty years ago the future of the industry, based on the then known facts, appeared to be pretty dismal. Fortunately for South Africa, the severe world depression of the early 'thirties brought about, somewhat fortuitously, a substantial increase in the price of gold. This gave the industry a new lease of life. In addition, with the advance of scientific methods of detecting subterranean metals, the goldfields then in existence were found to extend over a much wider area than at first appeared probable. As a result, the industry has not looked back since these developments, and has reached new heights of prosperity, assisted by further fortuitous developments such as the extraction of uranium from the gold ores.

A wise man takes stock of the situation when conditions are booming. So it should be with the gold-mining industry at present. Since the last war some twenty-odd new, large mines have been opened up, into which unprecedented capital sums have been sunk. These on the whole have proved highly profitable – particularly as most of them have also turned out to be uranium producers. The extraction of the uranium has not only increased the profitability of the new mines, but has also revived the flagging vitality of a number of the older mines. Over the past fourteen years the capital invested in the industry has in all probability exceeded £400 million – a large portion coming from external sources. In addition, considerable sums have had to be provided for ancillary services necessary for the opening up of new goldfields.

This capital expenditure in itself stimulated boom conditions in parts of the country, but the country would be guilty of excessive confidence were it to expect such a level of capital expenditure on the mines to continue indefinitely. In fact, this expenditure is already on the decline and is likely to fall to more modest proportions in the not-too-distant future. A few mines are still passing through the development stage and a few more prospects are on the horizon, but the tempo of gold-mining development must slacken considerably unless large new fields are discovered. South Africa has, however, been so fortunate in the past quarter of a century that it would be expecting rather much of Providence to continue such luck for very much longer.

The boom conditions of the past few years have rather obscured the steady corrosion that has been taking place over this period in the older section of the industry. From the point of view of future prospects the gold-mining industry should, in fact, be divided into two sections – the old and the new. At present there are just over fifty large mines in production, of which about twenty – mostly rich – would fall within the second category and thirty-odd – mostly marginal – within the first. The new mines are gradually working up to full production, while the old ones have in most instances, passed their zenith and are now eating into the developed reserves. To illustrate the position of the latter I have tabulated the developed reserves of twenty-eight of the older mines over the five-year period 1953-7. This reflects the steady fall in the available reserves :

DEVELOPED GOLD-ORE RESERVES OF TWENTY-EIGHT OLD MINES

Year	In Million Tons
1953	122·7
1954	114·4
1955	104·3
1956	92·3
1957	84·2

At the rate of decline of these reserves and under conditions similar to those experienced over the five years in question, it appears that the twenty-eight mines would be worked out within fifteen years. This would not necessarily mean that all twenty-eight would be out of production by 1972, but it does imply that a big majority would be, and that thereafter only a few stragglers nearing their end would remain. The significance of this decline lies in the fact that for the year 1957 the value of the gold production of the twenty-eight mines amounted to £97 million, while the production of uranium probably raised the total value of their output to approximately £110 million.

A loss of this magnitude, unless it could be replaced by the earnings of new mines, would be a very serious blow to the economy of the country – the more so as most of these mines are at present not highly profitable, which means that only a small proportion of their earnings leaves the country by way of dividend payments to outside investors. In this respect the old mines contrast sharply with the new ones, which in most instances are highly profitable and so will be required to pay out large sums annually to overseas shareholders.

Of course, new mines will be coming into production, but whether, over the next fifteen to twenty years, they will come in at a rate sufficient to replace the old is highly problematical. In reaching this conclusion I have borne in mind the fact that, under present conditions of gold price and capital equipment and development costs, a mine must yield nearly 7 dwt. per ton of ore in order to render a return on capital sufficiently high to make the investment attractive. To those who do not quite appreciate this statement it could be shown that, out of fifty-three mines at present producing in South Africa, only fifteen – or under 30 per cent of the total – are yielding 7 dwt. and over per ton of ore mined. A material increase in the price of gold would, of course, change this situation, but without such an increase it is clear that the country will be called upon to face a serious decline in gold mining over the next fifteen to twenty years. Even an increase in the price of gold cannot change the situation indefinitely, but merely lengthen the period of decline. The life of the industry is, therefore, a problem which sooner or later the country will have to face.

Effects of inflation

The next question that raises some anxiety about the future of the industry is the likely continuation of the inflationary trend experienced since the beginning of the last war. There is not much that can be said about this trend, except that it has steadily raised production costs of mining over the past twenty years, while the price of gold has not risen proportionately. The disturbing feature of this is that there is no clear indication as yet that it has run its course. On the contrary, there is a school of thought which holds that, under existing conditions of capitalistic enterprise, it is impossible to maintain full employment without a gradual inflation taking place. While I am not wholly convinced that this is the case, there are substantial grounds in support of this theory.

Over the past hundred years price trends have definitely been upwards, but during the period the heavy expenditure on

wars has undoubtedly contributed to this and it might well be
that, under more favourable conditions, these price rises might
not have occurred. On the other hand, the United States of
America recently experienced the extraordinary phenomenon
of a trade recession without a fall in price-levels – a recession
which was only mastered after heavy deficit financing, which
more likely than not will lead to a further round of inflation in
that country. Such a development is bound to influence conditions far beyond the borders of the United States. In South
Africa itself the inflation potential is still quite considerable –
particularly as regards non-White wage levels. As shown in the
preceding chapter, these levels have been unduly depressed in
the Union over the past fifteen to twenty years, in strong
contrast to conditions elsewhere, particularly in Africa, where
the non-White is demanding a larger share of the national
income. Therefore a strong possibility of further inflation in the
Union persists. Such a trend is a threat to the gold-mining
industry which we in South Africa dare not ignore.

The future of gold

Another important factor which is likely to influence gold
mining over the next generation or so is the future of gold
itself in the monetary affairs of nations. This is bound up with
the future price of the metal. Unquestionably, a substantial
increase in the price of gold would mean massive benefits to
the Union. Accordingly, every South African with a material
stake in the country should pray that such an increase will
come about before many of the older mines are forced to shut
down. While the availability of the gold reefs will ultimately
determine the future of the industry in South Africa, during
the next generation the price of the metal could markedly
influence the course of events in this country.

The Union should make every endeavour to get an increase
in the price of gold, but it should not be blind to those developments that, under existing conditions, are minimizing the
importance of the metal in the affairs of nations. By this I do not

mean that there is a likelihood of a fall in the price of gold. Such an eventuality within the next generation is extremely remote. In fact, a moderate increase is much more likely than a moderate fall, but this should not blind us to the fact that there are powerful forces at present at work that are gradually stripping gold of its importance in monetary affairs. These forces are part of the evolutionary process to which mankind is committed, and they cannot be side-tracked. Some people contend that the price of the metal should be increased at a time of depression when commodity prices are lower, on the grounds that such an increase would induce a general reinflation of price-levels and so a return to prosperity. Others contend that the gold price should be raised at a time of prosperity and high prices in order to ensure the liquidity of international monetary reserves. So, according to protagonists of an increase in the price of the metal, the price should be raised both in times of depression and prosperity – heads I win, tails you lose!

These arguments, however, touch on mere side issues, for the real determinant of the position of gold in monetary affairs is international confidence in the integrity of nations. According to some advocates of an increase in the price of gold, gold mining must always be related to the amount of world trade. Surely such a concept is sheer superstition, not far removed from that of 'Lobola'. (In parts of Africa the purchase price of a wife must be in livestock. This practice is called 'Lobola'.)

Indeed, as a medium of exchange, gold reached its heyday during the period of nineteenth-century rugged individualism. Then the individual carried gold on his person, for he had little confidence in the integrity of the financial institutions of those times. The development of banking and of central banking in particular changed all this, so that for some time now it has been conceded that gold is not essential for internal monetary purposes, but only as a means of settling international debts. This has meant considerable economy in the use of monetary gold. But society does not stand still and further developments have been taking place; in the international sphere a new outlook and confidence is gradually evolving. Ever since the First

World War the international power of the dollar has been growing, and since the last war it has even overshadowed gold as an international currency. Moreover, institutions such as the World Bank and the International Monetary Fund have been gaining in importance in international monetary affairs.

These developments have led to further economies in the use of gold. And the process, depending as it does on the development of confidence in the integrity of international arrangements, is destined to continue. The division of the world into Communist and Western spheres and the advent of nuclear power have had the effect of speeding international co-operation and solidarity. Tight controls have dispensed with gold for monetary purposes in Communist countries (the metal is used by these powers only for making purchases in the West), and, in waging economic warfare with the West, Russia has encouraged the Western powers to draw closer together. Nuclear power has helped to remove the danger of world-scale conflict, thus fostering confidence in international institutions controlled by the West. These developments in international solidarity among Western nations have added so greatly to the prestige and confidence placed in international monetary organizations that in time it is quite conceivable that this confidence could increase, as in the case of internal usage, to an extent where gold may become redundant for external purposes also. However, such a state of affairs is unlikely to develop in the foreseeable future, though fear of the U.S.S.R. will tend to increase solidarity in the West – and it should be remembered that it is only in this sphere that gold truly serves a monetary purpose.

Much of the credit for these developments must go to the United States of America, whose dominating position as a creditor nation since the Second World War has given rise to new concepts in international relations. It has now become obligatory upon the stronger creditor nations to assist the weaker debtor nations – by gifts if necessary – for only by this means can world trade be kept flowing at a healthy level. In addition, the policies of stock-piling of internationally-traded goods and of price support for local agricultural products have also played their part in keeping world trade on an even keel. These developments have brought about a stability in the economic affairs of Western countries which gold, no matter what its price-level, could never have achieved under the orthodox or so-called self-regulating system which goes under the name of the gold standard.

While gold will still have an important niche in monetary affairs for many years to come – even to an extent that we may see a moderate increase in its price in the fairly near future – gold-producing countries would do well to bear in mind these developments, for in the long run they are bound to have repercussions upon the gold-mining industry.

Uranium and the price of gold

Another consideration which may affect gold mining in the Union is the future price of uranium. At present the industry is extracting uranium oxide from gold-bearing ores under a ten-year arrangement with the Combined Development Agency – an Anglo-American organization. By this arrangement the Agency provides the finance for the erection of a number of uranium plants attached to certain gold-mines – 27 in all – and contracts to take over the output of these plants at predetermined prices for a period of ten years. These prices have been fixed at a level sufficiently high to redeem the capital costs of the plants over this period. The question therefore arises: what will the price of the oxide be after the termination of the arrangement, which expires at different dates for different mines in from four to seven years' time?

There can, of course, be no certainty on this issue, but it would be prudent to prepare for a considerable fall by the end of the period. In support of this it can be shown that production of the metal has increased enormously over the past few years and that its use is as yet rather circumscribed. So far the principal use has been in the manufacture of atomic weapons, the production of which might at any time be curtailed as a result of international agreement on nuclear disarmament. And there can be little point in piling up additional weapons if, as it is believed, those already in existence are more than sufficient to blow up the world. The future of the metal, therefore, appears to be in power production for use in peacetime. But as the world is still well supplied with cheap and conventional sources of power, it may be some time yet before nuclear power is used on any material scale. Fortunately for the Union the gold-mining industry could, on the whole, withstand a substantial fall in the price of uranium because it is produced as a by-product from gold ores, the cost of the mining of which is met by the proceeds from gold. Nevertheless, such a fall in price will embarrass some of the mines and adversely affect the country's economy.

Yet another factor likely to affect future gold mining in the Union is the growing necessity, in the interests of the country's economy, to increase substantially African wage levels. This matter has such wide implications that it will be discussed in a separate chapter.

From this it should be clear that gold mining will have many problems to face over the next generation or so. The industry in the Union is, however, highly efficient and vigorous and undoubtedly still has many years of prosperity ahead. Nevertheless, the situation must be faced that ultimately gold mining in South Africa is doomed to decline.

Ratio of White and Black labour

Before closing this chapter, I am including some significant figures. This table gives the ratios of White to non-White employees in various activities in the Union. These ratios illustrate the relative importance of non-White labour in the various spheres of economic activity. (*See following page.*)

The most significant conclusion that can be drawn from these ratios is that, in the categories of activity most exposed to outside competition, the proportion of non-Whites employed is highest. It is also clear that the more sheltered the occupations, the higher the proportion of Whites engaged: mining, whose

RATIOS OF THE NUMBERS OF WHITE TO NON-WHITE
EMPLOYEES

In Mining	1 : 7·5
In Agriculture	1 : 6
In Manufacturing	1 : 2·5
In Transport	1 : 1
In Commerce	1 : 0·65
In Public Services	1 : 1

products are largely exported, is virtually carried by non-White labour, while transport, commerce and public administration, which are largely free from outside competition, are heavily staffed by Whites. The irony of this situation is that in South Africa the jobs which on the average carry the greatest risks from external competition are the lowest paid, while the more sheltered are given, on the average, the highest rewards.

Gold mining is the rock upon which the economy of the country is built. This table illustrates the extent to which the gold-mining industry rests upon low-paid non-White labour. It follows, therefore, that the economy of the Union depends vitally upon non-White labour – that of the Africans in particular. But in an earlier chapter it was shown that the standard of living of the Whites in the Union ranks among the highest in the world. In the circumstances it is impossible to escape the conclusion that the affluence of the Whites in this country rests upon the poverty of the Blacks, for it is the earnings of the latter which, under present conditions, cushion the impact of external competition. And in the world at large it is this factor – ability to meet world competition – that in good measure determines the living standards of particular nations. This is certainly not a comfortable situation for White South Africa. Indeed, it is a particularly vulnerable one which carries with it the ugly implications of retaliation.

9

THE DYNAMIC PROCESS OF INDUSTRIAL GROWTH

IN discussing the factors likely to influence the future of gold mining in the preceding chapter, mention was made of the conflict of interests between mining and manufacturing industry in the matter of African wage levels.

Mercantilism

The system of free enterprise to which we in the Union subscribe has been undergoing evolutionary changes of a profound character. In the nineteenth century, capitalist enterprise was to a large extent based upon mercantilism. Under this system manufacturing industry was to a large extent concentrated in England and Europe generally, while the raw materials necessary for such industry were provided mainly by colonial and other industrially-undeveloped territories. This system led to the large-scale employment of low-paid, predominantly non-White labour on plantations or in mines.

Mercantilism without doubt served a useful purpose in opening up new territories and in bringing civilization to parts of the world where superstitious beliefs and practices thwarted progress. The exploitation of mines and plantations – the mercantilist system – has in recent years become identified with colonialism, which – somewhat unfairly – has come under heavy adverse criticism. While colonialism had unfortunate features, it was not wholly bad and was a constructive force in the evolutionary development of backward territories. The principal abuses under the system often arose out of the uneven distribution of the proceeds of colonial enterprise – the providers of the capital receiving too high a reward, while the mass of the workers were underpaid. However, in the heyday of the system it was almost invariably the case that, but for the work on the mines and plantations, large numbers in the colonial territories would have succumbed either from starvation or as a result of internecine strife or superstitious practices. So while the labour was, in fact, underpaid, it cannot be said that the employers were wholly inhuman or heartless. And during the eighteenth and nineteenth centuries there was also much suffering on the part of the workers in the industrial countries themselves, due to low wage levels. At that time labour was regarded in the same light as commodities – subject only to the law of supply and demand. Thus in the colonies, where the supply of workers was plentiful – often living under wretched conditions in their natural state – it was not unnatural that they were engaged at extremely low rates of pay.

Economic implications of industrialization

Economic concepts have undergone far-reaching changes since those years. These spread slowly at first, but since the close of the Second World War they have been rapidly gaining ground. These changes have their roots in industrialization and its spread to the far-off corners of the world. In the early days of the industrial revolution, the machine was regarded by many of the workers as a serious menace because it often deprived them of the jobs for which they had been specifically trained. But gradually the implications of the use of machines came to be understood and the inevitability of their employment accepted. Today the machine is being transported to the remotest parts of the earth.

Yet even in modern communities the economic implications of industrialization are not always fully understood. For industrialization does not merely mean the making or manufacture of goods, as so many believe; it has other equally important implications. From the point of view of the national economy, industrialization entails the use of machinery as an aid to human effort – the object being to boost the productiveness of the human so as greatly to increase output per unit of human effort. This process either lowers production costs or enables the manufacturer to increase his wage-rates.

Previously the emphasis was on cheaper production, but for various reasons it has now shifted to higher and higher rates for human labour. The reason for this switch is to be found partly in the destructive consequences, under present-day conditions, of the deflationary process, and partly in the power of trade unionism. Whether we like it or not, the capitalist system works more smoothly and equitably when subject to a gradual inflation than under deflationary pressure. This is so largely because of the *rentier* class of capital provider. When prices fall, this section of the public usually gets a larger share of the national income and consequently becomes a heavier burden on the national economy. Yet this class plays only a passive part in the productive process, not being responsible for management, labour or risk capital.

Under modern conditions of industrialization, therefore, the benefits of increased mechanization almost invariably result in higher earnings for both labour and capital rather than in lower prices. In any event, a *sine qua non* of industrialization, as more and more plant is brought into operation for the purpose of boosting human effort, is that real purchasing power must be increased to match the increasing outputs, either by means of falling prices or increased earnings. If this is not done, the economy of the country will not reap the full benefit of the increased mechanization. In other words, higher production must be matched by higher real earnings, so that these are sufficient to absorb the greater quantities of goods and services that result from the increased mechanization.

This feature of industrialization is complicated by the amount of savings and investment necessary to ensure full employment of the nation's human resources. But, subject to the right amount of savings and investment, the matching of buying power with output provides the dynamism that engenders industrial growth in the economy of a country. In practice, the matching of buying power and output means the spread of such power over as much of the population as possible, for the wider the spread, the greater the dynamism, and consequently the greater the affluence of the community.

Industrialization can therefore be said to be a function of the size of the market: its scope increases as the market increases. Under existing conditions, where markets are largely circumscribed by national borders, the scope of industrialization in any particular country is in direct proportion to the size of the local or national market. The local market, again, is primarily related to the size of the local population and its average standard of living. As a consequence, industrialization will be more effective and rapid and will also have greater scope in a country with a large population than in one with a small population – provided that the country is not overpeopled in relation to its material resources, as is the case in India and other Asiatic territories.

Unhealthy dependence of the manufacturing industries

In the Union, manufacturing industry has progressed rapidly, and large sums have been spent on its equipment and mechanization. But it has not advanced materially under its own dynamism; instead, it has been propelled predominantly by the large-scale development in precious mineral production that has taken place over the past twenty-five years, which means that South Africa finds itself in a rather anomalous position at present. Whereas throughout the world national economies previously based upon mercantilism have been, or are rapidly being, replaced by industrialization, the Union of South Africa, while ostensibly developing an industrial economy, still adheres to the practice of employing low-paid labour on a large scale – the characteristic of mercantilism. It would almost seem that South Africa, by this practice, is seeking the best of both worlds. Such a policy may be possible as an interim stage in the switch-over to industrialization, but in the long run it is bound to fail, and there is a distinct danger that, in seeking the benefits of both worlds, it may ultimately lose both. A nation cannot for long flout the dictates of evolution, which in its present stage prescribes industrialization.

We have seen, moreover, that a *sine qua non* of industrialization is the gradual raising of the buying power of the workers, and particularly that of the low-paid, so-called unskilled workers, in order that these may reciprocate by buying the products of industry – in this way generating the dynamic process of industrial growth. However, it has been shown earlier that the real buying power of the African in the Union has not been raised over the past fifteen to twenty years, despite the large sums invested in and the increased output of industry in the country during this period.

In consequence, the dynamism of manufacturing industry in South Africa has been short-circuited to a considerable extent. This, in turn, has largely prevented such industry from developing under its own steam. Fortunately for the country, progress has been possible as a result of the steam generated by the large-scale development in gold and uranium mining. In the circumstances, manufacturing industry has not so far been a substitute for precious mineral production in the economy of the country, but rather an offshoot vitally dependent upon such enterprise. This is not a particularly healthy state of affairs, as gold mining is a wasting asset and must sooner or later begin to fall away. In this event, manufacturing industry as at present constituted will decline in sympathy.

The situation as outlined is not irremediable, but, if it is to be overcome it will require a gradual and material increase in non-White wages throughout the country. In this manner the necessary dynamism could be generated in the country's industrial development. This would, of course, mean the acceptance of non-White labour as an essential contributory factor in the industrial build-up of the country, and would visualize a community at the present time of at least 15 million effective consumers, steadily increasing to something like 30 million or more by the end of this century. On such a basis, industrial development in the Union would be able to proceed under its own steam. Moreover, it would stand an excellent chance of healthy growth because of the major developments likely to take place throughout Africa in the next fifty years.

Conflict with the mining interests

Unfortunately, the adoption of such a policy would run counter to the country's gold-mining interests, whose profitability depends to a great extent upon the employment of a large, low-paid African labour force. Many of the mines are low-grade and past their prime, so that a moderate increase in wages would speed their closing down. This is what is meant by the conflict of interests between gold mining and manufacturing industry.

Many industrialists in the Union have recognized the defect in the country's policy of keeping down non-White wage-rates, and some are setting an example by increasing them. In so doing they are in conflict with the official policy of the Union Government, which is against the integration of African labour in the industrial economy of the country, so that in this matter the interests of the mining industry and Government policy go hand in hand. This is an unfortunate combination of the two most powerful interests in the Union. At present it would be virtually impossible to counter its influence in the affairs of the country, but in the end it will unquestionably undermine the economy, if not checked.

From the point of view of the mining industry, the attitude towards African labour is understandable as the industry is up against the facts of profitability: materially higher African wage-rates would greatly circumscribe the scope of its activities in the Union. Official policy, on the other hand, rests upon less excusable grounds. It is based upon the now universally-discarded concept that the non-White is an inferior being destined to fill only the menial and low-paid jobs. Thus, while the mining industry, because of the threat to its very existence, still operates under outmoded economic concepts, the Union Government actually seeks to uphold such concepts. Unless concepts that conform to evolutionary progress are adopted, the economy of the country is bound to suffer in the long run and, indeed, may suffer disastrously from the point of view of the white man.

There are even those in authority in this country who hold that African labour is not worth more than the subsistence rates it at present receives. Yet these people fail to see that African labour is, in the main, no longer of the unskilled pick-and-shovel variety of yesterday. In almost every sphere the African today operates power tools which provide the heavy labour, while the African's work as the operator of these tools is in the nature of semi-skilled labour. The African is also becoming more and more proficient in his new role; yet he has hitherto received very little recognition for this in the wages paid him.

This is bad enough, but what many do not appreciate is the fact that, by *not* increasing the earnings of the non-Whites as they enter the semi-skilled categories, we are defeating the whole object of equipping enterprise with power tools and mechanical appliances generally. In fact, much of the capital that goes into such equipment will be wasted, unless the people who operate it are given an adequate share of the benefits derived from its use. What is taking place in the Union is that industry is geared for about four million effective consumers, while it is operated by the adult workers drawn from a population of fifteen million. As a consequence, the economy of the country is lop-sided, resulting in waste and extravagant living on the part of its White population and inefficiency on the part of the non-Whites. This is substantiated by the following phenomena:

Decline in industrial share prices

Observers have, in recent years, been puzzled by the fact that the index of industrial share prices in the Union has declined to below 60 per cent of its 1948 level, while those in the United States of America and the United Kingdom have risen to about 300 per cent and 150 per cent respectively of the same (1948) levels. Why should this be? The only feasible explanation for this is the lack of dynamism in the country's manufacturing industry, which does not distribute sufficient buying power to the majority of its workers – the non-Whites – to enable them to buy the products of industry. Large capital sums have been spent on equipping manufacturing industry in the Union since the war, but, despite this, the profits earned are, on the whole, insufficient to pay 5 per cent on the replacement value of the capital assets employed, after meeting taxation and setting aside sufficient of the profits to enable industry to keep abreast of modern developments.

As a consequence, manufacturing industry in the Union is *not* an attractive investment. The necessity of appropriating profits for the purpose of keeping abreast of modern developments is not always appreciated, and, during periods of inflation such as that through which the world has been passing, this necessity can become particularly onerous. Furthermore, an industry that does not set aside a substantial proportion of its profits for technological development soon falls by the wayside under modern competitive conditions. Yet in the Union this setting aside of profits for development is actually penalized by an Undistributed Profits Tax. An industry that can pay no more than 5 per cent on the replacement value of its capital requirements is a poor investment; hence the depressed level of the industrial share index in the Union.

Import control

Another puzzling feature of the Union's economy is that, despite the country's amazing good fortune since the Second World War, it has been unable to meet its annual import commitments without import control. Here, too, the cause is to be found in the country's lop-sided economy – the high earning rates of the Whites against the low wages paid to the non-Whites. A study of the family budgets of non-Whites – those of Africans in particular – reveals the small extent to which these consumers draw upon imports. They exist almost exclusively upon South African produce and in this respect are the best South Africans. The Coloureds and Indians make more use of imported products than the Africans but do not compare with the Whites. In fact, imports are almost a monopoly of the Whites in the Union. If, as an estimate, 10 per cent of the annual imports of the country can be regarded as for the benefit of the non-Whites, then the balance of imports per head of White population has been running at about £165 per annum in recent years. Compared with imports per head in other countries, this seems an extravagant sum, and gives some idea of the extent to which White standards in the Union depend upon overseas supplies. The comparative figures are:

IMPORTS PER HEAD OF POPULATION

Country	£
United States of America	25
Germany and France	40
Great Britain and Australia	75
Switzerland and Sweden	90
Canada, Holland and Belgium	110
New Zealand	125

Nowhere has the figure approached that for the Whites in South Africa. In New Zealand, the nearest approach, the figure has been found to be excessive, necessitating drastic economy measures. Yet New Zealand is not industrialized to anything like the extent that South Africa is, for its economy is in some measure still tied to that of the United Kingdom.

It may be suggested that 10 per cent of total imports is too low a figure for the non-Whites' share, but I dispute this, because the standard of living of over 90 per cent of those people is extremely low and virtually independent of imports. The 10 per cent amounted to approximately £55 million per annum in recent years, or something like £4·5 per head of non-White population. Compare this with India's £1·25; Nigeria's £4·4; Iran's £5; Egypt's £7; and Mexico's and Japan's £10 per head of population. Of one thing there can be little doubt: if the distribution of earnings in the Union were more equitable there would be no need whatever for import control under present conditions. But of more importance is the irony of the present position. For whereas it is the labour of the non-Whites that in the main makes possible the earning of external currency, it is the high living and extravagance of the Whites that necessitates the appropriation of the bulk of those earnings.

The pattern of savings and investment

Another anomaly in South Africa's economic set-up is the pattern of savings and investment. Because of wage discrimination, White earnings are on the whole excessive, while non-White earnings are sub-economic. It has already been shown that the excessive earnings of the Whites has led to extravagance in the importation of goods. Moreover, the large earnings of the Whites as against the meagre income of the non-Whites has also meant that savings are virtually a monopoly of the Whites – non-White savings could hardly amount to 5 per cent of the total. As a consequence, investment has been predominantly in the interests of the Whites.

During the past few years savings and investments have averaged about £450 million per annum. Of this sum, over £250 million per annum has gone into buildings and construction generally – predominantly in the interests and for the convenience of White South Africa – and less than £200 million in plant and machinery. Of this latter amount, approximately £100 million has been invested in transport and other equipment of a secondary character, and only about a similar sum in agricultural, mining and manufacturing equipment. Of this £100 million only some £40 million represents investment in plant for manufacturing industry. Of the total of £200 million in plant and machinery, something like £145 million is, in effect, the cost of replacements resulting from depreciations. In reality, then, the total increase in mechanical equipment in recent years has averaged a mere £55 million per annum, of which manufacturing industry would probably have accounted for some £30 million.

These figures suggest that the country is spending excessive sums on building and construction and inadequate amounts on new industrial equipment. It can also be stated that a good proportion of the building and construction is of a luxury character: high-class dwellings and office accommodation and expensive roadways for the benefit of Whites only. On the other hand, by no stretch of the imagination can the £30 million spent annually on manufacturing plant be sufficient to ensure the ultimate replacement of mining by manufacturing industry. Indeed, this sum would hardly be adequate to ensure progress in industry sufficient to cope with the needs of the increasing White population. This figure of £30 million also confirms the low investment rating of manufacturing industry in the Union, for most of this sum represents the ploughing back of profits by industrialists – a very small proportion being from the savings of the man in the street.

The £250 million which has gone annually into building and construction represents an average annual increase in this form of investment of nearly 12½ per cent over the past five years. Comparing this with a White population increase of about 1½ per cent a year, one cannot escape the conclusion that the Union has been experiencing an unprecedented investment boom – largely in projects that are unlikely to yield increased earnings over the next decade or so. These abnormal increases in building and construction are likely to throw a heavy burden of fixed charges (rates, rents and taxes) upon the White community in the immediate future – a burden which adds materially to the potential inflation that at present threatens the country.

In a previous chapter it was pointed out that, in relation to power generated per head of population, South Africa compares with France. Yet while France has an income per head of £293, that for the Union is a mere £105. This suggests that labour in the Union is either underpaid or very much less efficient than in France. The truth, of course, lies midway between, for while non-White labour is underpaid it is also, particularly the African, very much less efficient than the French. Large employers of African labour believe, however, that, given adequate opportunity, African workers could become very much more efficient, as the African has already demonstrated his ability to operate power tools.

The principal causes of African inefficiency are, first, the migratory system of labour under which the African is never properly trained and under which he wastes a considerable amount of time in idleness at home in the Reserves, and secondly, the fact that as a rule he is inadequately fed and badly housed. If proper use were made of the labour resources of the country, both in training and equipment, and if, in addition, adequate payment were to be made and appropriate incentives given, the efficiency of this labour could be greatly improved. In such circumstances the income per head of population could be increased considerably and with it the national income of the country. But when any thought is given to higher African wage-rates, one immediately comes up against the gold-mining industry and, worse still, the official policy of the country towards this labour.

In this respect one cannot but view with uneasiness the nationally-approved policy of the mining industry of importing large numbers of Africans from outside the Union's border for labour in the mines. While ostensibly this importation is necessary because of the alleged labour shortage, this importation undoubtedly has the effect of depressing wage-rates for African labour in the Union. The policy is a relic of nineteenth-century capitalism, and where else in the world would it be tolerated today under twentieth-century industrialization? At some time or other it must break down under the impetus of twentieth-century concepts. And, with the continent of Africa moving rapidly towards twentieth-century industrialization, the end of this policy cannot be far distant. It would be well for South Africa if both the mining companies and the authorities faced up to this fact before it is too late.

★

Future outlook

Far too often one hears the comment that the economy of the Union is sound and the future of the country assured because of its untold natural resources. While it is true that the country could progress and prosper for many years to come, the analysis of its present economic situation makes it abundantly clear that the expected future prosperity will not come our way by mere wishful thinking. I have already pointed out a number of danger signals which we shall have to heed if the country is to continue its progress: the lack of dynamism in manufacturing industry, the excessive dependence upon imported goods on the part of the Whites, and the heavy unproductive investment in building and construction in recent years are all symptoms of the same disease. It is a disease which springs from a maladjusted economy – the result of the Union's excursion into twentieth-century industrialization without acceptance of its implications. In more specific terms, it is the result of a belief that the Union can enjoy the fruits of twentieth-century mechanization without the obligation of lifting the real earnings of the mass of the workers to effective twentieth-century consumer levels.

The remedy for insufficient dynamism in industry, for excessive importations, and for burdensome fixed charges can come only from one source, the broadening of the base of the Union's economy through the better and more enlightened use of its human resources. The country's material resources can never be properly exploited without the enlightened exploitation of its human resources. This means that South Africa must shed its reactionary policy of baasskap, under which only the Whites are able to enjoy the full benefits of the country's material resources. There is not much time left for this, for the consequences of the policy of baasskap are already adversely affecting the economy of the country.

Very soon the authorities will be confronted with the choice: whether to continue to regard the non-White population of the country as the white man's burden, or whether to see this population in perspective as the benefit it ought to be and indeed is. If the choice be the former, this population will soon become a very real and intolerable burden, sufficient to undermine the economy of the country and overwhelm its White population. On the other hand, if the non-Whites are allowed to fill their rightful and just place in the economy of the country, it is conceivable that White leadership could be an effective force in South Africa for several generations to come. The choice is simple and clear-cut, but unfortunately it depends largely upon the ability of Afrikaner nationalism to see the problem in its true perspective and to rise above deep-seated prejudices.

The question is, therefore, whether the *true* patriotism of the Nationalists will be sufficiently strong to overcome their worst prejudices. For the moment, their choice has been side-tracked by an obsession which they have come to believe is a policy capable of solving the country's racial problems – apartheid. So let us now examine its possibilities.

THE ECONOMIC CONSEQUENCES OF
APARTHEID

UNTIL some twelve years ago the word apartheid was almost unknown in Afrikaans; today it has acquired the international status not of fame but of notoriety. Literally, the word means 'separateness' or 'the state of being separate', but its real political significance is impossible to define at present, because to different people it means different things. As a policy it has never been clearly defined, but as an election cry its very vagueness has brought it success, for it could be given different interpretations satisfactory to a wide range of opinions.

It will be appreciated, therefore, that in describing or analysing the apartheid policy one cannot be too specific. Its meaning to Afrikaner Nationalists could be anything from outright baasskap – that is, perpetual servitude of the non-Whites because of their alleged inferiority as human beings – to complete independence of Africans in separately-assigned territories. In most instances the latter concept is held up as the ideal, but an ideal attainable only in some dim and distant future out of range of any intelligible explanations.

The segregation policy

When it is interpreted as outright baasskap, or even a modified form of it, apartheid will bring in its train those consequences which have already been described – the ultimate collapse of South Africa's economy and the likely eclipse of White leadership within the lifetime of our younger generations. Unfortunately, this interpretation of apartheid is accepted by a large number of the rank-and-file Nationalists – particularly the less enlightened elements. A prominent section of the intellectuals, on the other hand, envisage the policy as one implying complete territorial separation after the elapse of some fifty or more years. These people disapprove of baasskap on moral grounds and fear its probable consequences. They therefore seek a policy acceptable to their conscience but one that at the same time entails social, economic and political segregation – in particular a policy that will protect the white man against racial admixture with non-Whites. They recognize that such a policy would entail sacrifice on the part of the Whites and, up to a point, are prepared to face this, if it will assure the future purity of the White races.

The Tomlinson Report

In theory this latter policy would appear to be admirable, but its practicability will be shown to be another matter altogether. Indeed, on closer examination it is found to be not a policy but a make-believe solution of the racial issue that could only be feasible in a dream-world. However, it has this merit, that it serves to circumvent the prejudices and still the conscience of the dreamers – but at what cost only the future will tell.

Some years ago a Commission was appointed to examine the feasibility and to draw up a blue-print of a scheme for the separate economic development of the native Reserves. After an exhaustive inquiry, the Commission, under Professor Tomlinson, submitted a lengthy report. It made the best of an impossible task, but could not visualize the complete segregation of the Africans within the foreseeable future. In certain respects its recommendations were constructive, and the country would do well to adopt them. But its most significant finding was that, under the most favourable conditions, there would still be some six million Africans living in the areas reserved for Whites by the end of the present century, and many whose homes would be in the native Reserves would still have to seek employment in the White areas under migratory labour conditions, if their families were to be kept from starvation. Not a particularly encouraging outlook for the dreamers of complete territorial apartheid!

But this is not all, for a good deal of the Tomlinson Report is open to serious criticism. Indeed, quite a number of its findings would not stand up to enlightened examination. The most obvious weakness of the report is the warped perspective of its authors on the question of the Africans' value in the economic body of the country. The authors persist in the view that the African is a burden to the white man, who has to foot his bills for education and other amenities. They simply cannot see the great asset that the country possesses in its non-White labour; they take no account of the great contributions, past and present, made by the Africans to the economy, nor do they attempt to assess the greater potential benefits that these people could confer upon the country. Theirs is, therefore, a purely negative approach which can only give negative results, for if the African is to be regarded merely as a burden, he will indeed become a heavier and heavier burden with the passage of time until the dead weight completely overwhelms the White community financially.

The recommendations of the Commission relating to the agricultural development of the Reserves were on the whole sound – particularly the recommendation that the traditional tribal or communal tenancy of land should be replaced by a system of individual tenancy. This is in line with developments throughout Africa, but is unfortunately one of the recommendations discarded by the Government. A weakness in the proposals relating to the future farming of the Reserves, however, is the size of the proposed individual plots. They would not permit African families to maintain living standards much above those suffered at present.

In the appendix to this book it is calculated that the average income of families living in the Reserves ranged between £86 and £97 per annum in the year 1953/4. Of this, approximately £30 a year was derived from sources within the Reserves, and the balance from the earnings of adult males in the mines or the cities. The proposed agricultural plots under the Tomlinson scheme would have permitted an annual income per family of about £60. This – a mere £30 a year more than the existing income from agricultural operations – is all that the system of individual tenancy and improved farming methods would have offered an average African family, and even this would have been at a cost of the removal of 500,000 families from the land. Furthermore, the increased income of those remaining on the land would still have been below the average income per family under existing conditions, so that the families remaining on the land would still have had to augment their annual incomes by the migratory labour of the adult males, if they were to have maintained their present meagre living standards. But even a £30 a year increase, assuming migratory labour as in the past, would not be sufficient on which to build an industrial economy, for under present conditions the incomes are really too low to feed and clothe the families adequately.

It is therefore in the proposals for the industrialization of the Reserves that the report is weakest. To all appearances, the authors had no real idea of what it takes to industrialize a country or territory. In terms of the recommendations, there should be no more than 350,000 families settled on farms in the Reserves. In the year 1953/4, however, there were 850,000 families whose permanent homes were in the Reserves, so that at that time approximately 500,000 families would have had to depend upon occupations other than farming.

No purpose would be served by examining what conditions would have been like under the report's recommendations in the year 1953/4. Any such examination or calculation could be of value only if it were projected into the future to cover a time – say the year 2000 – when concrete results could be expected from the proposals. By that year, the total African population of the Union would be approximately 20 million, or roughly 4 million families. According to the Tomlinson Report, about 6 million of these Africans, or 1·2 million families, would still be living in White areas and 350,000 families would be earning a livelihood from farming in the Reserves. So 2.45 million families would have to be accommodated in the Reserves, in occupations other than farming. The problem to be considered, therefore, is what it takes in capital and other necessaries to place these families – in all, approximately 12·5 million people – in an industrialized economy.

Industrialization of African Reserves

It would be impossible at this stage to consider in detail every requirement for such a development; but primarily four essentials would have to be provided. These are 1, a supply of labour, suitably trained; 2, adequate capital; 3, suitable raw materials; 4, available markets. Now let us see to what extent these are available in the Reserves: labour is there in plenty, but raw and untrained; capital available for buildings, equipment and stocks, virtually nil; raw materials suitable for processing, an extremely limited supply; and markets for industrial products, next to nothing because of lack of buying power. Worse still, the Reserves themselves cannot feed the present population of under 4 million, let alone the 14 million that are to be accommodated by the end of the present century.

To give some indication of the inadequacy of the food supplies available in the Reserves, it can be shown that in the year 1953/4, of the average food consumption per family costing approximately £60 a year, only about a half came from sources within the Reserves. So that in 1953/4 the Reserves had to acquire food supplies from beyond their borders at a cost of over £25 million to feed their total population – resident and migratory. This position will, of course, be considerably worse by the year 2000. On the basis of present-day prices, and on the assumption that food supplies from the Reserves themselves will not have increased materially, the imports to feed the then population of 14 million even at the meagre standard presently existing will amount to approximately £125 million a year. In the light of this, it would be hard to imagine a less likely area in which to embark upon so ambitious an experiment as the industrialization of the Africans in the Reserves.

Capital requirements

It would be interesting, nevertheless, to examine these requirements in greater detail. Not much can be said about the labour supply other than that it is raw and untrained. It would take some considerable time and expense before it could be suitably trained and disciplined, though this should not be an insurmountable obstacle. The supply of capital is another question entirely. If capital is to be found by private enterprise beyond the borders of the Reserves, it would doubtless be forthcoming in limited amounts over a long period. But if it is to be attracted, the suppliers would certainly have to be given extensive guarantees. Included among these would be unhindered access to all Union markets, adequate supplies of power, water and transport, and assurances regarding taxation. The fulfilment of such guarantees would be costly and would most certainly adversely affect established industries in the Union's White areas.

But the attraction of capital in relatively small amounts for specific industries in the Reserves (or for that matter on the borders of the Reserves) would be a totally different proposition from the finding of capital for the thoroughgoing industrialization of the Reserves in a manner sufficient to ensure employment at reasonable rates of pay for all the African families, other than those in agriculture, that would have to be crowded into the Reserves by the year 2000 if the Tomlinson proposals were put into operation. It has already been noted that by the year 2000 the number of African families that would have to be accommodated in the Reserves, other than those on the land, would be in the vicinity of 2·5 million. As the ratio of men to women workers in industrial countries is something like 3 to 1, the figure of 2·5 million families suggests at least 3·5 million workers (allowing for female and unmarried male workers). I do not believe that the Commissioners ever gave adequate thought to the capital cost of placing 3·5 million workers in an industrial society.

To many people, industry means merely the making of goods – no matter how primitive the processes. Industrialization of a territory, however, is something entirely different. The making of goods can be by hand without the use of machines or power tools, but in most instances such production is extremely expensive, even if the labour receives only a pittance for wages. The snag about industry of this sort in the Reserves would be that the prices of the goods made would be beyond the means of those living in the areas. On the other hand, in the export markets the products would be hopelessly outclassed and outpriced by machine-made goods from Chicago, Birmingham or Johannesburg. Manufacture in the Reserves which does not entail the use of up-to-date machinery can only end in failure and heavy loss.

A *sine qua non* of industrialization is the extensive use of power tools and other machines, so that human labour may be replaced by mechanical horse-power, which is far more productive and hence cost-reducing. But the equipping of factories with machinery and plant is costly, involving vast capital sums, and an area cannot be satisfactorily industrialized without heavy capital expenditure in other directions such as the provision of power plants, water schemes, transport services, roads, housing, and other amenities. Industrialization without these services in a densely-populated area could end only in disaster, yet these secondary services, too, require heavy capital outlays.

In the Union, where industry is not as highly mechanized as in some other countries, the capital investment in factory buildings and plant is about £750 million. In addition, working capital must run to something like £250 million. So that, in all, capital employed directly in manufacturing industry in South Africa would be about £1,000 million. This capital outlay gives employment to approximately 300,000 Whites and 600,000 non-Whites. But this is not the whole story as far as capital costs are concerned, for, in order to keep this number of employees

in reasonable comfort and health, vast sums have been necessary for roads, railways, water supplies, houses, schools, hospitals,
etc., and it should be remembered that straw huts, cattle
tracks and well points could not possibly be tolerated in high-
density manufacturing areas, such as the Reserves would be if
they were to be industrialized.

From these figures and explanations it is clear that in the
Union the capital employed per worker (all races) cannot be
less than £1,500. It will doubtless be suggested that nothing
like this sum would be required to industrialize the Reserves.
To some extent this may be so, but there are also factors that
would operate in the opposite direction. For instance, thanks to
inflation, replacement values are today considerably higher
than actual capital costs. In addition, if industry in the Reserves
is to be dynamic in the sense that it generates its own expansion,
then the earnings of the African will have to be considerably
higher than they are at present in the Union.

It is hard to visualize any successful industrialization of the
Reserves (even if some of the industries are situated on the
borders of the Reserves) under a capital cost of £1,000 per
worker. This would mean a total capital cost of something like
£3,500 million by the year 2000. Spread over forty years, it
means an annual capital outlay of about £90 million, though
naturally the costs would be lower in the earlier years and heavier
as the population grew. Now compare these figures with the
estimates of the Tomlinson Commission: that body did not
extend its computations beyond the first ten years of the project,
and reckoned that £10 million per annum over this period of
ten years would see the industrialization of the Reserves well
and truly launched. Those sums fall fantastically short of the
true requirements of the project under review and could never
industrialize the Reserves to an extent that would enable them
to accommodate 14 million Africans as a viable community by
the year 2000. The Tomlinson calculations are based on 6
million Africans remaining in White areas by the year 2000
and the balance (14 million) being settled in the Reserves.

To be fair to the Commission, it did visualize private enterprise taking a hand in the industrial development of the Reserves. No doubt it believed that much additional capital would be provided from this source, but it never contemplated the investment of sums, from whatever sources, remotely approaching the figures given. This is because the heavy cost of the project removes it utterly from the realms of practicability. Not only would it be impossible to find the capital necessary for the purpose, but for further economic reasons the whole project is fantastically unreal and could never materialize without the complete destruction of the existing economy of the Union in the areas reserved for the Whites.

Raw materials

The third essential requirement of industry is the supply of raw materials. It has already been shown that the Reserves have such slender resources that they cannot feed their existing population of under 4 million people. At present the Reserves have to acquire about £25 million worth in food from outside sources; and by the year 2000 the figure will have grown to something like £125 million, if the Tomlinson plans are put into operation. Similarly, vast quantities of raw materials will have to be imported annually if any serious attempt is to be made to industrialize the Reserves.

To illustrate this, we need go no further than the experiences of the Union itself: for the employment of 300,000 Whites and 600,000 non-Whites, the annual cost of imported materials subject to processing in Union industries exceeds £200 million. Over and above this sum, the Union's manufacturing industries pay large amounts annually by way of interest and dividends to outside investors. In fact, it has been estimated that the annual payments by Union manufacturers for imported materials and outside capital supplies amounted to £260 million for the year 1955. Since the Union is far richer in raw materials and capital resources than are the Reserves, it can only be left to the imagination to assess the external payments that will be necessary to meet the industrial requirements of the

Reserves by the year 2000, if the 3·5 million African workers are to be given reasonable employment by that time. With the food supplies necessary to feed these people, the annual external commitments of the industrialized Reserves could hardly be less than £500 million, at present price-levels, by the year 2000, and the implications of the external payments would not be very different if some of the industries were situated on the borders of the Reserves.

It is here that any idea of the industrialization of the Reserves as a separate entity breaks down hopelessly. The development of the Reserves as a separate entity is really what is visualized by the apartheid of the Nationalist intellectuals. Their concept of separate development would be unintelligible if this were not so. But the development of a separate entity implies a separate economy for the Reserves, and this, in turn, will inevitably entail a separate external payments account. The obvious question then arises: how is this account to be balanced annually? Clearly it can only be achieved by the export of manufactured products. But the export of £500 million worth of manufactured goods is a staggering amount for so small and backward an area as the native Reserves of the Union. By comparison, the Union itself exports less than £150 million worth of manufactured products per annum, and then the bulk of this is favoured under preferential tariffs within the British Commonwealth.

Clearly, the necessary exports of the Reserves will have to be overwhelmingly to the Union itself, whose *total* imports under present conditions barely amount to £500 million. But if, by some fresh development, the Union were to purchase some £500 million worth of manufactured goods from the Reserves, the effect upon the Union's own manufacturers would be calamitous. Apart from construction, it would all but destroy manufacturing industry within the Union itself, that is to say the only economic activity that in the long run can sustain White standards of living in this country.

*

Markets

The fourth requirement of industry is markets and it can be stated emphatically that no industrial policy in relation to a particular area can possibly succeed without a substantial home market. The larger and more prosperous the local markets, the better chance there will be for any industrialization to succeed in them. Export markets inevitably take only the surplus production, and any plan of industrialization that ignores this fact will sooner or later land in difficulties. But in the African Reserves there is at present virtually no market for industrial products. The inhabitants exist very largely on unprocessed foods and the clothing worn is mainly primitive. The wants of these people are severely circumscribed by the low level of their earnings and of their production in the Reserves, so that they do not extend beyond a most monotonous and inadequate diet, primitive cover, and hutments of straw and clay. In consequence, any plan to bring industry into the Reserves must entail higher incomes and living standards in the Reserves themselves.

Under present conditions and price-levels, it should be obvious that industrialization of the Reserves cannot possibly succeed where the average family income is less than £300 a year. In 1953/4 the average family income for Whites in the Union exceeded £1,600 a year, so that a figure of £300 for Africans must be regarded as modest – even low. Moreover, on £300 a year an average African family could hardly make ends meet if it were to live under industrial conditions. Yet even at this low level the total income from sources within the Reserves would amount, at existing price-levels, to something like £1,000 million a year by the year 2000. In other words, by then the national income of the Reserves would have to be £1,000 million. Compare this figure with the total income derived from the Reserves for the year 1953/4 of £25·3 million. To achieve the population target set by the Tomlinson Commission, the national income of the Reserves would have to be increased from £25 million to £1,000 million in the relatively short span of forty-six years, i.e. by at least forty times.

This represents a consistent rate of increase in real income over forty-six years of nearly 8 per cent a year – an unheard-of rate anywhere in the world over such a period, even under the most favourable conditions, let alone in overpopulated, impoverished and badly eroded territories. By way of comparison, the relative rate of increase for the Union over the twenty years ended 1957 – a period of unequalled prosperity and progress in the history of the country – was only about 4 per cent annually.

The apartheid dilemma

From this analysis it becomes clear beyond any shadow of doubt that true apartheid, which entails the development of the native Reserves as viable entities in which the bulk of the African populations can work, live and prosper, is quite impracticable. The capital required for development and the ensuing problems of balancing the external accounts of the Reserves, and of progressing at the rate necessary to achieve the objective, make the project absurdly unreal and any policy that envisages it not strictly honest. Yet this is the policy on which past elections have been fought and won by the governing party. Moreover, the idea of a separate territory or territories for all Africans – a Bantustan, as it is sometimes termed (thus named because of its supposed similarity to Pakistan) – still grips the imagination of most Nationalists and is passionately believed in by the rank and file of the Nationalist Party as the ultimate solution of the country's racial problem.

Yet the Government itself is plainly on the retreat from such a solution. It is gradually realizing that the project advocated with so much enthusiasm in early years is an idle dream, and may soon become a ghastly nightmare. It is all too evident that the Government is in a nasty dilemma on this issue. It dare not disillusion the bulk of its supporters by telling them the facts, and it therefore seeks to buy time by nebulous promises of a

Bantustan in some dim and distant future, while tinkering with legislation and schemes that have little to do with true apartheid and are in effect nothing but the stricter and firmer application of baasskap, poorly camouflaged. Nor dare the Government disclose to many of its supporters the heavy costs that even partial apartheid will entail.

It has therefore been unable so far to accept the recommendation of the Tomlinson Commission to expend the modest sum of £10 million annually on the rehabilitation of the Reserves. The fact of the matter is that constructive apartheid – the version of the project which the Government seeks to pass off as its policy – is extremely costly while the application of baasskap – the true policy of the Government – is cheap in terms of money, and can in the main be achieved by legislation, which true apartheid cannot. But the Government will only be getting itself deeper and deeper into the mire by not facing up boldly to the facts of the situation. For the truth of the matter is that territorial apartheid can never be achieved in this country, and time is not on the side of those who believe that it can. The only people the Government can deceive by its policy of buying time are its own supporters. This may yet turn out to be the one bright spot in the ill-conceived policy of apartheid.

Present policy towards the Reserves

The latest contribution by the Government to the project of apartheid is almost pitiable. It is a further retreat from the policy of true apartheid. However defective the findings of the Tomlinson Commission may have been on the question of the industrialization of the Reserves, they did disclose the impracticability of complete territorial apartheid by indicating that by the year 2000 there would still be 6 million Africans in White areas. This suggested that in the Reserves there would then be something like 14 million Africans. The latest proposals of the Government, however, appear to suggest a population of only about 8 million Africans in the Reserves by the year 2000, leaving, presumably, about 12 million in the White areas by that time.

As the Africans in the White areas live and will continue to live under conditions of pure baasskap, it will be realized how Government policy is forcibly drifting away from apartheid to baasskap. First it was no Africans in White areas by the year 2000; then it was 6 million, and now it is 12 million. While previously the policy could, by a stretch of the imagination, be called apartheid, because theoretically it aimed at settling the bulk of the Africans in the Reserves, now it can no longer justify that euphemism, as the majority of Africans will have to live under baasskap conditions in the White areas. Yet even after the announcement of this new policy concerning Africans in the Union, the dream of a Bantustan lingers on, for we still hear cabinet ministers speak of the gradual return of the Bantu to their own territories. The lack of realism and the capacity for self-deception on this issue are truly staggering.

The policy now envisaged for the Reserves is the entrenchment of tribalism on the one hand, and a half-hearted attempt at industrialization on the other. Tribalism is to be enforced by an Act of Parliament – the Bantu Authorities Act – and is to be embellished by the appointment of secretaries-general in the various territories. There will be eight of these territories, each representing the homeland of a different ethnical group. The secretaries will be the representatives of the Union Government in the various territories, and in return the territories will have representatives in the large cities of the Union where African labour is concentrated.

The tribal heads in the respective territories will be given a certain amount of authority in the running of the areas concerned. Their contact with the Union Government will be via the resident secretaries to the Bantu Affairs Department and from there to the cabinet minister concerned. It is also expected that the tribal heads will be able to exercise a limited amount of authority over their subjects working in the White areas. This will be done through the territories' representatives in the big cities of the Union.

This pattern of authorities and representation is supposed to be a copy of the existing set-up of the British colonial administration in Africa. But when it is realized, first, that tribalism throughout Africa is on the wane and is gradually being replaced by representative government in varying degrees, secondly, that none of the territories in which tribal authority is to be entrenched is anything like viable, and thirdly, that the amount of authority to be exercised by the tribal heads will be less than that exercised by minor local authorities in the White areas, the whole set-up takes on the character of playing at soldiers. A few of the chosen chiefs or headmen will prize their regained authority, a few Whites will applaud the stage-setting, but the bulk of the South African population, White and non-White alike, cannot possibly be deceived by this farcical imitation of British colonial administration, which is described as political apartheid.

Equally farcical is the attempt that is to be made to industrialize these territories. No outside capital of White investors will be permitted to share in the development of the Reserves. This will be the function of a newly-established Bantu Development Corporation, initially to be financed by the Union Government. The capital of this body will, in the first instance, be £500,000, but ultimately it is expected that the Corporation will mobilize the savings of the Africans and in this way provide further funds for industrial development. But when the magnitude of the capital requirements necessary for any serious industrialization of the Reserves is compared with the paltry sum of £500,000, and when it is appreciated that the earnings of the average African family in the Union are insufficient to permit of any savings whatever, it will be realized to what extent the Government is likely to succeed in this venture. It might as well seek to shift Table Mountain by means of a couple of picks and shovels within the next forty years! Indeed, one might venture to predict that, with the means provided under the Bantu Industrial Development Act, the number of Africans likely to be profitably settled in the Reserves by the year 2000 will not reach 4 million, let alone 8 million.

The provisions are hopelessly inadequate for the job on hand, for the territories are already vomiting forth their populations, despite the fact that these are below 4 million, because of lack of resources, and it will take a great deal of careful planning and masses of capital to make the Reserves viable with their present populations, if migratory earnings are to be eliminated. Any objective assessment of the Government's latest policy must stamp it as ridiculous.

Even so, this would be kindly criticism, for the new proposals are capable of a more sinister interpretation. This was pointed out to me in all seriousness by a friend who is not, incidentally, a South African. He said it appeared to him that the Government's latest proposals had as their objective the herding of the bulk of the African population into the limited confines of the Reserves, there to become impoverished and to languish so that their spirit would be broken. In this way, he believed, they would become tractable to the wishes of the Government through mental and physical privation, and so by virtual banishment to the Reserves, cease to be a menace to the Whites. When I protested at the very thought of so sinister a motive, he retorted by asking: 'What other interpretation can be placed upon the proposals when it is the Government's oft-repeated intention to remove the Africans to the Reserves on the one hand, and hopelessly inadequate provision is made for the development of the Reserves on the other?'

Despite the obvious logic of this interpretation, as a South African I cannot possibly accept it. I have far too much confidence of the innate humanity of my countrymen. The true explanation of the inane policy of apartheid, in my opinion, is to be found in the complete lack of understanding on the part of the Nationalists of the implications of industrialization – of the industrialization of the Reserves in particular. Or perhaps the wanton refusal to understand these implications, the wish being father to the thought.

*

Impossibility of the Nationalist ideal

From the economic point of view apartheid is a one-way street leading to the collapse of the country's economy. A *sine qua non* of true or territorial apartheid is the industrialization of the Reserves as a separate economic entity. Whether such industrialization is a success or a failure, it can have only one effect upon the economy of the rest of the Union – disintegration and the undermining of White standards. Success – a most unlikely outcome – will mean a wholesale collapse of industries in White areas, while failure will result in the Reserves becoming a colossal liability that could only be sustained by ever more onerous subsidies – a veritable millstone round the necks of White South Africans.

It will doubtless be asked why I stress the idea of economic apartheid when certain ministers have recently stated that it is no longer the Government's aim to achieve such an objective, but merely political apartheid in the Reserves. I do so because political apartheid, as outlined in the recent proposals, is absolutely worthless unless the Reserves become economically self-supporting; otherwise it is tantamount to severing the head from the body. As more and more Africans are crammed within their borders, the Reserves (unless they become viable) will soon degenerate into vast concentration camps, bearing out the interpretation placed by my friend on the Government's recent proposals.

No matter what ministers may say, the vast majority of the rank and file among Nationalists still believe in and devoutly cherish the idea of Bantustans capable of separate development, where the bulk of the Africans may live in comfort and thrive without being a menace to White South Africa. The fact is that if these separate African areas cannot become economically self-supporting territories within the foreseeable future, the whole concept of apartheid as envisaged by the Nationalists breaks down completely and becomes a dismal failure. In such event the policy of the Nationalists can no longer be described as apartheid in the original sense of the word. It becomes unadulterated baasskap and perhaps even worse, as my friend has seen fit to interpret it.

The development of the Reserves into viable territories capable of supporting, at reasonably low living standards, the majority of the Africans who will be living in the Union by the year 2000, is a hopelessly impossible proposition. Even if the High Commission Territories are ultimately to be incorporated in the Union, the proposition will not be feasible. This is because both Basutoland and Swaziland are small, mountainous and thickly-populated areas, and the Bechuanaland Protectorate, while large in size, is three-quarters desert and the balance, where it is not swamp, capable of supporting only a small population under pastoral conditions. Moreover, the incorporation of these territories in the Union is by no means a foregone conclusion – especially in the light of recent developments inside and outside the Union. There can be no escaping the conclusion, therefore, that apartheid will prove a flop, and that the policy is the deception that Field-Marshal Smuts described it as being at the outset. The tragedy about this much-flaunted policy is that its bill of costs has not yet been presented, and it will be the generations to come that will have to meet it – not only in money, but also in heartbreak, sweat and tears, if not in blood.

Meanwhile, apartheid continues to be the official policy of the Nationalist Party, notwithstanding the Government's gradual retreat: the building crumbles, but the façade remains. So far, most of the Government's actions have been inspired by baasskap, but there has been always the promise that the true apartheid measures will follow some time in the future. Legislation involving racial differentiation has been mass-produced during the past ten years, but it would be difficult to single out a single Act which definitely favours the non-Whites. Invariably the measures deprive the latter of former rights or infringe their erstwhile liberties; or, where different treatment is prescribed, inevitably it is the non-Whites who get the worst of the deal.

No fair-minded person could possibly regard these measures as just apartheid or differentiation, under which a fair distribution of rights and obligations is provided. It is always the Whites who receive the privileges and the non-Whites the promises of benefits to come. Gradually even the promises are whittled away as they prove impracticable: Bantustan is a haven for dreamers, not a refuge for generations to come. It is baasskap, therefore, not apartheid in any constructive sense that emerges ever more clearly as the true policy of the Nationalist Government. Apartheid is merely a word with which the Nationalist leaders bemuse their more gullible followers.

But baasskap is a one-way street – though perhaps a bit longer than the Via Apartheid – that leads inevitably to the collapse of White standards in the Union. So whether Government policy is apartheid or baasskap or a mixture of the two, its outcome will be the same – the downfall of the Whites in the Union. To any unbiased, thinking person this is inevitable, for both baasskap and apartheid, as applicable in South Africa, run counter to Christian principles, universally-accepted ethical codes, the processes of evolutionary development and economic laws.

In one sense only could apartheid succeed, and in this sense the chances of success are slender indeed. This is in the sense of partition, where the Whites and the non-Whites are given full control of their respective areas, after an equitable division of the country. But such a partition must involve a division so that each of the separate parts becomes independently viable. The boundaries would be hard to define; it would also inevitably entail immense hardships and sacrifice on the part of the Whites. For this reason I do not believe that White South Africa could ever voluntarily accede to a partition of this nature. Against such a partition, the apartheid that the present Government visualizes can lead only to the collapse of the country's economy through the creation of hundreds of thousands of poor-Whites, and of millions of half-starved Africans.

CONCLUSION

II

THE NEXT FIFTY YEARS

I N May 1960 South Africa celebrated the fiftieth anniversary
of Union. The first fifty years of its existence as a united
country have witnessed steady, if not spectacular, progress
in its economy. These years could, on the whole, be regarded
as a half-century of good fortune – particularly the last twenty-
five. The country had its ups and downs during this period and
was involved in world wars on two occasions. Fortunately, it
emerged both times on the side of the victors and as a consequence gained much in wealth and experience. It gained in
territory, too, as South West Africa is today virtually a province
of the Union. Much of the progress must, however, be regarded
as fortuitous in that major discoveries of gold, diamonds,
platinum and uranium were brought to light and turned to
account during these years. Nevertheless, in other spheres also
progress has been substantial: agriculture has developed in
many directions and manufacturing industry has grown from
small beginnings to quite a substantial contributor to the
economy of the country – in fact, today it is the largest single
contributor to the national income of the Union.

Storm signals

While in the economic sphere progress has been substantial,
it is not by bread alone that a nation grows to maturity: the
spirit and temper of its people are of equal, if not greater,
importance to the welfare of the community. In 1910 there was
an immense fund of goodwill. The country had hardly emerged
from the misfortunes of the Anglo-Boer War, but it seemed that
the people generally were anxious to let bygones be bygones
and to make a new start and a co-operative effort for the

benefit of all. In this spirit the Union was launched, and by its momentum much has been achieved. But can it truly be said that this spirit has survived the past fifty years? According to the ruling Nationalist Party, race relations have never been better in the Union than at present. But then the Nationalists comprise only some 10 per cent of the country's population, and unfortunately this view is not shared by the remaining 90 per cent. In their view, relations have sadly deteriorated and the spirit of goodwill has all but vanished. Can it be that these diametrically-opposed viewpoints arise because the 10 per cent are the privileged few, while the rest in varying degrees are not so favoured?

The statistical analyses given in the appendix show that the country's prosperity has not been evenly shared by the different sections of the population. While the White peoples have come a long way since Union and are today enjoying a standard of life comparable with the best in the world, the non-Whites have not been so fortunate. During the past fifteen to twenty years, while the standard of living of the Whites has risen by some 40 per cent, that of most Africans has actually fallen, and in the main they are still living below the bread-line, despite the prosperity of the country. Moreover, ever since Union there has been a gradual whittling down of the previously-enjoyed citizenship rights of the non-Whites in the Cape Province. And in the past twelve years, under the impact of the Nationalist Government's so-called policy of apartheid this process of whittling down rights has been extended to the whole of the Union and expedited to a shocking extent. Surely this record of White stewardship can hardly have contributed to better race relationships between Whites and non-Whites, as the Nationalists aver.

Among the English-speaking South Africans there has arisen a growing feeling of disillusion. At the time of Union, which was only some eight years after the Treaty of Vereeniging, English-speaking South Africans in an act of faith readily accepted a constitution under which the Afrikaner vote outweighed theirs, not only in numbers but also in individual worth. This was due to the system of overloading town and city constituencies, where the bulk of the English-speaking lived, and underloading rural constituencies where the main Afrikaner vote was concentrated.

Instead of being grateful for this gesture on the part of English-speaking South Africans, the Nationalists have actually gone out of their way to distort the balance of voting power still more in their favour so as to entrench themselves as a ruling clique. This has left a rather nasty taste, for English-speaking South Africans have continued to give in as great a measure to the economic development of the country as have the Nationalist Afrikaners. But this is not all; now that the Nationalists have secured power by questionable means, they have proceeded to root out, one by one, sentimental ties with the British Commonwealth, which are dear to the hearts of English-speaking South Africans.

Do the Nationalists really believe that, by such behaviour, they are endearing themselves to English-speaking South Africans? So far the latter have taken these rather ungracious acts philosophically, mainly because in so many other ways South Africa (not the Nationalists) has treated them kindly. The beautiful country, the bracing climate, the benefits derived from non-White labour and the good fortune in precious mineral discoveries have enabled them to enjoy a standard of living and leisure unsurpassed anywhere else. But these benefits, and more besides, have been available to Afrikaner Nationalists also. And it is as well that they should realize that, should these benefits be whittled away – as inevitably they will be by the present short-sighted policies of discrimination and preservation of privilege – English-speaking South Africa will not be so complacent about Nationalist self-seeking and self-righteousness.

So we come to the end of the first half-century of Union: the country prosperous, but to a considerable extent fortuitously so and against a rising tide of racial friction, no matter what the Nationalists believe. Far from the optimism of 1910, the prevailing sentiments today are those of fear and doubt. Our reputation in the world at large has suffered; we have grave doubts about the future welfare of the country, despite the many blessings it has bestowed upon us in the past; and all around us great and rapid changes are taking place which daily shatter more and more of our beliefs and upset our complacency. The greatest problem that faces South Africa now that we enter on our second half-century of Union will be how to adapt ourselves to the rapidly-changing conditions in Africa and how, in so doing, we can win back that reputation that once we enjoyed the world over. For in the long run we dare not continue to flout world opinion.

The African awakening

For the first time in recorded history the continent of Africa is astir with ambition and hope. For centuries it had been the unknown, the dark continent, whose indigenous peoples had been living under primitive and barbaric conditions. The developments of recent centuries had passed them by, but now they are stirring as a result of the encroachments of scientific endeavour and achievement, and they are bewildered by what they see around them. They begin to feel that they are part of something greater than their tribal institutions, and stretch out to gain knowledge and some of the benefits to which the whole human race is heir.

What should be the attitude of the Union – the most advanced and wealthiest state in Africa – towards the awakening people of Africa? Should they receive encouragement and help in their efforts to gain knowledge and some of the benefits of Western civilization, or should they be returned to and maintained in their former tribal state? There is no doubt whatever where civilized nations – both West and East – stand on this issue. To them, Africans are part of the human race, which is caught up in the process of evolution, and are entitled to share in the benefits that science has bestowed upon the world. It is their view that Africans – however backward – should be helped, not hindered, in breaching the gap between primitive tribalism and civilization. In the circumstances, if South Africa is to win back its good name among the nations of the world, it will have no alternative but to help in bringing Western achievements and culture to African peoples.

There is overwhelming evidence that Africans, in their endeavour to reap the benefits of twentieth-century civilization, are becoming impatient and are seeking powers which they have not earned and to which their progress does not entitle them. In this impatience they are being encouraged by nations with ulterior motives, or by those who have but scant knowledge of Africa and the Africans. The latter are well-meaning, but they tend to overlook the fact that in Europe, America and elsewhere it has taken centuries for the white man to gain his present mastery over scientific facts and to fit him by experience, acumen and background to govern industrial societies under twentieth-century conditions.

Africans, prodded both by well-meaning and self-seeking peoples seek to run before they can walk or even crawl. All too frequently their feelings, which in many instances are still primitive instincts, become inflamed by an unbalanced picture of colonialism. The adverse features of this evolutionary process are stressed beyond all reason, and the constructive efforts and human achievements ignored or belittled. As a result, a somewhat unnecessary antagonism has been sparked off between Africans and the colonial administrations. This is rather unfortunate, as most colonial administrations have in recent times been neither unaware of nor unsympathetic towards African aspirations and the necessity for evolutionary changes.

That the Africans are anxious to supplant the colonial administrations by people of their own kind is understandable. It is only natural that they should wish to enjoy the fruits of twentieth-century developments in the same way as the Whites. What they do not understand, however, is that the reins of office, if held by their leaders, will not necessarily guarantee them the benefits of twentieth-century civilization. In many instances, the removal of the colonial administrations would only worsen their economic conditions – not improve them. This is particularly so in many territories which, under present conditions, are not viable and in consequence have to be supported from outside sources. In many instances, therefore, it would be in the interests of Africans to make haste slowly in their demands for self-rule.

Nevertheless, in territories where White and Asian colonial interests are relatively small, there would be little point in resisting demands for self-determination were it not for the ulterior motives of Communist countries, which seek African support in their cold war against the West. This can be illustrated by the Middle East, where Western powers, in acceding to Arab demands, have enabled Communist influence to fill the void. On the other hand, in countries where Whites have played the major role in their development, such as in the Union and the Rhodesian Federation, there can be no question, under present conditions, of acceding to African demands for democratic government on the basis of one man, one vote. Such action would mean domination by those least equipped to govern and virtual economic and political suicide for the White minorities.

Dangers of universal suffrage

Western critics who insist on universal adult suffrage for all African territories must realize that its adoption under present conditions would merely result in the inevitable surrender of such territories to Communist influences, since the mind of the African in recent years has been unbalanced both by Communist propaganda and by certain ill-conceived concepts of democracy. No doubt the one-man-one-vote variety of democracy functions reasonably well in highly-developed Western states, but by no stretch of the imagination can it be suitable for most African territories, where large masses of the population are just emerging from tribalism and are thus completely ignorant of the meaning and implications of democratic government. As is only natural, the Africans in the circumstances seek the rights and benefits of the system without having the necessary qualifications for it, and without any appreciation of the obligations involved.

The right to vote

On the other hand, White paramountcy or domination in African territories is hardly a tenable doctrine or policy for the future. The emancipated African cannot be expected to, and most certainly will not, submit to it indefinitely. He will inevitably bend all his efforts to overthrow it, and in this he will receive the rightful support of all civilized peoples. It is all too clear that his position in the body politic will have to be recognized and be given adequate representation in any future system of government. It would, of course, be desirable to base any such system on democratic concepts, but the power they confer should be related not to numbers only, but also to the qualifications of the voters – and in the initial stages a high qualification for all voters, White and non-White alike, would be desirable. The system should not be rigid but should permit of adaptation to evolving conditions.

Possibly the right to vote should be related in some way or other to the contribution made by the individual to the welfare of the state or community – the greater the contribution, the weightier the vote. Of course it would not be easy to apply such a system in practice, but it would not be impossible. A suitable system of representation and government is one of the most urgent problems in Africa today, because of the explosive conditions arising from the dormant African of yesterday being suddenly pitched into the scientific industrialization of tomorrow.

South Africa, the richest and most advanced country in Africa, should have taken the lead in evolving some such system of government. Instead, as this book demonstrates, it is deliberately running away from the problem. In the Rhodesias, on the other hand, a genuine effort is being made, through the policy of partnership, to meet the requirements of a multi-racial society where large masses are just emerging from tribalism.

Partnership is an adaptable concept and the Whites for some time yet will have to be the senior partner. But as the African's contribution to the economic welfare of the country increases, so will his share in the partnership – if the Rhodesians remain true to this concept. That the Rhodesians are having teething troubles is understandable, for they are involved in a far-reaching and explosive human experiment. All honour to them that they have had the courage to face up to it. Time will reveal their wisdom in tackling the problem at this stage rather than in leaving it to future generations, as we in the Union are doing.

It is clear that the implementation of any new system of representation and government will not be an easy matter, particularly in the present state of mind of the Africans, who have been encouraged by overseas opinion, both Western and Communist, to believe that they are equipped and entitled to govern themselves, irrespective of their limitations and of the rights of the White minorities. In the immediate future, administrators in Africa will have a delicate task in meeting African demands. At times when the demands are unreasonable, or when African opinion has been inflamed by self-seeking agitators, they will have to exercise their authority with firmness – even if it calls for the use of force. But such firmness can only be justified where it is based upon fair and generous treatment, and for the foreseeable future, the keynote of White authority in Africa in its implementation of any just system of government will have to be firmness backed by fairness in all its enactments and actions.

Those who know Africa will bear me out that, on the whole, the Africans will respond to such treatment, if they can be convinced of its fairness and justice. It would therefore be prudent for White administrations to err on the side of generosity in their implementation of economic policy. On the basis of firm but fair administration the authorities in Africa deserve the support of Western nations – particularly of the United Kingdom and the United States of America, for such support will not only assist administrations in Africa in guiding African opinion, but will redound in favour of the West in its efforts to stem Communist penetration.

*

Consequences of present Nationalist policy

African nationalism and African demands will inevitably figure prominently in the fifty years immediately ahead. The world is watching the rise of the African with a great deal of sympathy. It is vitally interested in a just solution of African problems and is prepared to render massive help in such achievement, the more so as certain Western countries are at present seeking outlets for their surplus energies and products. And where better to direct them than towards Africa, where there is vast scope for development through the advancement of the African?

The baffling enigma in this situation is the present attitude of the Union of South Africa. Whereas the country should be taking the lead in the development of African policy, it steadfastly declines to face the problem of the emergent African in the modern industrial set-up. Instead, it adheres to the outdated doctrine of baasskap and puts forward the make-believe policy of apartheid. This is the sum total of the Union's contribution to the most searching and vital African problem of the second half of the twentieth century. These policies certainly cannot be construed as offering justice and a fair deal to the non-White majority in the country, and therefore their implementation by firmness or force could never win the approval and support of the outside world. It has been the object of this book to demonstrate clearly that both these policies will have become untenable long before the expiry of the first century of the Union. Indeed, if these policies are not discarded, the collapse of the country's economy is forecast – not at some distant date, but within the lifetime of those alive in the country today.

This is certainly an unhappy augury for the next fifty years, for the collapse of the country's economy must soon end in the eclipse of White leadership in southern Africa. In the opening phases of such a collapse there would be a flight of capital, followed by an emigration of the best and most adventurous elements of the population. Then there would be a re-emergence of poor-Whiteism on a vaster scale than experienced before.

And in this parlous condition how could the country possibly stand up to a militant Black nationalism, backed by the whole of Africa and Asia and a large section of Europe and America? Such are the inevitable consequences of the policies of baasskap and apartheid which the Nationalists have foisted upon the country.

Future policy

South Africa – White South Africa in particular – deserves a better fate, and unquestionably could have one, if only it could pluck up its courage and shake off its prejudices, fears and selfishness which paralyse a section of its population. A people whose prime aim in life is the preservation of privilege can never reap greatness nor the best virtues of nationhood. Indeed by some twist of fate, the seekers of privilege invariably lose their all. And so it will be with those who worship baasskap or apartheid, which are only the modern versions of the old cults of privilege and isolationism. These policies are nothing else but privileges reserved for the benefit of the Whites in the country – privileges founded upon the mining of precious minerals, which will disappear as the mines become exhausted. On the other hand, great achievements are invariably the outcome of courage and generosity.

Only by a bold and generous policy of training and rewarding its emergent African population will it be possible for this country to face the future with confidence. As is generally accepted, the future of the Union can only be ensured if manufacturing industries are developed to replace mining, as the extraction of precious minerals declines. But these industries can never replace the mines if their economy is based upon baasskap or apartheid, for in that case manufacturing industry forgoes the dynamism which it can never achieve unless its African labour forces is properly trained and rewarded.

On the threshold of the second half-century of Union, White South Africa should therefore brace itself and squarely face the fact that this country is multi-racial and that its future will inevitably rest upon justice and equal opportunities for all its peoples – whether White or non-White. The policies of White domination and racial discrimination cannot possibly endure for any length of time: baasskap and apartheid, which in essence seek the preservation of White privilege, are clearly doomed and will not survive the next fifty years of Union. Those who see in apartheid a just solution of the racial problem through separate and parallel development are merely deluding themselves and will soon wake up with a nasty shock.

The crowding of the steadily-growing millions of Africans into the limited, impoverished and eroded native Reserves with but a mockery of self-rule can only create an even more frightful problem than that which the country declines to face at present. There is no alternative solution. The country will have to be developed economically as a unified whole, in which due cognizance is extended to all the elements of the population. In this competitive world our choice of course in the economic sphere is strictly limited, and a fundamental and essential condition of success in its present phase is the enlightened use of the country's human resources. Failure to exploit these resources will inevitably result in serious loss and ultimate decay. Therefore, if White South Africa is to look forward to further progress and happiness in the years ahead, it will have to alter its course at the earliest possible date and turn its back on the negative policies of the past that merely seek the preservation of White privilege. Instead, it should pursue a positive policy of full-scale development of the country's resources, both material and human – more particularly the latter.

Such a course will undoubtedly demand sacrifice on the part of White South Africans, and a change of heart and direction cannot be experienced overnight. We in South Africa have been moving in the wrong direction far too long for any change to flow from sudden and easy decisions. The change can only come about slowly and by degrees; but we dare not ignore the fact that time and opportunity are slipping by.

While it will ultimately be essential for South Africans to reorientate their views on non-White representation in the political field, the most urgent changes are in the sphere of economics. In this the country must, at the earliest opportunity, shed its negative attitude of indifference to the welfare of its non-White population and embark on an active programme of developing the skills and using the talents of those people, and of improving their living standards. This will entail considerable expense and a gradual breaking-down of all discriminatory practices such as colour bars, job reservation, differential wage-rates, etc., which means a complete reversal of present policy and – inevitably – some immediate hardships and disappointments. But failure to do so soon can only speed the country on its present course to economic collapse within the next fifty years. Crucial years, therefore, lie ahead of South Africa as it enters the second half-century of Union.

Equal opportunities

Many in this country believe that a policy of equal opportunity for all, White and non-White alike, will mean African domination in the foreseeable future. I do not share this view as I am a firm believer in White superiority. In the event of the extension of equal opportunity, South Africa will more than ever be in need of White leadership, but White leadership does not mean White domination or paramountcy. A policy of racial domination by one section will inevitably invite reaction against the dominant interests, and, by virtue of a form of Gresham's Law applicable to people instead of money, it will always be the dominated that will inherit the land. The ruling race inevitably rules itself out.

Equal opportunity in the economic sphere, however, does not mean universal suffrage in the political. This is something that White South Africa, with complete justification, dare not concede in the foreseeable future, because universal suffrage would at present be an abuse of democracy, and not an efficient and just use of the system. Instead, it should be possible to devise a modification of the democratic system of rule suitable to South African conditions – efficient yet fair to all sections.

On the basis of these radical changes the reins of government should, in the near future and for generations thereafter, remain predominantly in White hands, just as in industry and trade the principal executive positions will be held by Whites for many years to come. This is not because of the colour of their skins, but because Whites will be best equipped by education, experience, innate ability and background for these posts. The non-Whites – Africans in particular – have yet to display sufficiently the qualities of stability, sound judgment and acumen, and also the creative ability necessary for the management and control of big business, whether by state or private enterprise.

In essence, therefore, the policy of White leadership would be one where Whites hold the leading government and business positions because of merit, and not because of White privilege hedged in by protective laws. In business, this will inevitably be the case because the capital employed, which controls voting power, will be in the hands of Whites; and in the political sphere a suitable constitution could with ample justice prevent White leadership from being submerged by the more numerous but less well-equipped non-Whites.

The Rhodesian experiment

On this basis, the dangers of a policy of equal opportunities (not equal rights, for it is impossible to accept the hypothesis that all men are equal) would be more apparent than real. South Africans have shown themselves unduly timid on this issue. The Rhodesians, on the other hand, have displayed greater courage and vision, for their policy of partnership, if courageously implemented, does furnish scope and ample opportunity for the non-Whites for some generations ahead. In this policy the Federation deserves the active support, both moral and material, of the Western democracies, though it remains for Rhodesians themselves to implement the policy fairly and impartially and not to fail their far-sighted leader, Lord Malvern, as South Africa has failed her visionaries, Rhodes and

Smuts. The Rhodesians perhaps do not fully realize the immense importance of their experiment, for as things stand today, the success or otherwise of multi-racial co-operation in Africa largely depends upon its outcome. White South Africa, unfortunately, has shirked its duty and will have to pay the penalty if multi-racial co-operation fails in Africa.

Greater South Africa

Since my early youth British imperialism has been represented to me as the villain responsible for all South Africa's misfortunes. Rhodes, its principal architect in this country, has been reviled as an evil genius. But at this moment in the history of southern Africa it would be well to compare his vision of a great federation of southern African states with the inevitable position in the Union some years hence if the policy of apartheid is pursued to its logical conclusion.

Rhodes visualized a federation stretching from the borders of Tanganyika to the Cape of Good Hope. Had this materialized – and it certainly would have had he not been thwarted by Afrikaner isolationism – this federation would in all probability have held at the present time a White population of from five to six million; it would have possessed plenty of land for an African peasantry; the High Commission Territories would have been incorporated; the Africans would have been more advanced than they are today in the Union and their purchasing power immensely greater; industrialization, as a consequence, would have been further ahead and more dynamic; the Coloured population would have been more affluent and satisfied because of greater privileges; all in all, race relations would have been better and the name and fame of South Africa overseas would have been much more impressive. Indeed, this federation would have emerged as a powerful and respected country, comparable with Canada and capable of immense influence and progressive development on the African continent, capable too of speaking with authority for the Whites in Africa and commanding respect in the councils of the world.

By comparison, if the policy of apartheid is followed to its logical and tragic outcome, the Union will become a country greatly impoverished by the decline of its precious mineral industry, chronically short of capital, and gradually losing the most adventurous and affluent sections of its population; poor-Whiteism will have grown to an alarming extent and millions of Africans will be living on the borders of starvation, without hope, in over-populated and eroded Reserves, which will have become veritable concentration camps; bitterness, hatred and resentment will be rampant among the different races, and the Union will be detested throughout Africa and pitied by the world at large.

The contrast could not be greater; and in contemplating it one can hardly escape the conclusion that Rhodes and imperialism were not the villains of the piece after all. How could they be? The vision of Rhodes was conceived in a forward-looking, expansionist and generous mood, fitting into a system that has proved itself sensitive to evolutionary changes and to the wholesome aspirations of the different populations, while Afrikaner Nationalist extremism has its roots in the selfish isolationism of the past, its foundation upon sectional privilege, its purpose in flagrant opposition to evolutionary progress, and its spirit insensitive to the feelings and hopes of the vast majority of the South African population.

Hope resurgent

Will South Africa ever allow itself to be dragged down to so ignominious a level – the inevitable outcome of the policies of baasskap and apartheid? I cannot believe that it will, for I have far too much confidence in most of my countrymen – Afrikaners and English-speaking alike. The country has too much good sense ever to permit it. Despite surface appearances, there is an immense fund of goodwill among all sections in the Union. Although not much in evidence at present, principally because fortuitous prosperity in the Union has rather clouded the issue, this goodwill will come to the surface more and more as prosperity recedes under the impact of the short-sighted and destructive policy of apartheid. Indeed, any movement which is so utterly selfish and self-righteous as is Nationalist extremism in the Union, and whose main preoccupation in life is the quest for and entrenchment of privilege, must in the long run destroy itself – the more so as it exercises power by questionable devices.

For those who can see beyond the horizon of Nationalist extremism, the country still has a great future before it and an important role in African affairs. The vision seen by Rhodes, and by Smuts after him, still exists, although for the moment it is hidden by the mists of racial friction. As time brings greater maturity and understanding to the less enlightened – White and non-White alike – so will the spirit of co-operation and expansionism again assert itself. Time and evolution are unquestionably on the side of those who are big enough to think in terms of co-operation and generous enough to believe in sacrifice rather than privilege. For some years still the outcome of affairs in southern Africa will remain in the balance, and during this period the conflict between sectional domination and multi-racial co-operation will intensify, but in the interests of South Africa – White South Africa in particular – and also of the world at large, there can and must be one outcome – the triumph of a just multi-racialism.

At present, the forces of racial co-operation appear to be in retreat from those of sectional domination. Their lines are but slenderly held – mainly in the Rhodesias. But in the rear, throughout southern Africa, the reserves are massing and it needs only the unequivocal moral and financial support of the Western democracies to ensure their ultimate victory. In the meantime, the struggle in the Rhodesias is rather grim and all who believe in White leadership must pray that the front-line fighters will be able to hold out until help arrives. But when victory comes it will be great, for the concept of a great federation stretching from Tanganyika to the Cape of Good Hope will again become a live issue. The vision of Rhodes must materialize in the end, in the interests of all in southern Africa and indeed of the Western way of life. In the intervening years an apartheid republic will doubtless be established, but its early eclipse will not be the first occasion on which isolationist republics will have had to make way in southern Africa for something bigger and better.

In this great federation of the future, British traditions and ideals will enjoy their rightful place. So will Afrikaans culture and aspirations: in particular, Afrikaans may well become the official language in certain of the states; in others, Bantu tongues will receive full recognition. In the federation as a whole, industry will prosper on the ever-rising purchasing power of non-White skill and labour, which will be given every scope and will be justly rewarded. All sections of the population will enjoy representation in the various councils of the nation in accordance with their civilized status and their relative contributions to the national welfare. Social relationships among the races will be left to the good sense of the different peoples, who will naturally be attracted to, and will be encouraged (but not forced) to remain with, their respective groups. In a world rapidly moving in the direction of international co-operation, and even of integration of states, the establishment of this all-embracing multi-racial federation would not only provide the best and fairest solution to all the problems of southern Africa, but seems, indeed, to be inevitable. Only those whose vision is clouded by the mists and fears of racial prejudice will think otherwise.

While, in the territories to the north, African domination is bound to happen in the end, in southern Africa the only just and fair solution would be this multi-racial federation. It is to be hoped that the Western nations, in their own interests, will powerfully back its creation at the appropriate time, so that before the next fifty years of Union have run their course, we in southern Africa may be celebrating the birth of the great multi-racial federation stretching from the borders of Tanganyika to the Cape of Good Hope.

APPENDIX

STATISTICAL SURVEY
OF
EARNINGS, LIVING COSTS AND LIVING STANDARDS IN SOUTH AFRICA

I N this survey an attempt is made to arrive at a reasonably accurate indication of the living conditions of the different groups that make up the population of the country. Statistical presentation of the known facts is used to give this, but as the Office of Census and Statistics does not publish data relative to the different groups, concentrating principally on the country as a whole, the presentation given has necessitated considerable recasting of the information available. At times computations based upon informed estimates have had to be made, but on the whole only recognized statistical devices are used.

The information upon which the presentation is built is almost exclusively that given in official publications. On the whole, South Africa has a reasonably good statistical service – the only complaint of substance that can be levelled against it is that far too much time is taken in the preparation and publication of the information. Often much of its value has been lost through delay, and serious efforts should be made to speed up the service, even if short cuts have to be taken here and there.

Because of the tardy service, the most recent information given in this survey is for the year 1953/4. This is unsatisfactory, for considerable changes have taken place in the ensuing six years. Naturally, some statistical records relative to the facts presented are available for periods subsequent to the year 1953/4, but because certain essential information relating to later years is still missing, I have had to be satisfied with the year 1953/4.

The survey covers the years 1938/9 – the immediate pre-war year – and 1953/4. It therefore discloses and compares conditions after a lapse of fifteen years. The trends over this period are unmistakable, and it is virtually certain that they have continued into the years after 1953/4 and to the present time. Nothing fundamental has happened since 1953/4 to alter them, so that, despite the absence of full information since this time, the trends as disclosed by the survey are as true today as they were then, although later information would have enabled us to gauge the extent of the divergence in living conditions at the present time somewhat more accurately.

It is surprising that, with all the propaganda by the Government for apartheid or for separate development of races, no effort should have been made to present by statistical analysis the existing facts relating to the living conditions of the different peoples in the Union's population. Today, in all advanced communities statistics are compiled to keep track of all major events or movements. This is found to be essential, for without such information serious blunders could be made. It serves to keep the authorities from serious error in formulating policy or in steering the national course. It is hoped that the analysis given here will move Government statisticians to give more attention to the question of presenting the different living conditions of the distinct races in the Union. Government statisticians have much more data, and also powers to obtain necessary information, which would enable them to give a much fuller and more accurate presentation of the facts than I – an independent investigator – have been able to do.

In the following survey facts are given in respect of only three racial groups – Whites, Africans and 'Others'. The last-mentioned includes both Coloureds and Indians on the not very accurate supposition that the living conditions of these groups are largely similar. There are undoubtedly differences between these groups, but for practical purposes their being taken together should not detract much from the study. With fuller and more accurate details in the years ahead an attempt should be made to give separate figures in respect of these groups.

The tables here and the comments with them will, it is believed, give a fairly reliable picture of conditions relating to the races in question:

TABLE I

POPULATIONS AND FAMILIES (IN 1000S)

	1938/9	1953/4	1957
(a) POPULATION:			
Whites	2,100	2,780	3,000
Africans	6,920	8,940	9,600
Others	1,050	1,580	1,750
Total	10,070	13,300	14,350
(b) FAMILIES – NUMBER OF:			
Whites	488	646	700
Africans	1,462	1,858	2,000
Others	191	287	318
Total	2,141	2,791	3,018

The number of families has been derived from an official classification giving the marital condition of the population. From this it appeared that the average numbers per family were 4·3 for Whites, 4·6 for Africans, and 5·5 for 'Others'. A feature of this classification is the large percentage of widows among the African population. The percentages of families without male heads were: Whites 12·9 per cent, African 21·9 per cent, and Others 13·6 per cent. In the computation of African families, allowance has been made for extra-Union males working in the Union.

In order to determine the true improvement that has taken place in the welfare of individuals or families during the years under consideration, it will be necessary to correct the relative incomes in the following table by the increases in price-levels that have taken place over these years. This is normally done by using the cost-of-living index figures. But in the Union this index will not give an accurate reflection of the improvement in real incomes, because the different population groups live under very different conditions and standards; and the changes

TABLE II

NATIONAL INCOME, ALL GROUPS (in £1,000,000s)

(a) TOTAL INCOMES:

	Geographical	Due to Outside Interests	Net
1938/9	394·6	30·7	363·9
1953/4	1559·2	156·5	1402·7
1956/7	1930·7	229·0	1701·7

(b) PER HEAD:

1938/9	39·2	3·0	36·2
1953/4	117·2	11·7	105·5
1956/7	137·5	16·3	121·2

(c) PER FAMILY:

1938/9	184·4	14·4	170·0
1953/4	558·8	56·0	502·8
1956/7	640·0	74·0	566

that reflect increases in the cost of living of the average White family will by no means give a true reflection of the changes that have taken place in the average African family. It is in this respect particularly that the Union's statistical information falls badly short of the country's requirements – especially in view of the emphasis upon separate development of the races.

When considering non-White earnings, it is customary to apply the official cost-of-living index for any determination of necessary increases. The application of this measure, as this survey will show, has resulted in a grave injustice to the African population. African costs of living vary greatly according to where the respective families live – whether in the Reserves, on farms or in the cities – and it is a matter of the utmost importance that a detailed study of their living costs, and of the changes that have taken place since the last war, be undertaken. The official cost-of-living index reflects the standard of the average White working-class family and is influenced by many

factors which are alien to the living conditions of the Africans –
particularly those in the Reserves or on the farms owned by
Whites.

In this survey data are given which, as far as practicable,
reflect the living costs and standards of African families who live
under the different conditions applicable to them. These data
also, as far as the available information permits, disclose the
changes that have taken place in these costs in the fifteen-year
period from 1938/9 to 1953/4.

However, before giving this information, I must point out
what to my mind is a rather serious defect in the official cost-
of-living index as applicable to White families. This is in the
figures that purport to give the rises in rentals. The figures are
based upon actual rentals paid by Whites for houses falling
within specified categories. Unfortunately, these dwellings
represent only a small proportion of rented property, and therefore do not give a true indication of housing costs and the consequent increases. For instance, the index ignores rentals of
flats and leaves out of account the housing costs of the vast
number of families who own the homes they occupy.

The dwellings covered by the index are in the main houses
built some forty or fifty years ago, whose rentals have been
kept at a low level because they are old and because of the
operation of rent control. Since the last war, however, large
numbers of houses, and particularly flats, have been built to
which rent control does not apply. The housing costs in respect
of these affect a large number of families. Compared with the
relative pre-war costs, a material increase has taken place in
these cases, which can be measured by an index based upon
building costs, interest charges on mortgages, and municipal
rates. On this basis it has been computed that housing costs in
respect of this type of dwelling have risen between the years
1938/9 and 1953/4 by something like 165 per cent. It would
not, however, be accurate to use such an index in measuring
cost-of-living increases, as the rentals of most pre-war dwellings
have been subject to rent control and consequently kept at a
relatively low level.

The official index of rentals reflects an increase of only 53 per cent over the years from 1938/9 to 1953/4. This is the figure that has been weighted into the official cost-of-living index and its effect has been to depress unduly the increases that have actually taken place in living costs, whereas the straight average of the two increases – 53 per cent and 165 per cent or 109 per cent – would give a truer indication of the rise in housing costs over the fifteen years in question. If this average be adopted, then the cost-of-living index in respect of these years would reflect a rise of 108 per cent instead of the official 94 per cent.

As such a difference is material and fundamental, the index so amended is used in this study when measuring the increase in the living costs of the White population over the years under consideration – an index number for the year 1953/4 of 208 (instead of 194) on the basis of 100 for the year 1938/9.

As the object of this survey is to give statistical facts in respect of the different population groups, the first step is to divide the national income in such a manner as to give a reasonably accurate account of the earnings of the different groups. The bulk of these earnings, as far as non-Whites are concerned, is in the form of wages and salaries, either in cash or in kind. Fortunately, the published official figures give a considerable amount of information on this. Furthermore, in the Reserves and on farms owned by Whites, the Africans raise a considerable amount of produce on their own account, largely for home consumption. Official data in respect of the quantities of such produce are also available.

From this information a reasonably accurate account can be given of the earnings from employment of the different racial groups and of the value of the produce of African agriculture. This information is given in the following tables for the years 1938/9 and 1953/4 respectively. The totals, when added to income derived from sources other than employment, which (except for the value of African produce) accrues overwhelmingly to Whites, approximate the geographical national income. In the preparation of these tables, recourse was had, here and there, to computations based on unofficial data, but on the whòle the figures are derived from official publications. Only in respect of employment in domestic service is there little official guidance as to earnings, but a knowledge of the number of White families, nearly all of whom employ domestics, and of customary rates of pay for these services has, I believe, permitted the making of reasonably accurate estimates.

TABLE III

ESTIMATES OF SALARIES AND WAGES EARNED DURING THE YEAR 1938/9

	Numbers Employed (1000s)		Annual Rates		Total Earnings (£ million)
	M.	F.	M.	F.	
A. WHITES			£	£	
(a) Farming	60	—	150	—	9·00
(b) Mining	53	1	400	300	21·50
(c) Manufacturing and Construction	110	35	250	160	33·20
(d) Commerce and Finance	95	50	250	180	32·75
(e) Transport	70	3	200	200	14·60
(f) Household and Catering	5	20	250	80	2·85
(g) Public Administration	65	26	300	210	24·96
(h) Professional and Others	8	1	300	200	2·60
Total	466	136	£255	£168	£141·46
B. AFRICANS					
(a) Farming	400	180	30	15	14·70
(b) Mining	420	—	50	—	21·10
(c) Manufacturing and Construction	155	—	40	—	6·20
(d) Commerce and Finance	40	—	40	—	1·60
(e) Transport	40	—	44	—	1·76
(f) Household and Catering	200	200	50	30	16·00
(g) Public Administration	64	—	44	—	2·82
(h) Professional and Others	—	—	—	—	—
Total	1,319	380	£42	£23	£64·18

TABLE III—*cont.*

		Numbers Employed (1000s)		Annual Rates		Total Earnings (£ million)
		M.	F.	M. £	F. £	
C. OTHERS						
(a)	Farming	110	20	50	25	6·00
(b)	Mining	—	—	—	—	
(c)	Manufacturing and Construction	40	10	120	100	5·80
(d)	Commerce and Finance	20	—	150	—	3·00
(e)	Transport	20	—	70	—	1·40
(f)	Household and Catering	17	63	80	60	5·14
(g)	Public Administration	17	4	110	100	2·27
(h)	Professional and Others	—	—	—	—	
	Total	224	96	£80	£58·6	£23·61

TABLE IV

ESTIMATES OF SALARIES AND WAGES EARNED DURING YEAR 1953/4

		Numbers Employed (1000s)		Annual Rates		Total Earnings (£ million)
		M.	F.	M. £	F. £	
A. WHITES						
(a)	Farming	24	1	400	200	9·80
(b)	Mining	60	3	880	600	54·60
(c)	Manufacturing and Construction	215	45	725	360	172·00
(d)	Commerce and Finance	100	85	750	400	109·00
(e)	Transport	105	10	610	400	68·05
(f)	Household and Catering	5	10	600	350	6·50
(g)	Public Administration	105	60	730	460	103·50
(h)	Professional and Others	12	2	1,000	500	13·00
		626	216	£715	£410	£536·45

TABLE IV—*cont.*

	Numbers Employed (1000s)		Annual Rates		Total Earnings (£ million)
	M.	F.	M.	F.	
B. AFRICANS			£	£	
(a) Farming	600	200	50	25	35·00
(b) Mining	445	—	100	—	44·50
(c) Manufacturing and Construction	440	10	135	125	60·65
(d) Commerce and Finance	81	—	120	—	9·72
(e) Transport	110	—	110	—	12·10
(f) Household and Catering	200	400	120	80	56·00
(g) Public Administration	125	20	150	200	22·75
(h) Professional and Others	2	—	200	—	·40
	2,003	630	£99	£67	£241·12
C. OTHERS					
(a) Farming	90	25	90	50	9·35
(b) Mining	—	—	—	—	—
(c) Manufacturing and Construction	90	40	250	200	30·50
(d) Commerce and Finance	66	5	250	200	17·50
(e) Transport	15	—	250	—	3·75
(f) Household and Catering	10	50	250	120	8·50
(g) Public Administration	25	11	350	300	12·05
(h) Professional and Others	2	—	300	—	·60
	298	131	£210	£149	£82·25

TABLE V

ESTIMATES OF AFRICAN PRODUCTION IN RESERVES AND ON FARMS

	1938/9		1953/4	
	Reserves	Farms	Reserves	Farms
ANIMAL POPULATION (in 1000s):				
Cattle	3,722	1,380	3,449	1,325
Sheep and Goats	6,200	1,190	6,700	1,130

TABLE V—cont.

	1938/9		1953/4	
	Reserves	*Farms*	*Reserves*	*Farms*

MEAT PRODUCED AND CONSUMED (in million lb.):

	Reserves	*Farms*	*Reserves*	*Farms*
Beef	148·9	55·2	137·9	53
Mutton	18·6	3·6	20·1	3·4
	167·5	58·8	158·0	56·4

GRAIN PRODUCED AND CONSUMED (in million lb.):
(Average over 3 years in each case)

Maize	572	430	445	538
Kaffircorn	129	71	119	63
	701	501	564	601

MILK PRODUCED AND CONSUMED (in million gallons):

	67·0	28·0	67·0	28·0

EGGS PRODUCED AND CONSUMED (in million dozens):

	22·0	10·0	22·0	10·5

WOOL AND MOHAIR (in million lb.):

	10·46	·68	10·50	·65

VALUE OF PRODUCTS AT WHOLESALE PRICES (in £ million):

PRODUCT CONSUMED	*Prices*	1938/9 *Reserve*	*Farm*	*Total*
Meat	5d. per lb.	3·5	1·3	4·8
Grain	·8d. „ „	2·3	1·7	4·0
Milk	1·5d. „ pt.	3·3	1·4	4·7
Eggs	1s. 0d. „ doz.	1·1	·5	1·6
		10·2	4·9	15·1
PRODUCT SOLD				
Wool and Mohair	6d. per lb.	·3	·0	·3
Hides and Skins	4d. „ lb.	·2	·1	·3
		£10·7	£5·0	£15·7

TABLE V—*cont.*

PRODUCT CONSUMED	Prices	1953/4 Reserve	Farm	Total
Meat	1s. 3d. per lb.	9·8	3·5	13·3
Grain	2d. ,, ,,	4·7	5·0	9·7
Milk	3d. ,, pt.	6·6	2·8	9·4
Eggs	2s. 0d. ,, doz.	2·2	1·0	3·2
		23·3	12·3	35·6
PRODUCT SOLD				
Wool and Mohair	2s. 6d. per lb.	1·2	·1	1·3
Hides and Skins	1s. 4d. ,, ,,	·8	·3	1·1
		£25·3	£12·7	£38·0

These estimated quantities of meat, milk and eggs consumed may doubtless be questioned, but for the purposes of compiling an index for measuring increases in the cost of living of Africans over the years in question, they are accurate enough, and they are here used solely for the purpose of such an index.

An accurate reconciliation of the estimates of salaries and wages given in the foregoing table with the figures included in the Official Computation of National Income has not been found possible, as I am not in possession of all the data used in the Official Computation. The figures I give fall somewhat short of the official data and consist in some part of casual labour, which is not strictly comparable on an annual basis. The reconciliation, such as it is, would appear to be as follows:

	1938/9 £ million	1953/4 £ million
SALARIES AND WAGES (COMPARABLE):		
Whites	141·46	536·45
Africans	64·18	241·12
Others	23·61	82·25
	229·25	859·82

	1938/9 £ million	1953/4 £ million
OTHER INCOME:		
Whites (almost exclusively)	145	642·0
African farm income	15·70	38·0
	160·70	680·0
Differences*	4·65	19·42
National Income Geographical (according to Official Computation)	£394·60	£1,559·2

* The differences represent errors of about 1·2 per cent – not unduly significant.

The next step is a comparison of the real incomes per employee for the different racial groups. Such comparison is a measure of the improvement or otherwise of the standards of living of the respective groups. The real incomes are determined by correcting the average earnings per employee by the increases of the cost of living applicable to his group. The official cost-of-living index which applies to Whites has already been discussed and the conclusion reached that the increase in costs over the fifteen years in question should be 108 per cent, instead of the official 94 per cent. This increase does not, however, apply to the non-White groups, particularly the Africans, whose living conditions and standards are completely different. They spend their earnings in a very different manner; the food they eat is different; in the Reserves the women and children are clothed mainly in blankets; in these areas and to a large extent on the farms they do not pay rent, but live in huts which they build for themselves, and there also they have no transport costs to meet.

A measure of the increase in the living costs applicable to them requires a totally different index, and in subsequent paragraphs an index number is compiled to reflect the increase over the fifteen years 1938/9 to 1953/4. An index to measure conditions in the 'Others' group would be different again, for the Coloureds and Indians generally live at a lower standard than do the Whites, though the two modes of living are still comparable. As it would be a complex and onerous task to compile a special index for the Coloureds, which would not in fact be very different from that applicable to Whites, they will be included in the index for Whites, although it is believed that an accurate measurement of their costs of living would show an increase over the fifteen-year period somewhat higher than that given for the increase in respect of the Whites.

The increases in the earnings from employment and the purchasing power of the average employee (male and female) in the White and 'Others' groups are as follows:

TABLE VI

EARNINGS FROM EMPLOYMENT

	Average Money Earnings 1938/9 1953/4			Average Real Earnings in 1953/4 at 1938/9 Prices	
	£	£	Increase %	£	Increase %
Whites (average)	235	637	171	306	30
Male	255	715	180	343	34
Female	168	410	144	197	18
Others (average)	73·6	192	161	92·3	25
Male	80	210	162	101	26
Female	58·6	149	155	71·6	22

The figures disclose a substantial improvement in real earnings over the years in question for the Whites and 'Others' groups. The smaller increase in the real earnings of White women as against that of men is accounted for by the practice in the Union after the Second World War of paying materially lower cost-of-living allowances to single individuals and married women than to married men.

These figures do not, however, give a full account of the improvements which have taken place in the living standards of the groups in question. A far better indication would be a comparison of family incomes. In the first place the cost-of-living index is based on a family budget, so that its application

to the earnings of individuals would not be strictly accurate –
certainly not as reliable as when applied to family earnings.
Then, again, material changes took place in the pattern of
family earnings over the fifteen years in question: a larger
proportion of married women contribute to the family budget
today than in the pre-war years.

In the case of the Whites, income from sources other than
employment also materially increases family incomes and living
standards. This income, too, has undergone considerable
changes. The earnings of the Coloureds, on the other hand, are
almost exclusively from employment. In the case of Indians,
some are engaged as shopkeepers and agriculturalists on their
own account. But in the main these Indians are relatively poor,
so that earnings from sources other than employment are not
significant. At most, a few thousand families live on other than
earned income, and it is pretty certain that, in all, such income
from such proceeds did not exceed £2 million in the year
1938/9 and £6 million in 1953/4. If these estimates are used in
arriving at the total incomes that accrue to the 'Others' group,
then the total incomes that accrue to the White people could be
arrived at as follows:

TABLE VII

INCOME FROM ALL SOURCES ACCRUING TO WHITES
(IN £ MILLION)

	1938/9		1953/4	
NATIONAL INCOME GEOGRAPHICAL		394·60		1,559·20
Less: (a) Owing to non-Union Interests	30·70		156·50	
Less: (b) Paid to non-Whites:				
Africans – Salaries and Wages	64·18		241·12	
Africans – Agriculture	15·70		38·00	
Others – Salaries and Wages	23·61		82·25	
Others – Estimated Other	2·00		6·00	
Allowance for Casuals	3·00	139·19	8·00	531·87
		255·41		1,027·33

TABLE VII—*cont.*

	1938/9	1953/4
Add: Amount paid to ex-Union non-Whites included in (a) above	3·50*	16·70*
	£258·91	£1,044·03

* My own calculations put these figures (i.e. amounts paid to ex-Union non-Whites) considerably higher, but as they are the figures included in the Official Calculation of National Income, I have made use of them in this instance in order not to exaggerate family incomes.

If these incomes from all sources are divided by the number of families in the respective years, a fairly good indication of the average family income can be obtained.

TABLE VIII

AVERAGE FAMILY INCOMES

	1938/9	1953/4
Whites:		
Total Income (in £ million)	258·91	1,044·03
Number of Families (in thousands)	488	646
Income per Family	£530	£1,616
Others:		
Total Income (in £ million)	25·61	88·25
Number of Families (in thousands)	191	287
Income per Family	£134	£308

Correcting these income figures by the cost-of-living index, we arrive at the relative improvement in family incomes and standards over the years in question:

TABLE IX

IMPROVEMENTS IN FAMILY INCOMES (REAL)

		1953/4 *at* 1938/9	
	1938/9	*Living costs*	*Increase* %
Whites	£530	£777	46
Others	£134	£148	11

In the case of Whites, family incomes show a considerably larger improvement than do individual incomes (46 per cent against 30 per cent). This is accounted for (a) by the contribution to the family budget of the earnings of a larger proportion of married women in the latter year, and (b) by substantial increases in incomes from other sources. On the other hand, family incomes of Coloureds and Indians reflect a smaller increase than do the individual incomes of these people (11 per cent against 25 per cent). This is due to the fact that in 1953/4 a larger proportion of Coloured and Indian children were attending schools than in 1938/9, so that in the earlier year a larger proportion of the family contributed to its income. This is established by the official increase in scholars of the group during this period: over the fifteen years under review the numbers at school increased by 91·4 per cent, while the population increase was only 50·8 per cent.

I come now to consideration of the position of the African. As stated earlier, the mode of life of the bulk of these people is entirely different from that of the Whites. In fact, the pattern of life of the Africans in the Union can be divided roughly into three main groups – those whose homes are in the Reserves, those who live on the farms of Whites, and those who have taken up permanent residence in the cities and towns. The last group is a relatively recent development consequent upon the industrialization of the country, but it is frowned upon by the existing Nationalist Government.

As the Reserves cannot support – even at the customary primitive standard – the number of families that now reside there, the adult males find it necessary to spend long spells away from home working in the mines or in cities in order to augment the food supplies produced in the Reserves. Those males constitute part of the migratory labour force which keeps the wheels of industry turning in the Union. Male adults from families squatting on White farms also, to some extent, contribute to this migratory labour force.

Over 60 per cent of the African families who reside permanently in the Union live under conditions where their adult menfolk absent themselves for lengthy periods in order to maintain the family. The women and children in the Reserves live very much as they did before the coming of the white man, except that there are now some storekeepers (mainly Whites) who cater for those wants of the people which the Reserves can no longer provide, but which the cash obtained from outside employment now enables them to acquire. On the farms conditions are not quite so primitive for, in addition to the food supplies produced by Africans on these farms and the cash earned abroad, both men and women find employment as farm labourers or domestics.

In contrast to those who live in the cities, the Reserve- and farm-dwellers live close to nature: their wants, being simple, do not have to go through elaborate industrial and commercial processes. A cost-of-living index based upon White customs and standards would therefore be entirely inapplicable to their conditions. In fact, changes in their living costs would be influenced to a much greater degree by price changes of farm products than the official cost-of-living index, which reflects price movements in our complex industrial and commercial set-up. Taking that into account, the increase in their costs over the fifteen-year period 1938/9 to 1953/4 would be much in excess of the 108 per cent disclosed by the official cost-of-living figure as amended here. The official index number of producers' prices of farm products for 1953/4 is 420 as against the official cost-of-living index number of 194.

However, the use of the producers' index referred to would not be reliable either. In the circumstances, a study has been made in the following paragraphs of the incomes and living costs of African families in the Union. This, I believe, gives a fairly reliable indication of the changes that have taken place in the welfare of the African population over the fifteen years under review.

To obtain a comprehensive statistical picture of African living conditions, I found it necessary to examine such conditions under the three categories into which the family lives of Africans can be grouped – those relating to the Reserves, the farms, and the cities. This has entailed the breaking-down of population figures into the three specified groups. From such a break-down it has been found possible to determine (a) the number of families in each group, (b) the number of migratory labourers that affect each group, (c) the total earnings (cash and kind) per average family in each group, and (d) an index number that would measure changes in living costs in respect of each group. The computations employed in arriving at these figures are somewhat involved. I have therefore given them in some detail, so that they may be followed and checked in the event of their being disputed.

Step by step the details are given in the following analysis:

TABLE X

The Distribution of the African Population and the Earnings of African Families in the Years 1938/9 and 1953/4

		1938/9		1953/4
1. Population (in thousands):				
Total		6,920		8,940
Total Male		3,490		4,560
Non-Union Male	(estimate)	200	(estimate)	400
Permanent Union Male Residents		3,290		4,160
2. Effective Male Workers (15 to 60 years of age – in thousands):				
Total		1,885		2,462
Union Residents only		1,685		2,062
3. Wage-Earners (in thousands):				
Total		1,319		2,003
Union Residents only		1,119		1,603
4. Distribution of Effective Male Workers (Union Residents only – in thousands):				
In Reserves		566		459
On Farms		400		500*
In Cities and Towns		719		1,103*
Total		1,685		2,062

* Based upon the assumption that 100,000 non-Union workers on farms and 300,000 in cities and towns.

TABLE X—*cont.*

5. RATIOS OF EFFECTIVE MALE WORKERS TO REST OF AFRICANS (UNION RESIDENTS):

Ratios	1,685 : 5,035	2,062 : 6,478
Approximately	1 : 3	1 : 3·14

6. DISTRIBUTION OF AFRICANS (UNION RESIDENTS ONLY – in thousands):

In Reserves	3,160	3,440
On Farms	2,560	2,700
In Cities, etc.	1,000	2,400
Total	6,720	8,540

7. DISTRIBUTION OF AFRICANS (UNION RESIDENTS ONLY) OTHER THAN MALE EFFECTIVE WORKERS (in thousands):

In Reserves	(3,160 less 566) or 2,594	(3,440 less 459) 2,981
On Farms	(2,560 less 400) or 2,160	(2,700 less 500) 2,200
In Cities	(1,000 less 719) or 281	(2,400 less 1,103) 1,297
	5,035	6,478

8. NUMBERS OF EFFECTIVE MALE WORKERS WHOSE HOMES ARE (in thousands):

In Reserves	$\frac{2,594}{3}$ or 868	$\frac{2,981}{3\cdot14}$ or 940
On Farms	$\frac{2,160}{3}$ or 723	$\frac{2,200}{3\cdot14}$ or 708
In Cities	$\frac{281}{3}$ or 94	$\frac{1,297}{3\cdot14}$ or 414

9. NUMBERS OF MIGRATORY WORKERS (UNION RESIDENTS – in thousands):

From Reserves	(868 less 566) or 302	(940 less 459) or 481
From Farms	(723 less 400) or 323	(708 less 500) or 208
In Cities	(94 less 719) or −625	(414 less 1,103) or −689

10. DISTRIBUTION OF UNION AFRICANS – ACCORDING TO PERMANENT RESIDENTS (in thousands):

In Reserves	(3,160+302) or 3,462	(3,440+481) or 3,921
On Farms	(2,560+323) or 2,883	(2,700+208) or 2,908
In Cities, etc.	(1,000−625) or 375	(2,400−689) or 1,711
	6,720	8,540

11. DISTRIBUTION OF AFRICAN FAMILIES – BASED UPON RATIO 4·6 MEMBERS PER FAMILY (in thousands):

	Both Parents Living	Total	Both Parents Living	Total
In Reserves	(573)	753	(646)	852
On Farms	(477)	627	(478)	632
In Cities, etc.	(62)	82	(282)	372
	(1,112)	1,462	(1,406)	1,856

TABLE X—*cont.*

12. NUMBER OF WAGE-EARNER MEMBERS WHO CONTRIBUTE TO FAMILY INCOME:

(a) YEAR (1938/9).

	No. of Families (in 1000s)	Male Wage-earners		Female Wage-earners	
		No.	No. per Family	No.	No. per Family
Reserves	753	302 T.	·40	Nil	Nil
Farms	627	400 F.	·64	180 F.	·29
,,	—	323 T.	·51	100 D.	·16
Cities, etc.	82	94 T.	1·15	100 D.	1·22
(b) YEAR 1953/4					
Reserves	852	481 T.	·56	Nil	Nil
Farms	632	500 F.	·80	200 F.	·32
,,	—	208 T.	·33	100 D.	·16
Cities	372	414 T.	1·12	300 D.	·81

T. means Town Worker;
F. means Farm Worker;
D. means Domestic Worker.

13. AVERAGE FAMILY INCOMES, THEREFORE, DETERMINED BY FOLLOWING FORMULAE:

	1938/9		1953/4	
In Reserves	Income from land per family	+ ·40 of wage of Male Town Worker	Income from land per family	+ ·56 of wage of Male Town Worker
On Farms	Income from land per family	+ { ·64 Farm (M.) ·51 Town (M.) ·29 Farm (F.) ·16 Domestic (F.)	Income from land per family	+ { ·80 Farm (M.) ·33 Town (M.) ·32 Farm (F.) ·16 Farm (F.)

In Cities　　　1·15 Town Worker (M.)　　　1·12 Town Worker (M.)
　　　　　　+1·22 Domestic Worker (F.)　　　·81 Domestic Worker (F.)
　　　　　　　　　　　　　　　　　　　　　·08 Town Worker (F.)

14. AVERAGE FAMILY INCOMES (FROM DATA IN TABLES III, IV AND V):

In Reserves $\qquad \dfrac{£10\cdot7 \text{ M.}}{\cdot753 \text{ M.}} = 14\cdot21 \qquad \dfrac{£25\cdot3 \text{ M.}}{\cdot852 \text{ M.}} = 29\cdot70$

(a) Where Male
Worker in Mines　·40 × £50 =　20·00　·56 × £100 =　56·00

　　　　　　　　　　　　　　　　£34·21　　　　　　　£85·70

TABLE X—*cont.*

(b) Where Male Worker in Cities	$\dfrac{£10 \cdot 7 \text{ M.}}{\cdot 753 \text{ M.}} =$	14·21	$\dfrac{£25 \cdot 3 \text{ M.}}{\cdot 852} =$		29·70
	·40 × £48 =	19·20	·56 × £120 =		67·20
		£33·41			£96·90

On Farms	$\dfrac{£5 \cdot 0 \text{ M.}}{\cdot 627} =$	7·97	$\dfrac{£12 \cdot 7 \text{ M.}}{\cdot 632} =$		20·09
	·64 of £30 =	19·20	·80 of £50 =		40·00
	·51 of £48 =	24·48	·33 of £120 =		39·60
	·29 of £15 =	4·35	·32 of £25 =		8·00
	·16 of £30 =	4·80	·16 of £80 =		12·80
		£60·80			£120·49

In Cities	1·15 of £48 =	55·20	1·12 of £120 =		134·40
	1·22 of £30 =	36·60	·81 of £80 =		64·80
			·08 of £170 =		13·60
		£91·80			£212·80

15. INCREASES IN FAMILY INCOMES OVER 15 YEARS 1938/9 to 1953/4:
      Reserve Families   (a) 147·6 per cent (mines)
                            (b) 190·0 per cent (cities)
      Farm Families   98·2 per cent
      City Families   131·8 per cent.

COST OF LIVING – AFRICAN FAMILIES

The cost-of-living computations for these are based upon families in which both parents are living. The size of such families is 2 adults and 2·8 children, or 4·8 persons in all. For statistical purposes, this number is converted to consumption units in which the father represents 1 unit, the mother ·75 units and the children ·5 units each. So that, in all, an average family is comprised of 3·15 units.

From details given in Table V, African production in the Reserves and on farms has been estimated as follows:

	Year 1938/9		*Year 1953/4*	
	Reserves	*Farms*	*Reserves*	*Farms*
Meat	167·5 M. lb.	58·8 M. lb.	158·0 M. lb.	56·4 M. lb.
Grain	701·0 M. lb.	510·0 M. lb.	564·0 M. lb.	601·0 M. lb.
Milk	67·0 M. gals.	28·0 M. gals.	670·0 M. gals.	28·0 M. gals.
Eggs	22·0 M. doz.	10·0 M. doz.	22·0 M. doz.	10·5 M. doz.

TABLE X—*cont.*

Per family in the relative groups this production is as follows:

	1938/9		1953/4	
	Reserves	*Farms*	*Reserves*	*Farms*
Meat	222 lb.	94 lb.	185 lb.	89 lb.
Grain	930 lb.	800 lb.	662 lb.	950 lb.
Milk	730 pts.	360 pts.	680 pts.	360 pts.
Eggs	30 doz.	16 doz.	28 doz.	16 doz.

The computations below are based upon the following assumptions:

(i) The produce is consumed by families without passing through traders' stores.

(ii) Meat consumption per family for those in Reserves or on farms is throughout 222 lb. a year. Grain consumption is 600 lb. per family unit or 1,890 lb. per family.

(iii) Where production falls short of these figures, the families buy quantities to make up these figures at retail prices.

(iv) Where production is consumed direct, the prices are taken at wholesale.

TABLE XI

COST OF LIVING OF AFRICAN FAMILIES

1. FAMILIES IN RESERVES WITH MALE HEAD IN MINES FOR PART-TIME:

On this basis we have:

In 1938/9   Units of family in mines ·4   Units in Reserve 2·75

In 1953/4   „   „   „ ·56   „   „   2·59

FAMILY BUDGET   1938/9   1953/4

Food:

Maize	930 lb.	@ ·8d. =	£3	2	0	662 lb. @ 2d.	= £5	10	4
Maize Meal	720 lb.	@ 1·1d. =	3	6	0	892 lb. @ 2·8d.	= 10	8	2
Meat	222 lb.	@ 5d. =	4	12	6	185 lb. @ 1s. 3d.	= 11	11	3
						11 @ 1s. 6d.	=	16	6
Milk	730 pts.	@ 1·5d. =	4	11	3	680 pts. @ 3d.	= 8	10	0
Eggs	30 doz.	@ 1s. =	1	10	0	28 doz. @ 2s.	= 2	16	0
Sugar	240 lb.	@ 3·4d. =	3	8	0	223 lb. @ 5·3d.	= 4	18	6
			£20	9	9		£44	10	9

Other Food
(Groundnuts,
Beans,
Coffee)*   5 0 0   15 0 0

* Indices for these items show increases of 200 per cent at least over period.

TABLE XI—*cont.*

	1938/9					1953/4		
		25	9	9			59	10	9
Food in Mines ·4 of £18		7	4	0	·56 of £40		22	8	0
		£32	13	9			£81	18	9

Sundries:

	1938/9				1953/4			
Candles	12 pkts. @ 5d.	=	5	0	12 pkts. @ 13·5d. =		13	6
Soap	36 lb. @ 2·75d.	=	8	3	36 lb. @ 7·65d.	=	1	3	0
Tobacco	12 lb. @ 1s.	=	12	0	12 lb. @ 2s. 6d.	=	1	10	0
		£1	5	3			£3	6	6

Clothing:

	1938/9				1953/4			
Blankets	4 @ 6s.	=	1	4	0	4 @ 30s.	=	6	0	0
Other	·4 @ £5*	=	2	0	0	·56 @ £15*	=	8	8	0
		£3	4	0			£14	8	0

Total living expenses per annum		£37	3	0		£99	13	3

Percentage increase over period: 168 per cent.

*Indices for these items show increases of 200 per cent at least over period.

2. FAMILIES ON FARMS:

In 1938/9	Units on farms 2·64	Units in Towns ·51
In 1953/4	,, ,, 2·82	,, ,, ·33

FAMILY BUDGET   1938/9   1953/4
Food:

	1938/9				1953/4			
Maize	800 lb. @ ·8d.	= £2	13	4	950 lb. @ 2d.	= £7	18	4
Maize Meal	780 lb. @ 1·1d.	= 3	11	6	750 lb. @ 2·8d.	= 8	15	0
Meat	94 lb. @ 5d.	= 1	19	2	89 lb. @ 1s. 3d.	= 5	11	3
	120 lb. @ 6d.	= 3	0	0	136 lb. @ 1s. 6d.	= 10	4	0
Milk	700 pts. @ 1·5d.	= 4	7	6	750 pts. @ 3d.	= 9	7	6
Eggs	28 doz. @ 1s.	= 1	8	0	31 doz. @ 2s.	= 3	2	0
Sugar	230 lb. @ 3·4d.	= 3	5	2	247 lb. @ 5·3d.	= 5	8	1
		£20	4	8		£50	6	2

Other Food (Groundnuts, Beans, Coffee)		5	0	0	16	10	0
		£25	4	8	£66	16	2

TABLE XI—*cont.*

Sundries (as per Reserve families):		1 5 3			3 6 6
Clothes:		5 0 0			15 0 0
·51 of (City unit or £25)		12 15 0	·33 of (City unit or £58·3)		19 5 0
Total Living Costs:		£44 4 11			£104 7 8

Percentage increase over period: 136 per cent.

3. FAMILIES IN CITIES (FAMILY UNITS 3·15 IN BOTH YEARS):
ANNUAL FAMILY BUDGET:

Food:	1938/9			1953/4	
Maize Meal	1200 lb. @ 1·1d. =	£5 10 0	At 2·8d.	=	£14 0 0
Bread	730 lb. @ 3·5d. =	10 12 11	At 4·2d.	=	12 15 6
Meat	400 lb. @ 6d. =	10 0 0	At 1s. 6d.	=	30 0 0
Milk	730 pts. @ 3d. =	9 2 6	At 6d.	=	18 5 0
Eggs	20 doz. @ 1s. 9d =	1 15 0	At 3s.	=	3 0 0
Sugar	240 lb. @ 3·4d. =	3 8 0	At 5·3d.	=	5 6 0
Other Food (Beans, Coffee, etc.)		6 0 0			20 0 0
		£46 8 5			£103 6 6
Rent		12 0 0			30 0 0
Transport		5 0 0			12 0 0
Clothes		10 0 0			30 0 0
Coal or Wood (3s. per bag)		3 15 0	(4s. per bag)		5 0 0
Sundries		1 5 3			3 6 6
Total for family		£78 8 8			£183 13 0
Per family unit		£25 0 0			£58 7 0

Percentage increase over period: 134 per cent.

TABLE XII

COMPARISON OF STANDARDS OF LIVING OF AFRICAN FAMILIES

By correcting the incomes for the year 1953/4 by the relative increases in living costs over the fifteen years under review, we obtain the real purchasing power of such incomes compared with those for the year 1938/9. These comparisons are:

	1953/4	1938/9	% *Increase* or % *Decrease*
FAMILIES IN RESERVES:			
(a) Male head in mines	31·95	34·21	− 6·6
(b) Male head in cities	36·15	33·41	+ 8·2
FAMILIES ON FARMS:	51·06	60·80	− 16·0
FAMILIES IN CITIES OR TOWNS:	90·77	91·80	− 1·1

These figures disclose a fall in the standard of living of African families, except for those living in the Reserves where the head works in the cities. In the last-mentioned case their improvement is *not* due to improved productivity in the Reserves nor to the higher wage-rates in the cities, but solely to a larger proportion of adult males migrating to the cities in the year 1953/54 to augment the family income.

LIVING CONDITIONS OF AFRICANS AS A SINGLE GROUP

(a) The average increase (duly weighted) in living costs of Africans on the basis of the increases for the different family groups is 152.

(b) Over the fifteen years 1938/9 to 1953/4 the standard of living of the *Average African Family* has fallen by 7·3 per cent on the basis of the changes in the family groups considered.

(c) On the basis of the National Income of Africans, adjusted by the cost-of-living figure of the Average African Family, the decline in the Standard of Living of the Average African family is as follows:

National Income of Africans:

	1938/9 (*in £ million*)	1953/4 (*in £ million*)
Wages and Salaries	64·18	241·12
Casual Labour	3·00	8·00
Farm Income	15·70	38·00
	82·88	287·12

National Income of Africans: – cont.

	1938/9 (*in £ million*)		1953/4 (*in £ million*)

Less: Earnings of ex-
Union Africans: 100,000 @ £50
   200,000 @ £48   9·60   300,000 @ £120   41·00

               73·28   246·12

Less: Earnings of
families that moved
to cities during
period:

$$\left(372 - 82 \times \frac{130}{100}\right) \text{ thousand}$$

$$= (371 - 107) \qquad \text{thousand}$$

$$= \qquad 265 \quad \text{thousand} \quad - \qquad @ \text{ } £212·8 \qquad 56·39$$

               73·28   189·73

	1938/9	1953/4
No. of families	1,462	(1,856 − 265)
Income per family	£50·1	£119·2
Adjusted by cost of living	£50·1	£47·3
Percentage Decline:		5·6 per cent.

This verifies the figure determined by averaging the declines of the different family groups, 7·3 per cent, given under (b) above. The average of the two methods of computation is 6·5 per cent.

TABLE XIII

COMPARISON OF LIVING CONDITIONS OF THE DIFFERENT POPULATION GROUPS IN THE UNION

	Whites	Others	Africans
(a) Average family income 1938/9	£530	£134	£50·1

TABLE XIII—*cont.*

	Whites	*Others*	*Africans*
(b) Average family income 1953/4	£1,616	£308	£119·2
(c) Rise in living costs over 15 years 1938/9 to 1953/4	108%	108%	152%
(d) Average family income 1953/4 @ 1938/9 prices	£777	£148	£47·3
(e) Changes in purchasing power of family income over 15 years	£247 (increase)	£14 (increase)	£2·8 (decrease)
(f) Percentage increase (+) or decrease (−) in living standard	+46%	+11%	− 6·5%*

* In the comparison of living conditions among Africans over the 15-year period, the position of 265,000 African families has been omitted. These are the families that took up permanent residence in the cities and towns during this 15-year period. They have been omitted because there is no reliable means by which their living standard in 1953/4 can be compared with that in 1938/9 – their conditions having altered completely from those in the Reserves or on farms. The percentage fall of 6·5 per cent in the living standard applies to the 1,591,000 families.

These figures disclose that the Whites have enjoyed a very material gain in real income over the fifteen years under review; the 'Others' have also gained, but to a lesser extent; the Africans, on the other hand, have suffered a significant loss in real income, due principally to the following causes:

(a) the deterioration of the Reserves and farm-lands available to the African;

and

(b) the fact that, in fixing wage-rates of Africans, the full increases in African living costs have not been taken into account – their increases being measured by the index based upon White standards.

The latter reason is the more important of the two.

From this table it can be shown that, in terms of present-day money values, the average White family was £514 better off in 1953/4 than it was in the pre-war year 1938/9; the average 'Other' family was £29 better off; but the average African family was £7 worse off.

This discrimination is due to the uneven changes in the real incomes of the different population groups over the period in question. These uneven changes have occasioned a considerable shift in wealth in favour of the White group. Had the improvement in the living conditions of the different groups been uniform over the fifteen years (surely a not undesirable state of affairs), then, on the assumption that the national income of the country remained unaltered, the money incomes of the different groups (taken as groups) would have undergone the following changes:

MONEY INCOMES FOR THE YEAR 1953/4

	Actual	Estimated on basis of Uniform Improvement in Real Incomes	Differences
	£ Million	£ Million	£ Million
Whites	1044·03	955	−89
Others	88·25	94	+ 6
Africans	269·79	353	+83
National Income	1402·07	1402	—

It would appear, therefore, that the uneven changes referred to have had the effect of shifting £83,000,000 from the Africans and £6,000,000 from the 'Others' in favour of the Whites during the year 1953/4.

POSTSCRIPT

SINCE this book was written, an event of considerable significance has taken place in the Union. The United Party – the official Opposition in the Union Parliament – has shed its more progressive supporters. In the short run, this must be regarded as a rather unfortunate development, for it is likely to strengthen the Nationalists in Parliament in the immediate future. It is also to be regretted in that it means that the more reactionary elements have gained control of the United Party for the time being. In the long run, however, the split may have beneficial results, for it sheds a new ray of hope that at least a substantial section of the electorate is prepared to face the realities of the situation in Africa.

This belief is strengthened by the fact that the members who have had the courage to break away from the rather tepid policies of the official Opposition include some of the most enlightened and capable young men in Parliament today. That these young men will have to go into the political wilderness for some time is probably inevitable; but it is equally inevitable that the logic of events in Africa – the Union included – will ultimately draw them into the forefront of the political arena of the country. The powerful forces of world opinion, evolution, Christianity and economics are unquestionably ranged on their side, and against such forces a policy of White privilege can never prevail. Therefore, if the white man is to survive in Africa – the Union included – it can be possible only if he is prepared to adjust his way of life to the dictates of these forces.

It is my belief that if these young men remain true to their concepts, they, together with their counterparts in the Rhodesian Federation, will become the spearhead of a new force in Africa – a force which draws its inspiration from neither Nationalism nor Liberalism. Both these movements have their roots in earlier centuries and, as a consequence, are not attuned to conditions brought about by the scientific achievements of the second half of the twentieth century. The future of mankind in the face of the formidable forces released by nuclear power must inevitably rest on the one hand upon racial toleration and co-operation, and, on the other, upon positive leadership which seeks to harness those forces in the interests of peace and the betterment of living conditions – particularly of the under-privileged.

Neither racial domination on the part of certain peoples nor a policy of laissez-faire can achieve these objectives. And in Africa, where erstwhile White paramountcy is everywhere being ousted by Black nationalism, a new outlook and policy becomes imperative. This must seek as its prime objective the advancement of the non-Whites in all walks of life and the preservation of White influence and guidance with its rich heritage of achievement and culture.

It is along this road, if I am not mistaken, that the new Progressive group seeks to move, and, in some respects it would appear to diverge considerably from that previously pursued by the United Party. It is to be hoped, however, that, as the lessons of enlightenment and evolution reach down to the masses, these separate paths will tend to converge. I am not without hope that many Nationalists – particularly among the intellectuals, who in themselves can be a formidable force for good in South Africa – will in the not-too-distant future see their way clear to join forces with those who today have courageously accepted the challenge of the new era, based as it is upon twentieth-century scientific achievement and industrialization. Along this course alone can White influence rest secure in Africa.